# TEACHING DIVERSITY AND INCLUSION

*Teaching Diversity and Inclusion: Examples from a French-Speaking Classroom* explores new and pioneering strategies for transforming current teaching practices into equitable, inclusive, and immersive classrooms for all students. This cutting-edge volume dares to ask new questions and shares innovative, concrete tools useful to a wide variety of classrooms and institutional contexts, far beyond any disciplinary borders.

This book aims to instill classroom approaches that allow every student to feel safe to share their truth and to reflect deeply about their own identity and challenges, discussing course design, assignments, technologies, activities, and strategies that target diversity and inclusion in the French classroom. Each chapter shares why and how to design an inclusive community of learners, including opportunities to promote interdisciplinary approaches and cross-disciplinary collaborations, exploring cultures and underrepresented perspectives, and distinguishing unconscious biases. The essays also provide theoretical and practical strategies adaptable to any reflective teacher who wants to create a welcoming, inclusive classroom that draws in students whom they might not otherwise attract.

This long overdue work will be ideal both for undergraduate and graduate students and administrators seeking fresh approaches to diversity in the classroom.

**E. Nicole Meyer** (Ph.D., University of Pennsylvania) is a Chevalier dans l'Ordre des Palmes Académiques and Professor of French and Women's and Gender Studies at Augusta University. A recipient of the 2021 Louis K. Bell Research Award, she publishes on a wide array of topics, including contemporary French and Francophone women's autobiography, Flaubert, and French for Specific Purposes.

**Eilene Hoft-March** (Ph.D., University of California, Berkeley) is Professor of French and Francophone Studies and the Milwaukee-Downer and College Endowment Association Professor of Liberal Studies at Lawrence University where she also contributes to the Gender Studies and Global Studies programs. She has published works on a variety of late 20th and early 21st century French authors and genres.

# TEACHING DIVERSITY AND INCLUSION

Examples from a French-Speaking Classroom

*Edited by E. Nicole Meyer and Eilene Hoft-March*

NEW YORK AND LONDON

First published 2022
by Routledge
605 Third Avenue, New York, NY 10158

and by Routledge
2 Park Square, Milton Park, Abingdon, Oxon OX14 4RN

*Routledge is an imprint of the Taylor & Francis Group, an informa business*

© 2022 selection and editorial matter, E. Nicole Meyer and Eilene Hoft-March; individual chapters, the contributors

The right of E. Nicole Meyer and Eilene Hoft-March to be identified as the authors of the editorial material, and of the authors for their individual chapters, has been asserted in accordance with sections 77 and 78 of the Copyright, Designs and Patents Act 1988.

All rights reserved. No part of this book may be reprinted or reproduced or utilised in any form or by any electronic, mechanical, or other means, now known or hereafter invented, including photocopying and recording, or in any information storage or retrieval system, without permission in writing from the publishers.

*Trademark notice*: Product or corporate names may be trademarks or registered trademarks, and are used only for identification and explanation without intent to infringe.

*Library of Congress Cataloging-in-Publication Data*.
A catalog record for this title has been requested

ISBN: 978-0-367-64832-9 (hbk)
ISBN: 978-0-367-64827-5 (pbk)
ISBN: 978-1-003-12646-1 (ebk)

DOI: 10.4324/9781003126461

Typeset in Bembo
by Taylor & Francis Books

# CONTENTS

List of Tables viii
Acknowledgments ix
List of Contributors xii

Introduction 1
E. Nicole Meyer and Eilene Hoft-March

**SECTION I**
**Unscripting and Claiming Identities** 9

1 Queer Pedagogy for a Queer(er) Francophone Classroom 11
 CJ Gomolka

2 A Starter Kit for Rethinking Trans Representation and
 Inclusion in French L2 Classrooms 22
 Kris Aric Knisely

3 Disability Studies and the French Classroom: Toward a
 'Democracy of Proximity' 34
 Tammy Berberi

4 Why We Need to Talk about Race: Improving Racial
 Inclusivity in the French Language Classroom 44
 Kate Nelson

## SECTION II
## Inclusively Speaking     55

5  Inclusive Language Pedagogy for (Un)Teaching Gender in French     57
*Kiki Kosnick*

6  How Can We Teach French Inclusively?: Challenges and Resistance     68
*Dominique Carlini Versini*

7  A Classroom for Everyone: Creating French Courses that Embrace Learning Differences     77
*Kathryn A. Dettmer and Brenda A. Dyer*

8  Diversifying the Curriculum: From Structural Changes to Classroom Lessons     87
*Jessica S. Miller*

9  Embracing the Francophone World across the French Curriculum     97
*Stephanie Schechner*

10  Unlearning the Language of Divisiveness     106
*Eilene Hoft-March*

## SECTION III
## Embracing Cultures/Extending Contexts     117

11  Strategies for Teaching Diversity and Inclusion in Introductory Literature Courses     119
*Dominique Licops*

12  The Making of the Other Americas: Discovering the Francospheres of Latin America     129
*Lowry Martin*

13  Connecting French Studies to the World through Global Foodways     139
*Lauren Ravalico*

14  Lessons in Diversity from the Street: A Course on Hip-hop Cultures     149
*Kathryn St. Ours*

15 "We are all Negroes": Teaching Tolerance from a Haitian
   Literary Perspective                                         159
   *Lovia Mondésir*

16 Introducing Diversity into the Graduate Classroom: Teaching
   Jewish Francophone Writers                                   169
   *Nancy M. Arenberg*

17 Promoting Mutual Understanding and Inclusion in the French
   Classroom through French, Israeli, and Polish Post-Holocaust
   Life Writing                                                 178
   *E. Nicole Meyer*

*Essential Reads*                                               *188*
*Index*                                                         *191*

# TABLES

2.1 Non-binary French Forms (Knisely, 2021a)     26
8.1 Themes, Essential Questions, and Cultures Explored in FREN 201, Intermediate 1, with the subtopic "History" and the Target Proficiency of Intermediate Low     92
8.2 Themes, Essential Questions, and Cultures Explored in FREN 202, Intermediate 2, with the subtopic "Cultural Perspectives" and the Target Proficiency of Intermediate Mid     93
8.3 Themes, Essential Questions, and Topics Explored in FREN 401, Contemporary Societal Issue, with the subtopic "Social Justice" and the Target Proficiency of Advanced Low     93

# ACKNOWLEDGMENTS

Nicole would like to express deep gratitude to my son, Max Papadopoulos, whose love for me and mine for him fulfills my every day, as well as to my chosen sisters, Debra L. Nelson and Eva Meyer. The love and unwavering support of all three brings such light into my life. Working with Eilene Hoft-March has been both a privilege and a joy. Our daily phone calls are a highlight of my day and just one of the many delights of working with Eilene. The discovery of our complementary skills, as well as our amazingly shared vision of quality and understanding of the central issues of this volume cemented our already strong friendship in such beautiful ways. Eilene's stunning intelligence, exceptional tact, and knowledge of grammatical distinctions, such as that between which and that, and passion for sharing the bringing to birth this volume of which I have dreamed for so many years is priceless. In many ways, we are sisters—born of different parents, backgrounds and circumstances, the many traits that we carry from our parents are stunningly parallel in enlightening ways. Truth be told, the volume percolated within me for over five years. However, attracting the quality of essays contained within necessitated the passing of time, both to build upon the dream of its creation, and to establish a sense of safety for the diverse contributors, so that they would know their work had the right home and family. This volume integrates diversity and inclusion into every thread of its composition. It is the volume that I wished had existed—a chance to build outlooks and toolkits to teach diversity and inclusion with both an open heart and with the knowledge to support that teaching. My gratitude to each of the contributors for joining us on this journey and for trusting that their work is welcome, necessary, and at home is beyond words. Their openness to opening our dialogue to all will help so many others to grow as well. In addition, my sincere thanks go to the Augusta University Office of Diversity and Inclusion's for awarding me the

Diversity, Equity and Inclusion Research Grant, which proved invaluable in supporting the creation of this book. In their tireless leadership, Drs. Tiffany Townsend and Lindsey West have shifted the institutional outlook on diversity and inclusion in such a positive way. I look forward to continuing their vision through my role on the Council for Equity Leadership. My thanks also go to Walidah Walker, Luis A. Rodriguez-Cirilo and Wanda Prince, as well as the entire Office of Research at Augusta University. Julie F. Tolliver truly helped me in essential ways to bring this book to light and to realize my own personal path. Personal thanks go to my Women in French colleagues Colette Trout, Annabelle Rea, Cecilia Beach, Arline Cravens, and so many more, who have joined in the support of and growth of a wonderful organization that mentors so many. The American Association of Teachers of French's (AATF) inclusion of me into so many wonderful initiatives in so many meaningful ways means so much to me. Past President Catherine Daniélou, current President Anne Jensen, Randa Duvick, and so many other selfless AATF advocates for excellent teaching have my gratitude. I am also grateful to Lucienne Frappier-Mazur, Gerald Prince, and the late Frank Bowman, who each believed in my work; and to Susan Stanford Friedman, former Director of the Institute of Research in the Humanities at the University of Wisconsin-Madison, who supported my research through Fellowships that offered me community and resources. Her personal kindness to me will never be forgotten, nor will that of Cathy Nesci. Gratitude must also go to the Center for Instructional Innovation at Augusta University and to the libraries of the University of Wisconsin-Madison and of University of Wisconsin-Green Bay for their generous support of my research over so many years. Thanks also go to Augusta University colleagues, who are too many to list here, but includes Dr. Skip Clark, past Dean of Pamplin College, Guirdex Massé, Sandrine Catris, Kim Davies, current Interim Dean, as well as Rhonda Armstrong, Seretha Williams, Christina Heckman, and Jana Sandarg, for their encouragement of my research. Personal thanks go to a very special group of individuals who helped me to grow as I taught the course described within: Robyn Budenstein, Harriet Ehrlich, Katelyn Matthews, Nicole Perrin, Mary Sawilowsky, and Betty Sussman, and to Rabbi Sirull for his role. I gratefully acknowledge the Schusterman Center for Israel Studies Summer Institute for Israel Studies at Brandeis University for its generous grant that supported the creation of this course.

Eilene expresses gratitude to E. Nicole Meyer for inviting me to work with her on this volume. Nicole has led this project with passion, energy, intelligence, and purpose and has sought out strong new voices to join experienced ones to give this book authority and impact. Thanks and gratitude also go to Lawrence University colleagues David Burrows, Kathy Privatt, and Amy Kester, as well as the Andrew W. Mellon Foundation and the Milwaukee-Downer and College Endowment Association for their support. Finally, my thanks to two personal backers: my mother and first teacher, Shirley Hoft, and John, my partner in every way that matters.

We would both like to thank Ethan Fatheree and Alice Wynn for their assistance through this process. We would like to thank the Modern Languages Association, the American Association of Teachers of French, and South Atlantic Modern Languages Association for supporting pedagogical presentations related to this volume. And finally, we would like to thank the wonderful Routledge team, in particular Bryony Reece, Michelle Salyga, Reanna Young, and Driss Fatih. In addition, we wish to thank our indexer, Jay Knarr of KnarrEdit.

# CONTRIBUTORS

**Nancy M. Arenberg** (PhD, University of Arizona) is Associate Professor of French at the University of Arkansas. She teaches graduate courses in 17th- and 18th-century French literature and offers a variety of Francophone literature courses at the graduate and undergraduate levels. Her monograph entitled *Textual Transvestism: Revisions of Heloise (17th-18th-Centuries)* was published by Brill in 2015. Over the years, she has published numerous articles and book chapters on Francophone women writers, mainly from North Africa and Quebec. Presently, Professor Arenberg is conducting research for a monograph on Jewish migrant authors, focusing on absence, suffering, and fractured identities.

**Tammy Berberi** (PhD, Indiana University) is Associate Professor of French at the University of Minnesota, Morris and past president of the Society for Disability Studies. Co-editor for *Worlds Apart: Disability and Foreign Language Learning* (2008), Berberi continues to explore intersectional and inclusive teaching praxis and researches French disability studies in modern French literature and culture. She is a key member of the Morris Intercultural Education Initiative, as well as "Dreaming up the Change Disability Makes," a grant to develop critical disability studies at the University of Minnesota. In 2019 she was awarded the University of Minnesota President's Award for Outstanding Service.

**Dominique Carlini Versini** (PhD, University of Kent) is Lecturer in French at Durham University in the UK. She completed her thesis in 2018, in which she examines figures of excess in women's writing and filmmaking to question bodily frontiers, particularly in the texts and films of Marie Darrieussecq, Virginie Despentes, Laurence Nobécourt, and Marina de Van. Recent publications include a special issue on the role of sciences in Marie Darrieussecq's work in *Dalhousie*

*French Studies*, as well as articles in *Women in French Studies, L'Esprit Créateur*, and *Fixxion*.

**Kathryn A. Dettmer** (MA, Washington University in St. Louis, M. Ed. Temple University), an adjunct instructor, and **Brenda A. Dyer** (MA, University of Pennsylvania), an associate teaching professor, have worked together for so long that students send Brenda homework meant for Kathy and vice versa. This chapter is the result of many years of discussion about teaching and students. Kathy regularly teaches at Drexel University, Widener University, and the University of Pennsylvania.

**CJ Gomolka** (PhD, University of Maryland) is Associate Professor of Global French Studies at DePauw University in Greencastle, Indiana. His main area of interest is sexuality and gender in the Francophone world since the 19$^{th}$ century. His current book project entitled *(Don't) Call Me Queer: Nomenclature, Anxiety, and Identity in Contemporary France* examines the links between denomination, anxiety, and identity in the contemporary Francophone world. He is particularly interested in exploring how processes of naming operate in reference to social/cultural/political/linguistic anxieties and what this might tell us about social/cultural/political/linguistic processes of identification and disidentification for queer and non-queer identities. His publications include articles on contemporary decolonial feminisms, queer subjectivity, queer pedagogy, and AIDS iconography in France.

**Eilene Hoft-March** (PhD, University of California, Berkeley) is Professor of French and Francophone Studies and the Milwaukee-Downer and College Endowment Association Professor of Liberal Studies at Lawrence University, where she also contributes to the Gender Studies and Global Studies programs. She has received all three of her institution's teaching awards. She has published articles about contemporary French novelists and autobiographers, particularly women writers of the last fifty years. Her last co-edited publication was *Cixous after/depuis 2000* (Brill/Rodopi, 2017); her next project is a family memoir.

**Kris Aric Knisely** (PhD, Emory University, he/they) is Assistant Professor of French and Intercultural Competence and is an affiliated faculty member in the Second Language Acquisition and Teaching (SLAT) graduate interdisciplinary program at the University of Arizona. Knisely's research broadly considers gender and sexuality in language teaching and learning and, in its most specific form, focuses on the linguistic and cultural practices of trans and non-binary speakers of French, particularly as they can inform the articulation of trans-affirming L2 pedagogies.

**Kiki Kosnick** (PhD, University of Wisconsin-Madison) is Assistant Professor of French in the Department of World Languages, Literatures, and Cultures at

Augustana College in Rock Island, Illinois. Kiki's teaching and research interests include contemporary life writing, queer theories, inclusive language, and social justice pedagogy. Kiki's article, "The Everyday Poetics of Gender-Inclusive French: Strategies for Navigating the Linguistic Landscape," received the 2019 Florence Howe Award for Outstanding Feminist Scholarship. Kiki expresses gratitude to Augustana College for financially supporting this work—and for being a caring and affirming academic home.

**Dominique Licops** (Ph.D. Northwestern University) is Associate Professor of Instruction at Northwestern University, where she teaches language and literature courses. Her research interests are in Francophone literatures and the pedagogy of teaching French language literatures. She has published articles on Aimé Césaire, Maryse Condé, Gisèle Pineau, and Assia Djebar in *Nouvelles Études Francophones, Women in French* and in edited volumes. Chevalier dans l'Ordre des Palmes Académiques, she was a Digital Humanities Summer Fellow at the Kaplan Institute for the Humanities (2018) and has lead workshops on 'Developing Group Dynamics in the Language Classroom' across the Midwest, partnering with the French Consulate and the American Association of Teachers of French.

**Lowry Martin** (PhD, University of California, Berkeley) is Associate Professor of French at the University of Texas-El Paso. His primary fields of study are French literature during France's Third Republic, Francophone cinema, and the intersections of law, literature, and sexuality. He has written on Dumas, Colette, and Proust as well as Francophone and Israeli cinema. His book, *Sapphic Mosaics: Fantasy, Desire, and the Cultural Production of Paris-Lesbos 1880–1939* is currently under review, and he is working on a second monograph entitled *Imagining the Promised Land: Transnational Imaginaries and French Cultural Production*.

**E. Nicole Meyer** (PhD, University of Pennsylvania) is a Chevalier dans l'Ordre des Palmes Académiques and Professor of French and Women's and Gender Studies at Augusta University. Recipient of the 2021 Louis K. Bell Research Award, she publishes on a wide array of topics including contemporary French and Francophone women's autobiography, Flaubert, and French for Specific Purposes. An award-winning teacher, her latest being the Boundless Teaching Award from the Center for Instructional Innovation at her institution, her international leadership includes being named to the American Association of Teachers of French National Task Force on Diversity and Inclusion, and serving as Vice President of Women in French. Her most recent volume is the co-edited *Rethinking the French Classroom: New Approaches to Teaching Contemporary French and Francophone Women* (Routledge, 2019). Her current book project is *Fractured Families in Contemporary French and Francophone Women's Autobiographies*.

**Jessica S. Miller** (Ph.D., University of Illinois Urbana-Champaign) has been teaching all levels of French at the University of Wisconsin-Eau Claire since 2006 and has been a certified ACTFL OPI Tester since 2015. She received the Wisconsin-AATF Award of Recognition for professional dedication in 2016. Under her leadership, the UW-Eau Claire French section has been recognized twice as a National AATF Exemplary Program (2017 and 2020). Her professional interests include second language acquisition, phonetics, and oral proficiency.

**Lovia Mondésir** (D.EA., Université des Antilles; Ph.D., Emory University) is an independent scholar. She has received teaching accolades from the École Normale Supérieure of Port-au-Prince and the Agence Universitaire de la Francophonie. Her research focuses on the representations of women in the Haitian Revolution and in emancipatory movements in the Caribbean. Her article on women underground abolitionist work across economic and racial boundaries in Saint-Domingue appeared in *Nouvelles Études Francophones*. She has forthcoming articles on *Monsieur Toussaint* and *Mulâtresse Solitude*.

**Kate Nelson** is a PhD student at the University of Texas at Austin. Her research interests include critical race and gender studies, cinema, and women in the Maghreb and the Parisian banlieue. She has published and presented on translation, women in the French Revolution, and women's roles in Francophone cinema. She is currently working on the role of women in banlieue cinema and is interested in intersections of self and literary/filmic creation. Previous to arriving at UT, Ms. Nelson taught French and Francophone Studies at California State University Long Beach, Chapman University, and Humboldt State University.

**Lauren Ravalico** (PhD, Harvard University) is Assistant Professor of French and Francophone Studies and Faculty Affiliate in the Women's and Gender Studies Program at the College of Charleston. A specialist in modern French literature, art, and food studies, she enjoys teaching all levels of French language and cultural studies. Her published research focuses on the history of the senses, affect theory, women in the arts, gender and sexuality studies, and the social history of dialogue and networking.

**Kathryn St. Ours** (PhD, Catholic University of America) and is Associate Professor of French Transnational Studies at Goucher College in Baltimore County, Maryland. Her research career has taken her from the fantastic (book: *Le fantastique chez Roger Caillois*) to eco-criticism and the intersection of science and literature in the $20^{th}-21^{st}$ centuries (*Where Literature and Science Meet: The Earthy Writing of Jean-Loup Trassard*). She has also published articles about the film *The Story of the Weeping Camel* and the non-fiction text *Musher* by Franco-Canadian Julien Gravelle in the journal *Interdisciplinary Studies in Literature and Environment*.

**Stephanie Schechner** (PhD, University of Wisconsin-Madison) is Professor of French and Chair of Modern Languages at Widener University in Chester, Pennsylvania. She is Chair of the Board of Directors of the Guinean Alliance for Education and Development (Washington, DC). She has published on French and Francophone women writers, including Colette, Jovette Marchessault, Rachilde, and Nathalie Sarraute. She specializes in the work of the French lesbian working-class author, Mireille Best, and has translated Best's second novel *Camille en octobre* into English. She has also presented and published on pedagogical issues throughout her career.

# INTRODUCTION

*E. Nicole Meyer and Eilene Hoft-March*

Diversity and inclusion are the heartbeat of this volume.

When this project began, it was born of the desire to create the informative volume that we wished existed as we ourselves tackled how to become more informed pedagogues, and thus, to transform our own classrooms into an equitable, inclusive community of learners. Then came the coronavirus (COVID-19) pandemic in early 2020, just as social unrest that had long bubbled below the surface erupted into the streets in mid-2020 as witnessed by the senseless murders at the hands of the police of George Floyd, Breonna Taylor, and so many people considered "others." Truth be told, these violent deaths were not the first, and sadly, will not be the last. We need to recognize that the recurrent issues (and current events) permeating this volume are complex and difficult.

Thus, this volume speaks to our times—and to our teaching—in more ways than we could ever have imagined. Moreover, knowing that all educators would be remiss in not attending to these pressing issues, this collection addresses non-specialist and specialist alike. No matter our training or experience, we all need to recognize the devastating systemic concepts and practices that seep into our classrooms and our pedagogies. None of us can simply continue without questioning our varied blind spots, those of our students, and of our profession.

And, yes, our profession is in danger—the pandemic has hastened the rapid cuts of programs as administrators strive for financial survival while deaths accumulate across the globe. The threatened elimination of our livelihood, while relevant, is not the primary focus of our volume, however. More urgently, we need to understand the complex, troubling issues from both a long view as well as a short view. While the systemic practices that are addressed in this volume persist, the jump to eliminate programs such as French studies is often a short-term and short sighted decision. Just as pernicious, however, is the long-term

DOI: 10.4324/9781003126461-1

damage that would result from the loss of our ability to infuse teaching practices and materials with the perspectives of valuable "others." These mind-opening perspectives help in combatting the rampant ignorance burgeoning around us. The focus of this volume could not be more timely or more relevant to practitioners and administrators alike.

For people in the profession who do not know where to start, as well as for those already initiated, the essays contained within help us combat the resistance, both internal and external, that refutes change. The essays help our readers acquire tools and make incremental changes to their approaches to understanding, thinking, and teaching. We might not recognize the many ways that we resist being open to the revolution we need in order to thrive and grow.

The social, political, and linguistic revolutions that surround us demand that attention be paid to more complex understandings of diversity and the impacts of non-inclusion. Under the near-universal pressure of offering online education in order to reduce rates of infection and death, we might finally be paying the attention that it deserves to accessibility. Current circumstances have also broadened and concretized our understanding of equitable access, beyond that of the prevalent Quality Matters standards. In short, we can caption videos and change fonts—all excellent strategies—but we also need to change thinking about who is not able even to own a computer screen and how that got to be. Most importantly, we need to imagine, understand, and dismantle the exclusionary and anti-other systemic thinking that our own classrooms have perpetuated.

This is the challenge put to us by the writers represented in this volume. The French classroom they envision and model allows every student to feel safe to share their truth and to reflect deeply about their own identity and challenges, while learning of the diverse French-speaking world. Each chapter shares why and how to create such an equitable, inclusive community of learners. Our volume dares to ask new questions, and shares innovative, concrete strategies useful to a wide variety of classrooms and institutional contexts. In brief, in revisiting how we teach, why we teach, and what we teach through the prism of diversity and inclusion, we raise issues that affect *all* members of the French-speaking world, othered or not. We thereby create a welcoming, inclusive classroom that draws in students we might not otherwise attract. Whether new to the profession or seasoned educators, faculty will find innovative ideas to invigorate and diversify their pedagogical approaches.

The first section of this book, "Unscripting and Claiming Identities," addresses essential questions of teaching French with an enhanced awareness of who might be in the room. We must reframe our approaches to claim long silenced identities, all of which exist both in our classrooms and in the world around us. We must argue for a Queer(er), trans-affirming, POC-affirming (People of Color) classroom that not only accommodates, but amplifies the reclaimed identities through anti-racist, anti-ableist, anti-sexist pedagogical approaches. The essays in this section underscore the importance of this radical rethinking of what our classrooms can and should look like, as well as the intimate link between being and doing in a space that fights marginalization.

In "Queer Pedagogy for a Queer(er) Francophone Classroom," CJ Gomolka shares both the importance of and examples of successful pedagogies for creating a queer(er) French-speaking classroom. Gomolka proposes a practical manifesto calling for a queer-inflected pedagogy in the 21$^{st}$-century Francophone classroom. The pedagogy he advocates necessarily addresses students where they live: by visibilizing, legitimizing, validating, and interrogating the existential debates on cultural and political hetero- and cis-normativity that circumscribe queer and non-queer students' existence. Such a pedagogy promotes (self)reflexivity and empathic mindfulness and provides necessary tools and encouragement, as well as a framework for integrating inclusive and queer principles and content into the French curriculum from beginning French-language courses through more advanced courses. The following chapter, "A Starter Kit for Rethinking Trans Representation and Inclusion in French L2 Classrooms," introduces a toolkit that expands upon inclusion in the classroom. Here, Kris Aric Knisely argues for the essential inclusion of trans, non-binary, gender non-conforming (TGNC) bodies, lives, and concerns into the French L2 classroom. Not only does this chapter summarize existing frameworks for queering in the French language classroom, it offers concrete ways of awareness and respectful engagement with TGNC individuals and communities through French-specific TGNC resources, *realia*, assignments, activities, and pedagogical strategies to be integrated into both the language classroom and into the broader French curriculum. Knisely's chapter equips educators with the ability to provide all learners with an increased awareness of TGNC lives and concerns, and the means to respectfully engage with, and to better represent, include, and affirm the voices of trans individuals and communities.

In "Disability Studies and the French Classroom: Toward a 'Democracy of Proximity,'" whose timeliness is stunning, given 2020's COVID-19 nefarious effect not only on public physical health and safety, but on student (and faculty) anxiety, Tammy Berberi reflects upon the increasing depression, anxiety, and other mental health diagnoses among students, pointing out that inclusive teaching strategies support all learners' success. Her chapter cites the importance of focus on the intersectional disabled student—students who are both disabled *and*... deserve our understanding (pedagogical and other), and thoughtful inclusion of the challenges that they face in succeeding in a college environment that generally, and unthinkingly, excludes them. Berberi queries how the World Language classroom can respond to the changing demographics in our classrooms, and in particular, how the French classroom can not only include diverse peoples in terms of color, gender, and sexual orientation, but those who are disabled.

Any discussion of diversity and inclusion, especially in the generalization of the Black Lives Matter awareness of today, must include ways to aid French instructors in unpacking race and provide tools to talk about race in our classrooms. In the final chapter of this section, "Why We Need to Talk about Race: Improving

Racial Inclusivity in the French Language Classroom," Kate Nelson addresses the necessity of going far beyond the inclusion of Francophone texts into our classroom. She urges the reader to ask interesting questions and integrate materials and approaches to enrich discussions of race into our classroom. Nelson recommends applicable materials, guidelines, and practices to optimize success of achieving an anti-racist, inclusive, and safe classroom, best suited to deconstruct the dynamic manifestations of racism. Asking deeper questions and exploring anti-racist, anti-ableist, anti-sexist practices necessitate a more inclusive language, as we shall see.

"Inclusively Speaking," our second section, pushes us to model and expect sensitive, inviting, and validating language in our classrooms. We can no longer speak to the middle, buckle to resistance, ignore the margins, or sidestep the controversy. Similar to the impetus of the first section, this second section speaks from all those other places that have too long been passed over in silence.

In "Inclusive Language Pedagogy for (Un)Teaching Gender in French," Kiki Kosnick begins with a critique of the United Nations' adoption of a well-intentioned "gender-inclusive" language policy, noting that its failure to acknowledge that gender-neutral forms are often used to express non-binary genders amounts to avoiding gender rather than affirming it. A further consequence of such policy limited to the usage of the feminine and masculine forms is to risk the collapse of non-binary gender into a feminist cause. Arguing for an expanded coalition instead of collapse, Kosnick proposes a methodology for teaching French language that "creates multiple access points for the expression and validation of non-binary genders in ways that mutually reinforce interconnected linguistic and sociocultural struggles related to gender for women and non-binary people." These varied concepts build up a gender-inclusive approach to French language pedagogy that widens the circle to support non-binary learners and assert inclusive values. Approaching the problem of gender inclusivity historically (and even contemporarily), Dominique Carlini Versini helps readers understand the strong cultural resistance in France to *écriture inclusive* in the chapter, "How Can We Teach French Inclusively? Challenges and Resistance." This resistance has been on full and self-righteous display in the Académie Française's fierce opposition that has only recently culminated in capitulation to the social pressures to feminize French nouns and to adopt a typographical practice of inclusive writing. Taking the long view allows students to see the ideological forces at work on a living language, invites them to reflect on gender dynamics in society at large, and encourages them to think of language as a social phenomenon whose gender undercurrents they might influence as they engage linguistically.

Kathryn A. Dettmer and Brenda A. Dyer argue for greater attention to be paid to students with language-oriented learning disabilities such as dyslexia and audio processing disorders that discourage second language learning in the following chapter, "A Classroom for Everyone: Creating French Courses that Embrace Learning Differences." Basing their approach on Modern Language Aptitude Test competencies and principles of Universal Design of Learning, the authors model how the introductory French language classroom can be made both accessible, challenging, and rewarding for all students. They propose examples for acknowledging different paths to learning French, invoking prior knowledge, fostering collaboration, and modeling metacognitive tools. Finally, they espouse explicit goal setting, scaffolding, and alert responses to patterns in learning as a way of opening language learning to all. In the following chapter, "Diversifying the Curriculum: From Structural Changes to Classroom Lessons," Jessica S. Miller encourages colleagues—even those in small French and Francophone programs—to embark on curricular transformations that can achieve equity, diversity, and inclusion. Miller describes the use of backward and transparent design guided by student learning outcomes to do this otherwise daunting task. For those looking to make incremental modifications in their curricula, Miller models assignments and modules in both intermediate and advanced courses. These detailed examples demonstrate how instructors can lead students to examine cross-culturally questions of sexism, racism, ageism, and ableism or to focus on practices that originate or affect diverse environments and their under-represented populations in Francophone regions around the globe.

Seeing the challenge of representing a diverse French-speaking world as an invitation to give our classrooms a generous and accepting reach, "Embracing the Francophone World across the French Curriculum" encourages instructors of French Studies to use all the levers of diversity at our disposal, from course content to class membership. Stephanie Schechner also suggests addressing global issues such as migration or pairing "classic" French texts with comparable Francophone texts in order to deminoritize Francophone works and the issues they represent. Lastly, Schechner champions balancing the needs of heritage, native, and second language speakers in a diverse and respectful environment that is also cognizant of the current backdrop of political and social polarization.

It is precisely such schisms, coloring conversation in and out of our classrooms, that Eilene Hoft-March addresses in "Unlearning the Language of Divisiveness." She proposes a series of staged strategies in an advanced French and Francophone course designed to challenge stereotyping, break down divisiveness, and honor the principles of diversity and inclusion by underscoring respect, compassion, and engagement. Using the specific example of an undergraduate literature/cinema course on Franco-Maghrebian cultures within French culture, she advocates for a pedagogy of informed, civil discourse that is also sound language and culture pedagogy. This scaffolded practice promotes careful listening; alertness to historically, culturally, and politically loaded terms; understanding of ideological and systemic structures; and strategies for fostering civil dialogue without recourse to a stymying acrimony.

Our final section, "Embracing Cultures/Extending Contexts," expands our discussions to often neglected cultural contexts in order to deepen the understanding of diversity and inclusion to encompass questions of the arts, class, colonialism, immigration, the Jewish Diaspora, and other transcultural identities.

The authors engage students through interdisciplinary lens ranging from hip-hop to Global Foodways, with Francophone intersections with China, the Maghreb, Québec, Haiti, Latin America, Poland, and Israel.

Dominique Licops, in "Strategies for Teaching Diversity and Inclusion in Introductory Literature Courses," makes the case that the student-centered pedagogies stressing equity and inclusion that we use in language classrooms should be applied and enhanced in the foreign literature classroom. In the latter environment, diverse students have greater opportunities to explore difference, power, exclusion, and inclusion. Supported by the Intercultural Teaching Competence model (Dimitrov and Haque), Licops demonstrates a pedagogy that fosters awareness of our own and others' cultural blind spots and openness to diverse ways of knowing. Through her careful readings of text featuring senders and receivers of letters or stories, Licops demonstrates multilateral dynamics through which all participants can learn about "our respective worldviews, strengths, and vulnerabilities."

Lowry Martin's chapter, "The Making of the Other Americas: Discovering the Francospheres of Latin America," develops a perspective on lesser-known cross-cultural influences. Inspired by the students of Latina/o background in his classroom, he created a course on Francospheres, a concept that changes the discussion from one of a "Francophone world … based on imperial conquest, colonization, and decolonization" to the consequences of interculturality rooted in cultural and intellectual contribution and collaboration. The course also refocuses attention on the intertwined histories of France and Latin America and enhances student knowledge of the confluence of US and French histories. This unusual global perspective reminds us of the impact of vast cultural collectives over the serial sovereignties that are more commonly taught.

Two further chapters offer unusual entries into the global connectedness of Francophone cultures. French culture beyond traditional borders is featured in Lauren Ravalico's "Connecting French Studies to the World through Global Foodways." Ravalico discusses the transformation of a course on "The Culture of the French Table" as the basis of a university-wide interdisciplinary program, "Global Foodways," that engaged the academic and regional community in a yearlong exploration of food. The course comes under the aegis of global humanities, a critical field for the advancement of ethical, engaged citizenship and cross-cultural literacy. The chapter describes the design of both the French course and the interdisciplinary program, including the process of securing financial backing to support the high-impact, experiential pedagogical methods essential to understanding cultural diversity as an embodied, sensory experience. Ravalico also analyzes the pedagogical success of the course and its impact on recruitment, retention, and visibility on the campus and in the surrounding community.

Kathryn St. Ours describes an innovative manner to engage her students in a meaningful exploration of diversity, race, ethnicity, gender, sub- and counter-cultures, identity, and intersectionality through a study of Francophone hip-hop in her "A Course in Francophone Hip-Hop Culture." In so doing, her course includes a vast array of French-speaking cultures. This chapter explores street art found in the Maghreb, in France, in Québec, and in Haiti as part of a study of linguistic variations of slang, localisms, and poetic devices. Moving from protest rap to mainstream rap, St. Ours extends her interdisciplinary approach to additional Francophone countries. The chapter presents an engaging French language hip-hop culture course whose approach highlights Francophone transnationalism as well as the local particularities that support cultural sustainability.

Lovia Mondésir's chapter, "'We are all Negroes': Teaching Tolerance from a Haitian Literary Perspective," explores how fiction helps increase diversity and tolerance. Mondésir argues that Jacques Stephen Alexis's novel *Les Arbres musiciens* and Louis-Philippe Dalembert's *Avant que les ombres s'effacent* represent the anti-superstitious campaign of 1942 and the complexity of racial and political alliances in Haiti during World War II. The former focuses on the depiction of the persecution of Vodou practitioners by the Catholic Church. Alexis advocates for religious tolerance based on human dignity. He also portrays political corruption and colorism. Conversely, Dalembert emphasizes the persecution of a Jewish family in Nazi Germany and her immigration to Haiti. He depicts Haiti's involvement in rescuing hundreds of European Jews through immediate naturalization and immigration. Dalembert depicts tolerance as a newfound fraternity beyond racial, religious, and cultural identity. Mondésir's chapter first analyzes the ethical dimension of fiction and the intersectionality of race, religion, and class in Alexis's novel. Second, it investigates the fragility of identity and the figure of the foreigner, using examples of tolerance in Dalembert's work. Third, the chapter explores the anthropological shift introduced by the Haitian Creole word "*Nèg*" (Negro) in Dalembert's work. Mondésir confirms the relevance of both novelists' contributions to a study on tolerance and inclusivity for students, and their place in a course on Francophone Caribbean Literature and Culture.

Literature provides a wonderful entry into engaging students in meaningful discussions of diversity in the following chapter by Nancy M. Arenberg. While large research universities incorporate the language of diversity into their strategic plans, hiring initiatives, and graduate and undergraduate courses, Arenberg argues in her chapter "Introducing Diversity into the Graduate Classroom: Teaching Jewish Francophone Writers," that creating an engaging course that aligns with the oft-stated diversity objectives can challenge faculty. Her chapter focuses on a graduate French literature course that incorporates issues of ethnicity, tolerance, racism, gender, and identity into a survey of selected Jewish minority writers who write in French. Her multidisciplinary approach situates the texts historically to aid students in better understanding the political climate that fueled the rise in France in the 1930s and persists today. Exposing students to current feminist theories, the Jewish Diaspora, and Jewish "Otherness," Arenberg enables her students to interpret the included texts in insightful ways. They thus discover intersections of ethnicity, intolerance, gender, racism, and identity, which helps them better understand such issues in previous readings of canonical works. Her readings include diverse Francophone voices through the works of Patrick Modiano, Albert Memmi, Jean-Paul Sartre, Simone Veil, Colette Fellous, Monique Bosco, and Chochana Boukhobza. Arenberg's chapter provides practical ideas to generate stimulating questions related to oft-neglected salient issues, and thus creates a more global learning environment.

In the closing chapter, "Promoting Mutual Understanding and Inclusion in the French Classroom through French, Israeli and Polish Post-Holocaust Life Writing," E. Nicole Meyer presents an interdisciplinary course that includes narratives of multiple origins (including those of the Holocaust) to help students to move beyond stereotypes and the hate-filled speech of their current world. Designed to inform and address an area where students are often misinformed, the course explores memoirs, autobiographical texts, short stories, and poems that voice pain and suffering further providing an entry point to increased empathy. In short, Meyer aims to ask important questions through an intercultural, interdisciplinary lens that directly confronts memory, history, identity, anti-Semitism, and mutual understanding, and requires looking within the self for answers. In addition, Meyer explains how she expands student audiences to include the voices of non-traditional students aged 60 through 85, thus adding another level of diversity through building a more inclusive classroom community. Such a course increases mutual understanding and serves as a model of how to infuse a diversity of voices while engaging traditional and non-traditional students through reading the experiences of others from places and backgrounds they have never experienced.

In "Essential Reads," E. Nicole Meyer compiles suggestions for "must reads" for anyone interested in creating a bookshelf of diversity and inclusion reflecting perspectives from the various viewpoints represented in our book.

Diversity and inclusion have finally entered the academic conversation in meaningful ways, due to pivotal changes in our society leading to the understanding that systemic structures, thinking, and reflexes must be addressed. The variety and depth of the essays contained within this timely volume explore important, often neglected perspectives on teaching essential questions related to diversity and inclusion. Now is the time to take on the deep-seated schisms in our profession and our societies. No longer can we avoid seizing the cultural opportunity to teach desperately needed ways of addressing the many facets of diversity and inclusion. Ignorance of the tools contained within this volume is no longer acceptable. We must become aware. We must help our students, colleagues, and administrators to understand the absolutely crucial nature of change.

# SECTION I
# Unscripting and Claiming Identities

# 1
# QUEER PEDAGOGY FOR A QUEER(ER) FRANCOPHONE CLASSROOM

*CJ Gomolka*

It is worth the risk, I believe, of a perhaps overly dramatized reductionism to say that my pedagogy is wholly informed by my queerness. As a student, from undergraduate to doctoral work in literary and cultural studies, I often ceded to the corrosive, ultimately self-effacing abnegation of any expectation that course material would mirror my experiences. Even today, queerness in pedagogical and methodological exploits is often conspicuously absent leaving queer students with fewer resources, or at best, heteronormatively inflected ones, that might evince, reflect on, or reify their lives. A direct consequence of this is the promotion of a sense of entitlement for straight- and cis-identified students who consistently see their histories, languages, and cultures unfolded before them in ready-made formats specifically designed for maximum legibility to themselves and that rarely, if ever, challenge these positions of epistemological and representational hegemony. A pedagogy that intentionally centers queer experiences is important not just because it would envision these resources as no less than tools for survival for queer-identified students. It would also imagine its core components as working toward community and alliance-building, epistemological razings and restructurings, as challenging queer-eradicating impulses and therefore (re)tuning students' awareness to the neglected frequencies of historical, cultural, and linguistic contributions of queers. There is, to my mind, a decided urgency to this queer-focused pedagogy in French and Francophone Studies, a discipline that has historically assumed especially truculent stances against the communitarian encroachment of identity-based politics and disciplines often imaged as so many epistemological bombardments on an otherwise unshakable universalist foundation.

The queer pedagogical approach that we must adopt in our courses envisions the 21st-century French and Francophone classroom as one that must necessarily address students where they live. To do so, this pedagogy must visibilize,

DOI: 10.4324/9781003126461-2

legitimize, validate, and interrogate the existential debates on cultural and political hetero- and cis-normativity that circumscribe queer and non-queer students' existence. It must provide mirrors and windows for (self)reflexivity and empathic mindfulness. It must attend to a growing interest in and concern for the globalization of certain identitary structures and their attendant linguistic, cultural, and ideological constructs. It must recognize and problematize the processes of normalization happening within queer and non-queer communities both locally and globally. This queer pedagogy must do all this while providing the tools and encouragement necessary to access a linguistic platform from which to hold these broad conceptualizations, and the materials used to think through them, palpably accountable. Finally, this pedagogy must amplify the voice and purpose of anti-racist, anti-sexist, anti-imperialist, anti-ableist, and decolonial pedagogies to claim any legitimacy. Any queer pedagogy lacking these intimately linked ideological orientations can only hobble towards a liberatory vision of education and will always already fail to be queer.

This queer pedagogy as well as the resources and materials curated to mobilize it provide a dynamic interface between the acute needs and perhaps more supple epistemological frameworks of queer-identified students and the threadbare, socially tailored tapestry of preconceptions and assumptions, or in many cases absence of knowledge, that many queer and non-queer students bring, unwittingly or not, to courses with or without a queer focus. Admittedly, this type of pedagogy requires an exhaustive and perhaps unruly commitment to the generative and dynamic properties of queerness to knock students from the gravitational pull of heteronormative, cisnormative, ableist, race-neutral, imperialist ubiquity. To my mind, the vitality of the demand that students bring to the classroom for this type of pedagogy makes it no less than an academic and intellectual imperative.

## Queer(ed) Outcomes

Thinking about queer pedagogies and queering pedagogies in this way allows us to contemplate critically the, in some cases, awesome failures of French and Francophone programs and departments to teach to the presence of the queer bodies and identities that populate, or could potentially populate, our classrooms. Both Stacey Waite and bell hooks have centered the importance of bodies in conceptions of pedagogy and pedagogical praxis. By bodies they include the "bodies of knowledge" with which we engage and that we valorize in our classrooms, but also the physical bodies that might embody that knowledge, those bodies' relation to power systems and structures, institutional understandings and imprimaturs of what counts as a "body of knowledge," as well as our contributions to the unintelligibility of certain bodies (both physical and of knowledge) because of the pedagogical and methodological choices we make or do not make.

A quick glance at many French and Francophone curricula reveals that we have, for a long time, made pedagogical and curricular decisions that exclude the queer bodies of knowledge that many of our students embody, not conceptualizing our courses and materials with them in mind. This is also to say, of course, that we have ignored how these queer bodies, and the battleground scars of living outside dominant and normalized modalities of being, testify to a history of profoundly meaningful experiences, intimacies, geographic and epistemological odysseys, and identitary experiments that might bring to our discipline important and prismatic cultural, linguistic, global, and translocal values and literacies. Perhaps just as importantly, these values and literacies will challenge us to rethink our pedagogical role in forming and informing holistically educated student populations as well as help us to reconceptualize how our courses and classrooms could more successfully stand as passports to understanding global citizenship, examples of humanistic training, cross-listed investments in diversity and inclusion. Our courses and classrooms, of course, already do many of these things, but we can do them better. And we must, because how could we possibly expect our classes to serve as cultural and linguistic interfaces between our students and the Francophone world if we fail to expose the beautiful queerness of that world?

A queer(ed) pedagogical orientation to the French and Francophone classroom will produce 1) more globally engaged polyglots; 2) more critically aware intellectuals; and 3) more historically and culturally informed Francophiles. A queer Francophone classroom will produce globally engaged polyglots who recognize the critical importance of being (poly)linguistically capable, globally oriented, and socially engaged citizens in a contemporary society that includes, but often violently excludes, queer representation and identification. I understand (poly)linguistically capable in its broadest sense to include capacity for linguistic expression in another language, but also aptitude to engage linguistically and empathetically with queer discourses, vocabularies, and identities. This necessitates an education that centers the processes of globalization, and concurrent localizations, happening contemporarily, but also historically, in the Francophone world, with all its attendant political, literary, cultural, and linguistic developments and evolutions and what this means for queer and non-queer populations. A queer Francophone classroom will produce more critically aware intellectuals who approach linguistic and socio-cultural content through a variety of critical and analytical frameworks mediated by the recognition of the inherent biases embedded in the power systems and interpretive models that inform these frameworks. To do this, a queer Francophone classroom will need to place a high premium on the development of a model of a Francophone intellectual that is both liberally educated about and linguistically and culturally sensitive to the structures and patterns of hetero- and cis-normativity that exist in the languages, cultures, histories, and epistemologies of the Francophone world and that we often unconsciously teach. Lastly, a queer Francophone classroom will produce historically and culturally informed Francophiles who understand the linguistic and cultural specificity of the Francophone world and how this specificity intersects with broader topics of contemporary and historical interest in such areas as gender and sexuality studies, post-colonial and decolonial studies, feminisms, critical race, and anti-racist studies among others.

As Francophiles ourselves, we cannot underestimate the importance of this position of linguistic and cultural ambassadorship and the privileged responsibilities that come with it: providing pluralistic cultural and linguistic context to socio-historical information; decentering and decolonizing master and canonic narratives that paper over and/or marginalize non-white, non-heterosexual, cis-representations of Francophone identity; and allowing for the amplification of the queer histories, stories, languages and vocabularies, epistemologies and ideologies that have historically and contemporarily spangled the Francophone world.

## Queering Lower-Level Introductory French Courses

Most lower-level French language manuals follow a similar methodological path: themed chapters proceeding through familiar units on family, friends, professions, and areas of study, food, housing, travel, the arts, and health that often awkwardly comingle language acquisition and cultural competency. As a consequence, the cultural points to be presented in these chapters are habitually tethered to granular sub-sections that often reduce content to digestible, if perfunctory, cultural fragments. This can lead to superficial presentations of well-known cultural stereotypes like café culture, the number of *bises* (kisses) given in different Francophone regions, types of *pâtisseries*, or outdated and heteronormative information about "traditional" family units and gendered language use. And while many of these aspects of French and Francophone cultural production are important, more contemporary discussions on France's continued imperial structures, queer identities, trans★ grammars, decolonial activism, Afro-feminism, *banlieue* culture and spatial discrimination, curational activism and representational ethics, among others are omitted because of the more complicated linguistic structures needed to respectfully discuss them in French or because their abrasive content sits uncomfortably within units meant to attract students to the discipline, rather than be divisive. These omissions that shy away from the presentation and examination of difference in favor of more conservative, generalizable presentations of French and Francophone cultural material have as a salient consequence the reproduction of the cherished and sacrosanct universalist ideologies of neutrality that no doubt inform the choices of the authors and editors of these manuals, something that also deserves discussion and critical attention. It is important to consider how these informational lapses in our lower-level courses do a disservice to our students who get a more "approachable" version of French and Francophone culture *ab initio*, one that ultimately subdues "disorderly" content through glossy descriptions of France and the Francophone world, leading to students, in many ways, unprepared for the more complex topics of our upper-level courses as well as unaware of the myriad ways that our courses intersect in interesting ways with other disciplines and studies programs.

What follows are preliminary suggestions for adding some queer(er) discussions into your lower-level French and Francophone classrooms ending with a simplified architecture for an intermediate/advanced-level course on contemporary French and Francophone podcasts informed by queer pedagogy. While the discussions in lower-level classes, and the articles used to prompt them, are mainly in English, they provide important opportunities to offer unique French lexicons that will no doubt enrich the lower-level manuals we use; to practice question and sentence formation in the target language; to consider cross- and trans-cultural language use and linguistic lived experience; and to discuss grammar, all of which, of course, contribute to language acquisition, cultural competency, and, in many cases, global and trans-local linguistic sharings and transfers.

## *Chapitre préliminaire: Présentons-nous! (Preliminary Chapter: Let's Get Acquainted!)*

Preliminary chapters in most lower-level French manuals often pay scant attention to the gendered nature of the French language, shrugging it off as the inconsequential by-product of a process of diachronic linguistic morphology that deserves little real critical attention in lower-level courses. The very fact that most explanations of grammatical and identitary gender use in French are found in some variation of a "forms and functions" section reduces linguistic gender use to its structural, meaning grammatical, components. To be sure, these reductive explanations of linguistic gender use risk blithely excising the socio-cultural, epistemological, and performative identitary function of those very structures. That these explanations are often rehearsed in introductory sections focused on self-presentation, and therefore self-affirmation and determination, without even a soupçon of information on French linguistic inclusivity or the fluid and novel uses of gendered pronouns and trans★ grammars by trans, genderqueer, and non-binary French and Francophone individuals seems at best irresponsible, at worst violently exclusionary and existentially disbarring. Rather than running roughshod over the identitary and self-determinative complexities of gendered grammatical constructions, these simplistic sections could provide felicitous opportunities for our students to engage with queer linguistics in a variety of ways including the intersection of feminist social justice discourses and language use (Timsit); inclusive language use and writing in French (Benjamin; Deborde; Haddad); the existential and linguistic challenges produced at the intersection of genderqueer, trans, and non-binary identification and discourse in a highly gendered language (Crouch; Bonneville); the traditionalist battleground stance of the Académie française opposite ever-encroaching French-language evolutions, international imports, and phonetic modifications (Chazan; Daldorph); the constellation of trans, non-binary, and queer Francophone Youtubers whose narrated lived experiences expose the ways in which (English and French) language(s) forms and informs the conditions of possibility for self-affirmation, determination, and identification (Badler; De la Vega; Léon; Lveq).[1]

## Chapitre: La famille et les relations (Chapter: Family and Relationships)

I am often surprised by the traditionalist bent of most lower-level chapters on the family and familial relations in France. While many updated editions of lower-level language manuals perfunctorily point to the 1999 PaCS legislation and the 2013 *Mariage pour tous* (Marriage for All) decision as socio-cultural inflection points linked to broader conversations concerning family and filiation in France, without every really saying as much, few use the opportunity to take deeper dives into the socio-cultural, epistemological, and ideological frameworks that provide the architectural blueprints against or for such decisions. Indeed, the counter-arguments churned up during debates on marriage equality by groups like *la Manif pour tous*,[2] still very much alive in France today, are strikingly absent from these chapters. Socio-political movements against the PaCS legislation and particularly the 2013 *loi Taubira*[3] produced an array of demonstration posters that can be used over the course of a class period to discuss the types of discourses (communism, socialism, neoliberalism, "reproductive futurism" (Edelman), racism, (post)colonialism, religion, economic liberalism, universalism, biological determinism, "traditionalism," homophobia, transphobia, genderism) often mobilized against marriage equality in France.[4] These posters are particularly useful as the language summoned for counter-messaging (grammar, vocabulary, and syntax) is simplified for visual and aesthetic purposes allowing students to contemplate the ways in which visual and material culture are affected by lexical choice and linguistic constraint. Perhaps more importantly, the aesthetics of the posters and the specific discourses mustered against marriage equality that adorn them have rhizomatic genealogies linking students to expanded branches of socio-cultural information that could be used to nourish conversations about France's continued (post)colonial epistemologies. These include a racially exaggerated image of former Minister of Justice, Christiane Taubira, disciplining a child with the *code civil*, hyperbolically marqueed with a reproductive futurist slogan: *sauvons les enfants de la loi Taubira* (Let's save the children from the Taubira law), the intertwining of universalist and ecumenical-traditionalist, socio-political positionings (an image of a rabbi, a priest, and an imam attest: *croyants, non croyants peu importe la confession: un père + une mère pour la filiation* (Believers, or non-believers, regardless of confession: one father + one mother for filiation), as well as France's socialist history and its relationship to sexual revolution (four raised fists brandishing the colors of the French flag: *touche pas au mariage, occupe-toi du chômage!* (Hands off marriage, Get a handle on unemployment!). Finally, the 2016 documentary *La sociologue et l'ourson*, written and filmed by Étienne Chaillou and Mathias Théry, is another approach to introducing and engaging with this topic: dynamically and ludically staged through puppets, the film tracks the moments leading up to the 2013 marriage debates from diverse perspectives, but namely that of the documentarist, Mathias Théry, and his relationship with his mother,

Irène Théry, a sociologist called upon to professionally testify to the historical ecology of family, filiation, and the social in France during the debates.[5]

## *Chapitre: Les traditions et la tenue (Chapter: Traditions and Clothing)*

A basso continuo of most lower-level French chapters on clothing is the intoning of tradition in primarily Hexagonal, white, bourgeois terms. Difference, when present, often calls out in a strained *sotto voce* from the distant margins of the page where *la mode* or *les traditions africaines, antillaises, maghrébines* (fashion or African, Antillean, Maghrebi traditions) is positioned, through chapter appendices or sidelined boxes, as always already existing outside Hexagonal borders, rehashing polarized binaries between the West and non-West, and situating students as voyeuristically peering into "untraditional" expressions of Francophone identity. The very structure and editorial choices of many of these chapters—the clothing presented; how they are presented; who is wearing them; assessment strategies and pedagogical practices on these traditions suggested by the manuals (are assessment questions to be answered through multiple choice or critical thinking? how are we asked to present material?); the lexical choices used to present them; the percentage of presentation space in reference to more "traditional" sartorial choices and traditions—could spark dynamic and informative debates concerning how methodological and pedagogical decisions are often of a piece of a politics of inclusion and/or exclusion that centers, erases, and/or stereotypes certain identities and cultures as opposed to others. For example, with 20 percent of the some 66 million people living in France being immigrants or children of immigrants, two-thirds coming from outside Europe, and the almost 6 million Muslims living within the *hexagone* (Fleming), we might legitimately question the absence of the hijab or burka as common sartorial possibilities in these chapters, not to mention, with their representational erasure, the elision of their histories, their uses in decolonial feminist traditions and socio-political positionings, as well as France's continued juridical rebuff of them within the public sphere. More recently, the "veil question" resurfaced during the COVID-19 pandemic when, after a mandatory mask policy was adopted across France, "an observant Muslim woman want[ing] to get on the Paris Metro … would be required to remove her burqa and replace it with a mask" (McAuley). The irony of this sartorial dilemma was not lost on journalist and host of the anti-racist podcast *Kiffe ta race*, Rokhaya Diallo, who stated that the mandatory mask policy has revealed:

> that the so-called 'burqa' ban has nothing to do with the incompatibility of face coverings with the French way of life and everything to do with the state's reluctance to include visible Muslims into the French national identity.
> *(Diallo)*

These important discussions find queer expression in Franco-Moroccan performer/artist 2Fik and his work. Through a series of interconnected, fabricated identities and identitary experiences (a total of 15), *tableaux vivants*, and street performances in *dramatis personae*, 2Fik stages an artistic coup meant to challenge the socio-cultural stereotypes associated with Muslim populations both within and without the Francophone world.[6] His work wrests open a space from which to question how traditional understandings of Islam and gender might be reinterpreted through queer art and performance as well as through practices and strategies of disidentification (Muñoz). Moreover, 2Fik's work could be used to explore the intersection of gendered and sexualized structures and frameworks with culture and religion. Finally, his photography and interactive performances allow us to contemplate queer constructions of identity as an interesting way to recast obscurantist formulations of Islam as well as the novel and ludic ways queerness might be expressed through Islamic traditions and cultures.

## (Novel) Voices of the Francophone World in Upper-Level Courses

If we understand the voices of marginalized populations as critical vectors through which social justice discourse and activism emerge, we might be more apt to saturate our courses with them. Podcasts can provide a felicitous bridge between our classrooms, these voices, and social justice activism. The popularity, in the social media landscape and among our students, of podcasts that tackle a diverse array of contemporary and historical issues from multivalent perspectives cannot be understated. Besides providing information through a dynamic and transportable medium, many of these podcasts approach topics from a social justice perspective encouraging students to develop empathetic listening skills that are translatable to everyday human interactions, especially the complex and challenging social interactions on college campuses. In the French and Francophone classroom, podcasts can be used as required listening for given topics, suggested listening to expand the limits of a given topic, or as the foundational architecture for courses on contemporary French and Francophone issues.

"Speaking from the Margins: Podcasts Changing the Way We Understand the Francophone World" is an upper-level course that uses a constellation of podcasts to teach contemporary French-language use, oral and aural French skills, critical analysis and cultural competency all through the voices of historically marginalized populations. The course is structured around 5 podcasts: *Camille* (Binge Audio),[7] *Kiffe ta race* (Binge Audio),[8] *Les couilles sur la table* (Binge Audio),[9] *Miroir, miroir* (Binge Audio),[10] *Parler comme jamais* (Binge Audio).[11] Each podcast has a central topic of investigation and exploration (sex and gender, race, masculinities, aesthetic media and societal standards, and language respectively) refracted through a variety of viewpoints. Podcasts can serve as individual units of a course spread out over the semester. Specific podcasts can also be supplemented with articles, blogs, websites, and YouTube videos/discussions (often mentioned on the podcasts) to make larger units. In addition, discrete episodes easily complement already prepared courses on literature, culture, history, language/linguistics, especially when using survey-type manuals that often focus on canonical information and representation.

Assignments are varied and might include: 1) mini-, bi-weekly podcasts created by the students based on the topics and discussions of episodes; 2) written op-eds that incorporate outside research on a given episode; 3) more expansive research-style papers on a given topic mentioned in a podcast; 4) comparative written papers or oral presentations that find common cause between represented marginalized groups; 5) transcultural examinations of shared socio-political struggles; 6) critical analyses of the form and function of the podcast medium more generally; and 7) full-length final projects that require the creation of an imaginary podcast. Examples include the podcast's website and description, proposed episodes with linked articles and information, a sample episode created with a classmate, or if your geographical location allows for it, interviews with Francophone identities, as well as a report on the topic's relevance to contemporary questions in the Francophone world.

## Conclusion

Providing a space in our classrooms for these conversations and representations is all the more important when we consider our pedagogical choices as partially fashioning the cultural and identitary backdrop that students will expect when visiting a Francophone country and that they will use to (mis)judge what they see and experience there. Remembering that our pedagogical platform is also a social justice platform, one that has the power to (dis)orient world views, opinions, and attitudes of our students, it is incumbent upon us to do this important work.

## Notes

1 Some of these resources would be more appropriate for upper-level classes as they are in French; for a short discussion on introducing French queer studies in the Francophone classroom, see Gomolka, 2019.
2 The *Manif pour tous* or Protest for All is a heterogenous, counter-protest group often, but not always, from conservative political ideologies who oppose(d) France's "Gay Marriage" law.
3 The 17 May 2013 *loi Taubira* provided same-sex couples the right to marriage equality.
4 These posters can be found at https://genere.hypotheses.org/385 and http://leplus.nouvelobs.com/contribution/845577-mariage-gay-le-gouvernement-a-laisse-les-opposants-dire-n-importe-quoi-sur-la-filiation.html among other sites.
5 A meritorious documentary that, unfortunately, fails epically to consider the racialized aspects of *le mariage pour tous* and the notion of LGBTQ community.
6 2Fiks website offers professors a treasure-trove of artistic productions, interviews, and commentary (both in French and English) that can be used at all levels of French instruction: https://2fikornot2fik.com/fr.
7 *Camille*, hosted by Camille Regache, focuses on deconstructing ideas about gender and sexuality.
8 *Kiffe ta race*, hosted by Rokhaya Diallo and Grace Ly, explores questions related to racialized identities in France and in the Francophone world.

9 *Les couilles sur la table*, hosted by Victoire Tuaillon, interrogates cultural, social, historical, and juridical discourses related to masculinity.
10 *Miroir, miroir*, hosted by Jennifer Padjemi, focuses on understanding and deconstructing imposed standards of beauty, worth, and ability in the media and society.
11 *Parler comme jamais*, hosted by Laélia Véron and Maria Candea, explores the relationship between language and its users.

## References

2 Fik. *2fikornottofik*. 2fikornot2fik.com.
Badler, Laura. "Parlons non-binarité." YouTube, April 23, 2018, www.youtube.com/watch?v=r_FEl0eC0x0&list=PLBO9SfbIevIxzLKJ1P5pwEWR4xpxLeNd4&index=2.
—. "Naître dans le mauvais corps." YouTube, June 15, 2018, www.youtube.com/watch?v=h7-JBOGft7E&list=PLBO9SfbIevIxzLKJ1P5pwEWR4xpxLeNd4&index=2.
Benjamin, Alex. "Le Langage Neutre en Français: Pronoms et Accords à L'écrit et à L'oral." *Genre!*, April 19, 2017, entousgenresblog.wordpress.com/2017/04/19/quels-pronoms-neutres-en-francais-et-comment-les-utiliser.
Bonneville, Floriane. "Why Some French-Speaking Non-Binary People Don't Seek Treatment in Their Language | CBC News." CBCnews, January 23, 2019, www.cbc.ca/news/canada/windsor/why-some-french-speaking-non-binary-people-avoid-treatment-in-french-1.4984997.
Bryson, Mary and Suzanne de Castell. "Queer Pedagogy Makes Im/Perfect." *Canadian Journal of Education*, vol. 18, no. 3, 1993, pp. 285–305.
Candea, Maria and Laélia Véron, hosts. "Parler comme jamais. Binge Audio." www.binge.audio/category/parler-comme-jamais.
Chaillou, Étienne and Mathias Théry, directors. *La sociologue et l'ourson*. Docks 66, 2016.
Chazan, David. "Gender-Inclusive French Is a 'Mortal Danger' to the Language, Académie Française Warns." *The Telegraph*, 27 October 2017, www.telegraph.co.uk/news/2017/10/27/gender-inclusive-french-mortal-danger-language-academie-francaise.
Crouch, Erin. "What Happens if You're Genderqueer—But Your Native Language is Gendered?" *The Establishment*, 7 September 2017, theestablishment.co/what-happens-if-youre-genderqueer-but-your-native-language-is-gendered-d1c009dc5fcb/index.html.
Daldorph, Brenna. "Académie Française Rejects Push to Make French Language Less Masculine." France 24, 27 October 2017, www.france24.com/en/20171027-academie-francaise-gender-inclusive-spellings-mortal-danger-french.
Deborde, Juliette. "Écriture Inclusive: Le Genre Neutre Existe-t-Il Vraiment En Français?" *Libération*, 28 November 2017, www.liberation.fr/france/2017/11/28/ecriture-inclusive-le-genre-neutre-existe-t-il-vraiment-en-francais_1613016.
De la Vega, Adrian. "Adrián de la Vega, Youtubeur Trans. " YouTube, April 24, 2018, www.youtube.com/watch?v=7XtH6k-bfCo.
Diallo, Rokhaya. "Coronavirus Exposed the Real Reasons behind France's 'Burqa Ban.'" *Al Jazeera*, May 15, 2020, www.aljazeera.com/indepth/opinion/coronavirus-exposed-real-reasons-france-burqa-ban-200514105218122.html.
—. "Visages masqués, la contradiction à visage découvert." *Slate*, May 20, 2020, www.slate.fr/story/190779/covid-19-loi-voile-integral-niqab-obligation-port-masque-contradiction-assimilationnisme.
Diallo, Rokhaya and Grace Ly, hosts. "Kiffe ta race." Binge Audio." www.binge.audio/category/kiffetarace.

Duggan, Lisa. *The Twilight of Equality? Neoliberalism, Cultural Politics, and the Attack on Democracy*. Beacon, 2004.
Edelman, Lee. *No Future: Queer Theory and the Death Drive*. Duke UP, 2004.
Fleming, Crystal Marie. *Resurrecting Slavery: Racial Legacies and White Supremacy in France*. Temple UP, 2017.
Gomolka, CJ. "Queering the Francophone Classroom: Towards a More Inclusive Pedagogy." *Rethinking the French Classroom: New Approaches to Teaching Contemporary French and Francophone Women*. Edited by E. Nicole Meyer and Joyce Johnson. Routledge, 2019, pp. 150–159.
Haddad, Raphaël. "Manuel d'écriture inclusive: faites progresser l'égalité femmes/hommes par votre manière d'écrire. Mots-clés", www.motscles.net/ecriture-inclusive.
hooks, bell. *Teaching to Transgress: Education as the Practice of Freedom*. Routledge, 1994.
Léon, Clö. "Quel est mon genre? #2 (être genderfluid, le regard des autres, coming-out)." YouTube, May 9, 2017, www.youtube.com/watch?v=IAtnfXVbTIM&list=PLBO9SfbIevIxzLKJ1P5pwEWR4xpxLeNd4&index=2.
Luhmann, Susanne. "Queering/Querying Pedagogy? Or, Pedagogy is a Pretty Queer Thing." *Queer Theory in Education*. Edited by William F. Pinar. Taylor and Francis Group, pp. 120–132, 1998.
Lveq. "A Propos De L'expression 'Trans Binaire'." La Vie En Queer, 9 September 2018, lavieenqueer.wordpress.com/2018/07/04/a-propos-de-lexpression-trans-binaire. Accessed 18 September 2020.
Mayo, Cris and Nelson M. Rodriguez, editors. *Queer Pedagogies: Theory, Praxis, Politics*. Springer, 2019.
McAuley, James. "France Mandates Masks to Control the Coronavirus. Burqa's Remain Banned." *The Washington Post*, May 10, 2020, www.washingtonpost.com/world/europe/france-face-masks-coronavirus/2020/05/09/6fbd50fc-8ae6-11ea-80df-d24b35a568ae_story.html.
Muñoz, José Esteban. *Disidentifications: Queers of Color and the Performance of Politics*. U of Minnesota P, 1999.
Naze, Alain. *Manifeste contre la normalisation gay*. La Fabrique, 2017.
Padjemi, Jennifer, host. "Miroir, miroir. " Binge Audio, www.binge.audio/category/miroirmiroir.
Regache, Camille, host. "Camille." Binge Audio, www.binge.audio/camille.
Timsit, Annabelle. "The Push to Make French Gender-Neutral: Can Changing the Structure of a Language Improve Women's Status in Society?" *The Atlantic*, November 24, 2017, www.theatlantic.com/international/archive/2017/11/inclusive-writing-france-feminism/545048.
Tuaillon, Victoire, host. "Les couilles sur la table." Binge Audio, www.binge.audio/category/les-couilles-sur-la-table.
Villaverde, Leila E. and Dana M. Stachowiak. "Introductions/Orientations: Queer Pedagogies, Social Foundations, and Praxis." *Queer Pedagogies: Theory, Praxis, Politics*. Edited by Cris Mayo and Nelson M. Rodriguez. Springer, 2019. pp. 127–44.
Waite, Stacey. *Teaching Queer: Radical Possibilities for Writing and Knowing*. U of Pittsburgh P, 2017.

# 2

# A STARTER KIT FOR RETHINKING TRANS REPRESENTATION AND INCLUSION IN FRENCH L2 CLASSROOMS

*Kris Aric Knisely*

In language teaching, just as in the broader world, we cannot separate language from the people using, doing, and continually (re)shaping the language. In this way, identity is an inherent part of language learning and use. Mounting professional calls for diversity and inclusion (e.g., ACTFL) echo, at least in part, this assertion. To respond, educators can and should explicitly attend to identity (re)construction in their pedagogical approach. This is in keeping with research demonstrating the ways in which identity-focused pedagogies facilitate second language (L2) development (Darvin and Norton). As is the focus of this chapter, this creates space for educational stakeholders to recognize and contend with the profound importance of critical and respectful engagement with gender and sexuality in contemporary society. Framing and often driving this conversation in L2 teaching, scholars in queer applied linguistics (ALx) have begun to directly attend to sexual and gender diversity in L2 curricula, textbooks, research, and pedagogy (e.g., Nelson; Paiz; Sauntson). However, trans, non-binary, and gender-non-conforming (TGNC) bodies, lives, and concerns remain marginalized in L2 teaching and learning and are even more scantly treated in French specifically (e.g., Kosnick; Provitola). Owing largely to a lack of training and materials, most instructors, students, and institutions alike are ill equipped to treat TGNC topics and to meet the needs of TGNC learners.

As such, this chapter aims to provide a jumping-off point for educators new to queer pedagogies, broadly, and to French ALx[1] specifically. It is critical to make clear that the work of social justice[2] is always ongoing. There is no end to the process of liberation and, in following, process and product are always entangled (Spade, *Normal Life*, etc. 1–2). The idea that equity and justice can be achieved through checklists, toolkits, and examples is a desire rooted in whiteness and in normativity (Ahmed). We must release this idea that things can be fixed so as to

DOI: 10.4324/9781003126461-3

learn to sit with any discomfort we might feel and to learn how to begin to exist in community with TGNC people, including our students. It is in and through learning to be accomplices in equity and justice[3] that you will learn to move beyond the suggestions, resources, and examples herein. My ultimate goals are to provide sources for further reading alongside initial insight into concrete ways that materials, pedagogical strategies, and the broader curriculum can be adapted to provide equitable opportunities for TGNC language learners, affirm TGNC lives, and increase respectful engagement with TGNC people.

## Queering L2: Classrooms

There are numerous possible equity-focused pedagogies that could guide gender-just language teaching. Critical social justice and feminist pedagogies, for example, share an attention to making explicit the hidden curriculum, power structures, and personally held biases and can be useful in searching "for gender liberation within and alongside of anti-racist and decolonial pedagogical strategies, as these forms of oppression are inextricably linked" (Nicolazzo, 129). This chapter, however, is framed by trans-affirming, queer inquiry-based pedagogies[4] (TAQIBPs), so as to foreground both gender and language. In TAQIBPs, educators seek to collaborate *with* students to create space for marginalized voices and restively problematize all identities, discourses, and normativities. At their core, TAQIBPs must seek to "shift the hegemonic ways in which we communicate, or are expected to communicate, gender" (LeMaster and Johnson, 192) and sexuality, making explicit the role of language in indexing and performing identities (Paiz). This is foundational to equipping individuals with the linguistic and symbolic resources needed for self-congruent self-representation and to advocate for themselves and others in the L2. Knowing how to use language critically, thoughtfully, and fluently with regard to gender and sexuality is akin to contemporary literacy, given their omnipresence as organizers of social life. As exemplified later, these goals lend themselves to myriad strategies.

Regardless of the particular strategies used, educators must actively work to dismantle marginalization, violence, and oppression, without reifying discourses that limit understandings of TNGC people to said domain as "we may be from oppression, but are not solely constituted of oppression," (Nicolazzo, 123). At its most basic level, this implies resisting cis-normativity and assuming that trans individuals are present, whether we are aware of it or not.[5] As we develop structures, practices, and critical habits of mind that create visibility and value around TGNC lives, it becomes evident that *everyone* benefits from thoughtful, sustained engagement with myriad culturally and linguistically situated experiences of gender. In these practices, however, we must forgo any urge to perform the role of LGBTQ+ expert in favor of focusing on a deep, critical, and sustained engagement with queer lives (Paiz). TAQIBPs call for de-centering power in the classroom by exploring *with* students, and thus an iterative, self-reflective, and co-constructed pedagogy[6]—*not* exhaustive knowledge—is needed to create conditions for meaningful inclusion and representation. This focus on critical, self-reflective practice for *everyone* further makes clear that queering the L2 classroom is a continuous, collective responsibility, which cannot be left to community insiders alone.[7]

Centered on these underpinnings, the subsequent sections illustrate possibilities for situating trans knowledges in French L2 classrooms. As there is no one way to embody queerness or TAQIBPs, each reader will need to adapt these principles, strategies, and commitments to be locally relevant. This implies collaboration, co-construction, and dialogue with all stakeholders and necessitates prioritizing TGNC students, without tokenizing or putting the onus of queering the classroom on them, whether or not they choose to disclose.[8] Just as visibility alone is not liberatory, we need not know someone's existence as TGNC in order to unscript gender in our pedagogies and curricula.[9]

## *Mapping French ALx*

Teaching *to* and *about* TGNC individuals requires us to draw upon that which is culturally and linguistically familiar to students (gendered normativities and the discourses that subvert them). We must simultaneously connect these familiar localized, individual, and societal conceptions of gender with those that might be less familiar. If for some the familiar is restricted to binary, cisgender, heteronormative, North American, Anglophone articulations of gender, others might be able to draw upon a broader repertoire (e.g., non-binary, trans, non-Western, non-Anglophone).[10] As we lay bare L1 and L2 normativities and explore alternatives, we must model respectful engagement and equip students with linguistic forms[11] to index and perform TGNC-ness in readable ways.

Facilitating this task, an emergent body of literature[12] has academically codified what has long been known and experienced by many: TGNC individuals live in Francophone contexts and make up a nascent linguistic community, even if French-speaking societies have been slow to adapt (Ashley). Where traditional French grammar produces violent non-binary erasure, TGNC people are subverting the language to more readily encode non-binary experiences of social gender (Knisely, "Teaching Trans"). This dovetails with mounting recognition of TGNC individuals as a non-trivial part of the US population. Singular they and neopronouns, which have a long history of use in queer communities, are increasingly present in inclusive educational practices and students' L1 repertoires, lived experiences, and expectations (Clarkson; Spade).

To respond to the need for L2 equivalents, we can leverage studies that outline myriad forms used by TGNC Francophones[13] in order to offer linguistic *possibilities*, rather than prescribing norms that would reproduce the violence they are intended to subvert. Framed by explicit conversations about normativity in language,[14] linguistic autonomy, and the right to self-definition, we can dialogue with students about the nascency and variability of non-binary language and present forms that have been empirically among the most frequently used: *iel, iels, læ, un.e, ellui, elleux, cellui, celleux, maon, taon, saon*, and avoiding differentially marking gender (e.g., *une personne* or *quelqu'un* as the subject of the sentence) or using inclusive punctuated suffixation (e.g., *Iel est allé.e*) (Table 2.1). However, we should clearly and consistently articulate the intentionality of this multiplicity, how forms were chosen for curricular inclusion, and the availability of myriad others.[15]

As educators, we must recognize the evolving nature of language and make clear to students the importance of gender in the process of (co-)constructing an L2-self. In keeping with TAQIBPs, this can help us to de-sensationalize TGNC content and co-create a space of collaborative exploration where we model respectful engagement. In and through this process, we can and must make clear that we see, value, and respect TGNC people, take TGNC concerns seriously, and "are available to help each student find the strategy that works best for them" (Provitola, 8).[16] TAQIBPs would further encourage systematically teaching these forms from the first-semester forward—as each structure is introduced—and reviewing them often throughout the curriculum. For example, you might list "*elle (féminin)/il (masculin)/iel (non-binaire)*" initially in verb charts and later remove *all* qualifiers. Similarly, *Mx* (honorific) and *adelphe* (sibling) should be added when covering related lexical items. You can further scaffold by leveraging the fame of well-known Anglophones who use non-binary pronouns (e.g., Sam Smith, Asia Kate Dillon) in introductory examples followed by non-binary Francophones. At any level, we must reject the idea of a trans day in favor of seeking out all moments where trans lives and concerns can be woven into the curriculum in direct connection with language learning goals. This connection helps us to consistently highlight their value and relevance in language learning as well as to avoid tokenization, marginalization, and sensationalism.

Linguistic inclusion must be a part of a broader ethos regarding gender in the classroom. For example, do we use stereotypes of colors (e.g., pink, blue) in ways that erroneously conflate grammatical and social gender? Could we choose alternatives that do not risk reifying normative conceptions of social gender? Do we critique such normativities *with* our students when they do appear, asking: What is the status quo? Why is it this way? Who benefits? Who is disadvantaged? And what maintains it?[17] Do we *invite* sharing pronouns[18] and agreements, via private, voluntary first-day surveys, for example, as opposed to making public demands? Does this systematically carry into assessment (e.g., including name, pronouns, and agreements on assignments)?[19] Inclusionary pedagogy is about seeking out, laying bare, and upending all forms of normativity.

As we explore how the normativities that underlie our experiences can creep into our pedagogical practice, it becomes evident that linguistic forms alone are not liberatory; they are a critical but singular part of trans-affirming classrooms. If we are to make visible the relevance of TGNC-ness throughout the curriculum we must engage with the actual lives and concerns of the people we are linguistically representing and, ultimately, come to treat gender as the structural social

**TABLE 2.1** Non-binary French Forms (Knisely, 2021a)

| | Form | Frequent positive evaluations | Frequent negative evaluations | Departure from binary | Partial departure from binary | Common | Infrequent use | |
|---|---|---|---|---|---|---|---|---|
| Singular third-person pronouns | iel, iels★ | X | X | | X | X | | Can mark absence of gender using ol. |
| | Ol | X | | X | | X | | |
| | Ul | X | | X | | | X | Orthographic departure from binary. |
| | Yel | | | | X | | X | Inadequate oral/aural departure from binary. |
| | Ille | | X | | | | X | See ille |
| | El | | X | | | | X | |
| | Im | | X | | | | X | Extremely rare. |
| | Em | | X | | | | X | |
| Agreement | Avoidance of differentially marking gender★ | X | | X | | X | | Use wherever possible, e.g., via invariable une personne (a person, F) or quelqu'un (someone, M) as sentence subject. |
| | IPS (ex. e.e)★ | X | | | X | X | | Periods most frequent (versus e-e, e/e, e·e), despite ideological discontents. |
| | Alternative suffixation (ex. –t) | | | X | | | (X) | Less frequent than IPS, greater variation in comprehension. |
| | Absence of suffixation | | X | X | | | (X) | Variation in comprehension. Reticence. |

# A Starter Kit for Rethinking Trans Representation

| Category | Form | | | | | | | | Notes |
|---|---|---|---|---|---|---|---|---|---|
| Direct object pronouns | læ★ | X | | | X | X | | | |
| | Léa | | (X) | | X | X | | X | Confusion with the name Léa. |
| | le.a | | X | | X | X | | X | Læ preferable to avoid punctuation. |
| | Lo | | X | | | | | X | |
| Disjunctive pronouns | ellui, elleux★ | X | | | X | X | | | |
| Demonstrative pronouns | cellui, celleux★ | X | | | X | X | | | |
| Possessive determiners | maon, taon, saon★ | X | | | X | X | | | |
| | man, tan, san | | X | | X | | | X | Concerns about English *man*, some incomprehension. |
| | mo, to, so | | X | | X | | | X | Concerns about typo of/misheard as M form. |
| Definite article | læ★ | X | | | X | X | | | |
| Indefinite article | un.e★ | | (X) | | X | X | | X | Ideological discontents. Periods most frequent (versus *un-e*, *un/e*, *un·e*). |

*Note:* Combining existing binary forms is often described as common, easy, and accessible but simultaneously yields ideological discontents due to the false ideas this might engender about non-binary people. ★ = most frequently used and rated as most comprehensible among participants.

and political issue that it is, a task for which educators tend to be "woefully unequipped," (Provitola, 3). Academic work might help to culturally situate and historicize[20] these discussions, by giving insight into popular media[21] and artistic[22] representations of trans lives and forms of online media that hold importance in TGNC communities.[23] There are infinite ways that we might use this and related literature to bring TGNC people and topics into the full spectrum of coursework we teach. For example, in Business French, we might leverage trans-focused materials (e.g., fondationemergence.org/proallie) to discuss diversity in the workplace. Not only can this facilitate intercultural and linguistic work in our courses, it sets up expectations for TGNC presence and models possibilities of being. As we consistently return to TGNC content, it is made clear to students that TGNC people are present in all areas of life. For some students, this is a reminder that we see and value them, that their gender modality is not and should not be taboo, and that they can be successful as learners and in the other social roles we discuss. For other students, this sets up an important counter-narrative to their own (cis)normative expectations. This approach can be extended to all domains (e.g., education,[24] politics,[25] the arts). As we include TGNC authors and artists,[26] we must pay careful attention to thematic reoccurrences, as they can afford us opportunities to lay bare the structural social and political issues that inflect TGNC lives. Engaging in collaborative, critical close reading and analysis can also help us to draw particular attention to the role of language and assumptions in constructing our realities and normativities.

Although useful, academic articles are regularly outpaced by rapidly shifting TGNC cultures (Mackenzie, 13) and are not immune to transphobia, which, in conjunction with a history of mistreatment by researchers (Tebbe and Budge), can undermine meaningful representation. We can and must guard against any possibility of reliance on voices whose eminence derives from the very cis-normative, transphobic, and/or transnormative structures that we claim to interrogate. This entails engaging with locally relevant, real-world TGNC experiences and language *ourselves* while we collaboratively question the very ways that knowledge and authority are constructed and work to upend normativity with our students. If it is by amplifying and centering TGNC voices that we have begun to (re)articulate the field of French ALx, it is by learning to hear and bear witness to TGNC lives and concerns *ourselves* that we continue to address the perennial problem with access to trans-inclusive materials and trainings designed for French L2 contexts.

## Extending French ALx

Actively practicing respectful, intentional listening can help educators to come to know TGNC people in ways that prioritize in-community voices. This better equips educators to create conditions for learning that are more equitable, just, and affirming with regard to gender. This listening to, building connections with, and peripherally participating in L1 and L2 TGNC communities and organizations can be among the best strategies for finding resources and *realia*, but must be deliberately and unequivocally ethical. Particularly for those who are not trans, non-binary, or gender nonconforming (GNC) themselves, it is important to safeguard against common pitfalls while seeking to be accomplices in equity and justice. Specifically, under no circumstances should you ask TGNC people to educate you, if they themselves have not chosen to be activist-educators in the context in which you are interacting with them. Honor that being publicly trans, non-binary, and/or GNC often comes at great personal cost. Further, take care not to insert yourself into conversations and spaces that are intended only for members of a community to which you do not belong. Listen more than you speak. Minoritized individuals might be unheard, but are *not* voiceless. And, when you make a mistake, apologize succinctly (e.g., I'm sorry. Thanks for correcting me.) and move forward (e.g., use correct pronouns, avoid the transphobic phrase). Do not make an excuse or ask others to take on your resulting feelings. Existing in solidarity means listening, being accountable, owning the need to engage in self-reflection, and committing to doing better as you learn.

Mindful of these principles, there are several strategies that educators can use to connect with TGNC individuals and organizations. First, examine your sources of information about TGNC people. Subscribe to LGBTQ+-focused media and listservs (open to non-community members, if applicable) in all relevant language (s), according particular value to those that are owned and/or authored primarily by TGNC people. This might include broadly queer publications (e.g., *Têtu, Komitid, them.*), streams from larger publications (e.g., *Libé LGBT+*), and organizational newsletters. Similarly, examine who is in your online social networks. Follow activists, artists, scholar-educators, and organizations who have explicitly chosen to educate the broader public. You might start with broad-reaching associations[27] and well-known individuals[28] and then expand via platform-suggested connections[29] and hashtags (e.g., #trans, #nonbinaire, #iel).[30]

By ethically investing in TGNC lives, you will grow, over time, in your ability to exist in solidarity with TGNC people and familiarity with topics that inflect TGNC lives. In TAQIBPs, students should be invited into this learning through activities, assignments, and discussions. For example, embedded in a larger discussion, students and educators could conduct a WebQuest exploring inclusive and non-binary linguistic strategies using the above principles and a starting list of hashtags, usernames, websites, and/or questions (Knisely, "Teaching Trans"). With this and all strategies, however, we must be careful to align with our theoretical underpinnings and de-sensationalize TGNC-ness, perhaps by also using WebQuests to explore other forms of linguistic diversity (e.g., slang, regional differences). Similarly, in courses engaging with particular genres of media (e.g., comics, blogs), include TGNC Francophones so as to bring together existing foci with new understandings gained from the creator's voice (e.g., Assignée garçon [Assigned Male] by Sophie Labelle, lavieenqueer. wordpress.com, entousgenresblog.wordpress.com). In a writing-focused course the above could be framed by genre and/or multiliteracies pedagogies, wherein work by TGNC Francophones is included alongside others. In any course with presentational speaking, the genre of a TED Talk (e.g., Antonin Le Mée TEDxRennes, Hely Ventura TEDxNouméa, Jeanne Lagabrielle TEDxQuébec) could be similarly treated. We might also leverage videos like Fondation Émergence's *devoir de mémoire* [duty of remembrance] (fondationemergence.org/devoir-de-memoire) or aging campaign (fondationemergence.org/pour-que-vieillir-soit-gai-outils) in courses treating these topics. The ways in which gender diversity can be made relevant to French L2 classrooms are as limitless as the ways in which gender inflects the lives, cultures, and languages of those *to* whom and *about* whom we teach.

In conclusion, if we are to realize locally relevant pedagogies and classrooms that are increasingly better at representing, including, and affirming the limitless linguistically and culturally situated ways of being a gendered person in the world, we must recognize the universality of feeling boxed-in by the gendered boundaries that have been placed around our bodies and, simultaneously, lay bare and unscript all such normativities *with* our students. Gender-just teaching entails an unequivocal investment in trans lives and concerns and a parallel divestment from systems and practices that lead to oppression. We must embrace liminality, infinite possibility, fluidity, and flexibility. We must accord value to the lives of people who unapologetically contain multitudes and/or exist in the in-between, be comfortable with discomfort, and see incompleteness as whole. In short, if we, as scholars in a field, are to leverage TAQIBPs to truly realize equitable and just language education, we must all come to know, value, and center the voices of trans individuals and communities.

## Notes

1 For a general introduction: TSER (transstudent.org), GLAAD (glaad.org/amp/beginners-guide-being-ally-to-trans-people), the Trevor Project (thetrevorproject.org/wp-content/uploads/2020/03/Guide-to-Being-an-Ally-to-Transgender-and-Nonbinary-Youth.pdf), and the 2020 documentary *Disclosure*.
2 See Adams and Bell for a sourcebook.
3 Allyship is too often understood as static or passive. Accomplice evokes undertaking the active work of dismantling oppressive structures, as directed by the stakeholders in the marginalized group.
4 See Paiz for an introduction to the diverse collection of queer inquiry-based approaches.
5 Living TGNC-ness visibly or privately is an individual, context-dependent decision. It is entirely valid to share particular aspects of ourselves in all, some, or no contexts. Visibility *can* signal a vehicle for students to see possibilities of being, as a part of upending gendered normativities, but does not override personal privacy and autonomy. We can create visibility *without* demands for disclosure by creating value around trans possibilities of being: Were we to embrace trans invisibility as a strategy of liberatory pedagogical practice, I imagine we may not wait for trans students to 'come out' before we invest in their lives. I imagine we would learn about and feel committed to trans students' success, and we would find ways to affirm gender exploration … We do not need to know trans people exist in our midst, or that a certain

A Starter Kit for Rethinking Trans Representation    31

number of us are present, in order to create educational environments that are accessible, humane, and liberatory (Nicolazzo, 127–129).
6  See Knisely, "Teaching Trans" for guiding questions.
7  These strategies have been previously outlined by Paiz, particularly as related to sexuality, and are adapted here to focus on gender.
8  It is with reticence that I use the largely cis-centric concept of *disclosure*, which is often perniciously leveraged against trans people to set up an erroneous expectation that there is something that *needs* to and *must* be shared with cisgender interlocutors. Regardless of any desire to know a person's gender modality, no *right* exists.
9  "When we see other trans people, we can begin to fashion possibilities for who we can become […]. However, when all we have is what we see, then we miss the potential of leveraging that which we do not, could never, or need not attempt to see" (Nicolazzo, 130).
10 Intersections with other subjectivities (e.g., race, class) are also always at play. See Knisely 2020 for further discussion of the cultural self-positioning of TGNC Francophones.
11 Students and teachers will necessarily vary in their familiarity with and linguistic abilities for encoding TGNC-ness, in both L1 and L2 contexts.
12 Europe and North America are over-represented herein, likely reflecting the criminalizing of queerness in numerous contexts and larger hegemonic forces in academia. Educators are encouraged to explore LGBTQ+ rights throughout the Francophone world *with* students. *Dans mon pays* may be one useful resource (fondationemergence.org/2018-afficher-ses-couleurs).
13 E.g., Alpheratz, Ashley, Elmiger, Greco, Knisely.
14 Discussing linguistic diversity and corpus-based approaches to selecting instructed forms, as opposed to standard language ideologies, may be useful in laying bare the ways that power and prestige influence language attitudes.
15 See Knisely, "Le français non-binaire" on form variation.
16 Each non-binary person may use a singular or multiple, binary or non-binary pronoun(s).
17 These questions were posited by Paiz as a tool for resisting heteronormativity and have been noted elsewhere (Knisely, "Teaching Trans") as useful for resisting cis-normativity.
18 The transphobic qualifier *preferred* should not be used. The pronouns and name an individual uses are the only acceptable way to refer to them and not a matter of preference. Instead, ask "What pronouns do you use?" and list "Pronouns:" on forms.
19 Make clear that this voluntary, *temporary* pinning-down of grammatical structures can facilitate providing relevant, assumption-free linguistic feedback. The *invitation* should honor each individual's right to self-definition and to change forms-in-use.
20 E.g., Bolter.
21 E.g., *Plus belle la vie* (Mackenzie).
22 E.g., Sophie Labelle (Swamy); *Requiem* (Alpheratz); *Sphinx* (Kosnick).
23 E.g., *La vie en queer* and *En tous genres* (Mackenzie); Rowland.
24 E.g., Ashley; Knisely.
25 For example, by engaging with the careers of politicians (e.g., Camille Cabral, Marie Cau, Julie Lemieux, Petra De Sutter). We must, however, be careful to never allow the existence and happiness of LGBTQ+ people to become a classroom debate topic.
26 E.g., actors, musicians (Christine and the Queens, Lucas Charlie Rose, Trans Trenderz), film-makers.
27 E.g., The International Lesbian, Gay, Bisexual, Trans, and Intersex Association, Coalition des groupes jeunesse LGBTQ+, Le réseau Enchanté, ÉGIDES, Trans PULSE Canada.
28 E.g., Alok Vaid-Menon, Laurier The Fox, Mx. Cordélia (Princ(ess)e–LGBT).
29 E.g., "you might like" or "who to follow" on Twitter and "pages liked by this page" or "related pages" on Facebook.
30 Multiple hashtags narrow results. Locations may prove useful (e.g., #belgique).

## References

ACTFL. "Position Statement on Diversity and Inclusion in World Language Teaching and Learning." May 17, 2019, www.actfl.org/news/position-statements/diversity-and-inclusion-world-language-teaching-learning.

Adams, Maurianne and Lee Anne Bell, editors. *Teaching for Diversity and Social Justice*. 3rd ed. Routledge, 2016.

Ahmed, Sara. *On Being Included: Racism and Diversity in Institutional Life*. Duke UP, 2012.

Alpheratz. *Requiem*. CreateSpace, 2015.

—. *Grammaire du français inclusif*. Vent Solars, 2018.

Ashley, Florence. "Qui est-ille? Le respect langagier des élèves non-binaires, aux limites du droit." *Service social*, vol. 63, no. 2, 2017, pp. 35–50.

—. "Les personnes non-binaires en français: une perspective concernée et militante." *H-France Salon*, vol. 11, no. 14, 2019, h-france.net/h-france-salon-volume-11–2019/#1114.

Bolter, Flora. "'Le masculin l'emporte': évolution des stratégies linguistiques dans les associations LGBT+ en France." *H-France Salon*, vol. 11, no. 14, 2019, h-france.net/h-france-salon-volume-11–2019/#1114.

Clarkson, Nicholas L. "Teaching Trans Students, Teaching Trans Studies." *Feminist Teacher*, vol. 27, nos 2–3, 2017, pp. 233–252.

Darvin, Ron and Bonny Norton. "Identity and a Model of Investment in Applied Linguistics." *Annual Review of Applied Linguistics*, vol. 35, 2015, pp. 36–56.

Elmiger, Daniel. "Au-delà de la binarité: le trouble entre les genres." *GLAD! Les genres récrits*, vol. 3, 2018, www.revue-glad.org/961.

Greco, Luca. "Linguistic Uprisings: Toward a Grammar of Emancipation." *H-France Salon*, vol. 11, no. 14, 2019, h-france.net/h-france-salon-volume-11–2019/#1114.

Knisely, Kris Aric. "Le français non-binaire: Linguistic Forms Used by Non-Binary Speakers of French." *Foreign Language Annals*, vol. 53, no. 4, Winter 2020, pp. 850–876.

—. "Subverting the Culturally Unreadable: Understanding the Self-Positioning of Non-Binary Speakers of French." *The French Review*, vol. 94, no. 2, December 2020, pp. 149–168.

—. "Teaching Trans: The Impetus for Trans, Non-Binary, and Gender Non-Conforming Inclusivity in L2 Classrooms." *How We Take Action: Social Justice in K-16 Language Classrooms*, edited by Kelly Davidson, Stacey Margarita Johnson, and L. J. Randolph. Information Age, Forthcoming, 2021.

Kosnick, Kiki. "The Everyday Poetics of Gender-Inclusive French: Strategies for Navigating the Linguistic Landscape." *Modern & Contemporary France*, vol. 27, no. 2, 2019, pp. 1–15.

LeMaster, Benny and Amber L. Johnson. "Unlearning Gender—Toward a Critical Communication Trans Pedagogy." *Communication Teacher*, vol. 33, no. 3, 2019, pp. 189–198. doi:10.1080/17404622.2018.1467566.

Mackenzie, Louisa. "Beyond 'French-American' Binary Thinking on Non-Binary Gender." *H-France Salon*, vol. 11, no. 14, 2019, h-france.net/h-france-salon-volume-11–2019/#1114.

Nelson, Cynthia D. *Sexual Identities in English Language Education: Classroom Conversations*. Routledge, 2008.

Nicolazzo, Z. "Visibility Alone Will Not Save Us: Leveraging Invisibility as a Possibility for Liberatory Pedagogical Practice." *Queer, Trans, and Intersectional Theory in Educational*

*Practice: Student, Teacher, and Community Experiences*, edited by Cris Mayo and Mollie V. Blackburn. Routledge, 2020, pp. 120–132.

Paiz, Joshua M. *Queering the English Language Classroom: A Practical Guide for Teachers*. Equinox, 2020.

Provitola, Blase. "'Faut-il choisir?' Transgender Access to the French Language Classroom." *H-France Salon*, vol. 11, no. 14, 2019, h-france.net/h-france-salon-volume-11-2019/#1114.

Rowland, Olivier. "Les genres non binaires sur Internet et Facebook." 2015, observatoire-des-transidentites.com/tag/genre-non-binaire.

Sauntson, Helen. *Language, Sexuality and Education*. Cambridge: Cambridge UP, 2018.

Spade, Dean. *Normal life: Administrative Violence, Critical Trans Politics, and the Limits of Law*. Duke UP, 2015.

—. "Some Very Basic Tips for Making Higher Education More Accessible to Trans Students and Rethinking How We Talk about Gendered Bodies." *Radical Teacher*, vol. 92, no. 1, 2011, pp. 57–62.

Swamy, Vinay. "Assignée garcon." *H-France Salon*, vol. 11, no. 14, 2019, h-france.net/h-france-salon-volume-11-2019/#1114.

Tebbe, Elliot A. and Stephanie L. Budge. "Research with Trans Communities: Applying a Process-Oriented Approach to Methodological Considerations and Research Recommendations." *The Counseling Psychologist*, vol. 44, no. 7, 2016, pp. 996–1024.

# 3

# DISABILITY STUDIES AND THE FRENCH CLASSROOM

## Toward a 'Democracy of Proximity'

*Tammy Berberi*

Written when Swiss philosopher Alexandre Jollien was only 23 years old, *L'Eloge de la faiblesse* recounts Jollien's adventures inside a residential facility for disabled children. Jollien's entire memoir consists of an imagined dialogue with Socrates. When Socrates asks Jollien whether he can explain his notion of mutual support, he replies:

J: "Paradoxically, I find it hard to explain. With Adrien, conversation was limited to "Nice sweater. Nice pants. How are you?"
S: "Small talk?"
J: "Precisely the opposite! The question, 'how are you' was vitally important for us."
S: "Really?"
J: "With a 'how are you?' we entered the existence of another, taking on their suffering and thereby communicating our friendship."*(43; my translation)*

Throughout Jollien's memoir, attention to the present moment and immediate surroundings is intense—and intentional. The boys perform for adults during the day, striving to overcome their limitations; left to their own devices, they're aiming for community, friendship, and liberation. Jollien's text reminds us of the complexities of forging relationships through communication that is labored and limited, highlighting varying abilities as well as unfaltering loyalty and mutual regard. We readers may at first reject Jollien's childhood experiences and indeed the parameters of his existence, as being radically different from ours. However, Jollien's reliance upon Buddhist philosophy and friendship bridges this psychological distance. The spare prose, spare conversation, and spare furnishings of the dormitory reflect an emptying of conventional priorities and plenty of room for possibility.

DOI: 10.4324/9781003126461-4

This possibility is no small matter, forming the basis for new modes of interaction and for a renewed social contract. Julia Kristeva officially took up the cause of disabled civil rights not long after the publication of Jollien's French-language edition, first with a reasoned, direct appeal to then President Jacques Chirac, and later in *La Haine et le pardon* [*Hatred and Forgiveness*].[1] For Kristeva, the vulnerability that is inherent in the notion of disability holds important potential for social transformation. As she explains:

> My ambition, my utopia, consists of believing that this vulnerability, reflected in the disabled person, forms us deeply, or if you prefer, unconsciously, and that as a result, it can be shared. Could this humanism be the cultural revolution with which to construct the democracy of proximity that the postmodern age needs?
>
> (30)

Understanding that this is more than a misuse of disability as metaphor is the task, predicated on deep inter-relationality, that Kristeva puts before us: to build together a "respect for vulnerability that cannot be shared" (30).

In his history of the French Disability Rights movement, *Les Métamorphoses du handicap de 1970 à nos jours* [*Metamorphoses of Disability from 1970 to Today*, untranslated] Henri-Jacques Stiker deepens Kristeva's formulation, exploring the psychology of inter-relationality with disabled people. Reframing specific rights (such as the right to access or employment) as the fundamental immutability of human dignity, Stiker develops an intersubjective ethics of recognition that entails embracing unabashedly an unceasing and unpredictable dynamic of acceptance and rejection, distance and proximity, knowledge dawning and ignorance renewed, that is rooted in the psychoanalytic process of interaction. Grounded in the promise of psychological intimacy vis-à-vis oneself and others, this dynamic cultivates a boundless and inter-relational human present.

Jollien's abiding loyalty, Kristeva's humanist utopia, and Stiker's mutual regard form the ethical basis for my exploration of inclusive praxis; highlights from an American disability rights movement serve to anchor specific practices. Studying another language and culture is always an invitation to play with, rearrange, and share the building blocks that comprise the world we have come to understand. If we went about this work as though we believed we were changing the world, we just might. At the heart of this enterprise is the simple awareness that what young people believe about their own potential, and what I have been given to believe about mine, is a matter of critical importance: we must not let society be imposed upon us. Two parts praxis, one part personal, this essay writes its way through difference in a language classroom in an effort to spur the recognition of difference within the self.

Although most students have never had a disabled teacher, they cheerfully adapt to my need for some assistance. However, much of what I share in this essay emerged by necessity, as strategies for overcoming tensions among some students. I realize now that these are usually a by-product of our shared hesitation to admit vulnerability. It took me longer to realize another source of my unease: over the past few years, my classroom has come to feel increasingly foreign to me. It is not the physical environment, since that has improved dramatically since the days when dreary and smeary transparencies alone supported grammatical explanations. These days, I have a very snazzy "Zoom room" with a computer station, an adjustable chair, and three screens that can synch or display different content. What has made the classroom feel like foreign terrain is the shift in higher education from process to mastery and an imperative, seemingly omnipresent, to reduce difference and eliminate imperfection before it manifests.

Trajectories of optimization and perfectibility have proved especially harmful to disabled people. I am advancing an argument that these epistemologies are harmful for everyone, and for society as a whole. Critical disability studies (CDS) makes a home for imperfection, challenging a traditional understanding of disability that relies uniquely on medical and eugenic logic to justify normalizing, curing, or removing disabled people from the everyday. CDS draws upon the arts, humanities, and social sciences in forging new epistemologies that explore disabled experiences as well as the normative forces that give rise to them. By displacing the locus of inquiry from the individual to the disabling environment, CDS decenters impairment, undermines bio-certification as the basis for embodied legitimacy, and invites solidarity across identities in order to redress the impact of systemic, intersectional inequities.

More students are pursuing college—and demographically, they are more diverse—than ever before. Despite the proliferation of support programs intended to mitigate the impact of entrenched social disparities, graduation rates have scarcely improved at all since 1990, when the US began measuring them (Gabriel, ch. 1). The reasons for this seem to bloom in all directions, engaging disability, race, gender, and class and reflecting complex systemic inequities. For example, while two-thirds of affluent students finish a four-year degree by age twenty-five, only one-third of low-income students do. Low-income, first-generation students are four times as likely as non-first generation to leave college after their first year (Roksa and Kinsley, 415). While roughly equal numbers of disabled and non-disabled people complete some college or an Associate's degree, far fewer disabled than non-disabled people complete four-year degrees. This disparity spawns a host of others, including a poverty rate among disabled people that is more than 2.5 times higher than that of non-disabled people ("Disability Status Report").[2]

It is also true that nationally, only about one in four students who had an Individualized Education Plan in K-12 requests accommodation in college (Scott and Edwards, 5). As David Connor, Beth Ferri, and Subini Annamma, the editors of *DisCrit: Disability Studies and Race Theory in Higher Education* note, reasons for non-disclosure are also complex and intersectional. African American K-12 students are three times as likely to be labeled mentally retarded, twice as likely to be labeled emotionally disturbed, and one and a half times as likely to be labeled learning disabled, compared to their white peers (11).³ Alicia Broderick and Zeus Leonardo's research, published in the same collection, demonstrates that within the regulatory system of K-12 schools, constructions of "goodness" and "smartness" begin to circulate as early as kindergarten and readily interpolate with constructions of race, in order to maintain white privilege (55–67). To highlight the ways that deficit notions of race, disability, and class undergird broader patterns of social privilege is not to validate those diagnoses. Nor is it to place experiences of race and disability in easy parallel. Rather, it is to highlight the norms that give rise to their construction and the social prerogatives they serve. All of this complexity is always in play in our classrooms—the impulse to maintain the status quo (arguably, this was the substance of my pedagogy training) as well as the imperative to recognize these patterns and their consequences and to strive to redress them.

The body of research correlating a heightened sense of stigma with diminished performance and satisfaction is well-known in social psychology. This pattern is consistent whether a Latina/o engineering student recalls her minority status before an exam or a disabled student must manage greater self-doubt upon disclosing a disability to their adviser. Abigail Stewart and Virginia Valian discuss the compounded impact of repeated microaggressions (for some) and accumulated advantage (for others), demonstrating how easily the so-called molehills become the mountain (ch. 3). Yet for disabled people, too, stigma may begin before we get in the door: a lack of physical access, whether a flight of steep stairs or a broken electronic door button, amounts to microaggression, likewise diminishing one's sense of adequacy and belonging.

My relationship to France is illustrative of the kind of change that can happen over half a lifetime. I took my first trip over spring break in 1984, in eighth grade. I was rarely permitted to leave the tour bus, "for my own safety." I visited the Eiffel Tower, Notre Dame, Mont Saint Michel, and other marvels from the inside of a coach while my grandmother (who had agreed to chaperone) took photos and herded other students around, then returned to the bus to tell me about it. Lonely does not begin to describe the sense of disconnection and isolation I felt. My experience studying abroad in 1989 was much the same: doting and overprotective, my host family drove me everywhere and afforded me little autonomy. It was again a deeply lonely time, but my solitude paired well with my love for reading and resulted in terrific, even literary, French. Social change crystallized for me when, many trips later, my family returned to Paris to permit my university research. Mobility that summer was complicated by my advancing pregnancy and by a toddler who tired easily. My husband had tricked out my manual chair with a standing platform affixed to its anti-tip bars and a canvas sling attached to its push handles. As he pushed the lot of us, our son, then four, could stand up to look around, and relax into his sling for a nap on the go. We thus joined the ranks of rollerbladers, *vélib'* users, and caddy-pullers. One day as we rolled through the center, a Parisian twenty-something whizzed past on a bike, yelling backwards to me, *"Où t'as trouvé ça? C'est cool!"* ("Where did you get that? It's cool!") We had rented an apartment on the fifth floor and I was counting on the elevator to work for an uninterrupted month. It was a miniscule triangle, a vintage retrofit wedged next to the staircase. Whether riding up or down, I stepped in and spread my feet apart so my son could crouch between my legs. I'd inhale and hold my breath so that the steel doors would close just inches from my growing belly; he'd push the chunky, chocolate-colored button and off we'd go… until it broke down a few days into our stay. Soon after, as I gripped the railing with one hand and half-crawled with the other, making my way around the first bend in the long staircase above me, a regular tenant zipped past me in the other direction, *"Je les appellerai aujourd'hui, Madame. Ne vous inquiétez pas."* *"Merci,"* ("I'll call them today ma'am. Don't worry!" "Thank you,") I called after him, grateful but not expecting much, as such tasks ordinarily take weeks rather than days to accomplish in France. The next day when I saw him, I asked how he had convinced the repair staff to service the elevator so promptly. "Well," he answered, "They weren't going to come so we all (the building's regular tenants) went downtown together to insist that they come fix it for you. *"On aime bien manifester, vous savez!"* ("You know how we love a protest!"), he smiled. While such examples of solidarity have not been rare in my travels, this one stops me still. Never before had I felt such a sense of home in this city of never-ending stairs. The privilege my experiences reflect is not lost on me. My family did not have a lot of money, so every time I wanted to travel, I sold my car, or housesat, or picked up another part-time job, and left. One thing I did have, though, that may be lacking in some of our students, was a sense of deservingness—an understanding that I was worthy of experiences that would enrich my mind and life, whether or not these choices made sense to others. I dearly desire the same liberation for my students.

With the recent *Disability and World Language Learning: Inclusive Teaching for Diverse Learners*, Sally S. Scott and Wade A. Edwards offer a useful and deeply affirming handbook of specific practices to cultivate a community of diverse learners. Using the nine principles of universal design (UD) as the basis for their approach, Scott and Edwards begin by highlighting the ways UD principles already reflect the values we enact in world language learning: self-expression, flexibility, community, and a comparatively high tolerance for error.[4] A series of case studies and reflective prompts cultivates our inclusive, disability-centered problem-solving skills. Findings indicate that teacher disposition is paramount to student success and persistence: optimism, approachability, and a willingness to partner are its key features. Since universal design will never eliminate the need for accommodations for some students, Scott and Edwards offer clear guidance about working with disability resources to understand what is possible. Students—and especially new college students—may not be aware of what is possible, or even fully understand or be able to articulate their own needs in this new environment. Only in retrospect do I realize how deeply the strategies I have developed over the years are informed by basic tenets of the American disability rights movement and disability studies. These are a great foundation for the shared project of reimagining our classrooms, higher education, and the world we want for each other and the future. I offer them from where I teach, with tenure, at a public liberal arts college with small classes and strong relationships. Your teaching context (and values, etc.) will differ, so the strategies you develop will, as well.

## Crip Time

Crip time refers to the time it takes for disabled people to navigate expectations that were not created with us in mind. Alison Kafer writes "rather than bend disabled bodies and minds to meet the clock, crip time bends the clock to meet disabled bodies and minds" (28). In fact, crip time bends and flexes to all sorts of diversity. My strategies include: 1) scheduling emptiness—a few catch-up days scattered throughout the semester. We always make good use of them; 2) encouraging students to schedule a few wellbeing days for themselves each semester, using the excused absences permitted in their courses and timed so as not to interfere with exams and major assignment due dates; 3) implementing spanned due dates. Rather than creating a due date for each assignment, after which I penalize students, I accept a given assignment anytime in the week in which it is due. In honor of the French *semaine de huit jours* (eight-day week) the span typically stretches through the following Monday; 4) creating reasonably paced exams. A student who has not finished a test by the end of class can finish their exam any time before the following day, either in my office or at a study table in the hall. This enables students to let go of associated anxiety and achieve better results; 5) beginning each class session with two minutes of meditation, as a way of coming together and settling into the day's material. Research suggests that even brief bits of meditation have wonderful benefits for focus, cognition, and emotional regulation, in addition to achieving something akin to diminished affective filter.[5]

## Interdependence and Community

My own identity development as a disabled kid was greatly advanced by two years I spent in a dedicated special education class for kids with mobility impairments. There I found my joy, and was encouraged to do things through, not in spite of, my disability. We were made to understand that these differences in ways of doing made us unique and fun. We were unable to manage many activities by ourselves, but together we were able to realize whatever we could imagine— which was a lot. Strategies I use to foster interdependence and community include: 1) crafting a unique welcome for each of my syllabi each semester and asking students to write their own. Inspired by Saran Stewart's suggestions for teaching a diverse student body, I aim to introduce myself, learn more about students, humanize our shared enterprise, and demystify my successes; 2) managing absences with care: three absences over the course of the semester, no questions asked, also seems standard. I let everyone know that I appreciate hearing from them when they know they will be away. When a student exceeds this limit or disappears, I write to them to reframe their absence as a missed opportunity for *us*. I let them know that we count on their contributions and enjoy learning from them. This may not yet be true, but it is always possible. I have found that a kind reminder prompts growth; 3) implementing a community notes archive, assigning to two or three students the task of taking class notes (in French), typing them up, and uploading them to the course site within two days. This activity produces strong French and fascinating opportunities to think about how our minds work differently; 4) acknowledging course preparation by means of a reader's journal and brief reflective writings as a reasonable alternative to earn the dreaded 'participation' grade. I have come to understand student reticence to speak as a symptom of internalized perfectionism. They do come 'round to talking, and appreciate multiple means of engagement while they gain confidence at understanding advanced material and analyzing it with short bits of writing; 5) expanding the university-approved disability statement. Disability disclosure per standard university procedures can be terribly fraught and isolating, so I contextualize the statement and invite partnership. Part I of the statement, "what I do for every student" is an opportunity to showcase good teaching. Part II, "What we can do if the elements of part I don't seem to be enough" comprises the official statement and an invitation to visit with disability resource staff, together. Part III, "What I am unable to do if you opt away from opportunities in this class," includes clarity about whether I accept work retroactively, etc. This wraparound serves to reframe a need for support as partnership and interdependence.

## *"Nothing about Us without Us"*

A ubiquitous slogan for disability rights, "nothing about us without us" captures succinctly the determination to be oneself, to see oneself, and to participate fully in the world around us. It invites us to take leave of diagnoses that reduce people to their deficiencies and to declare oneself an agent, rather than the object, of knowledge and world-making. To honor it, we must together overcome several environmental deficits, the most important of these being French language textbooks, which present an ever more technological, homogenized view of what it means to be human. The kinds of content I have developed to enrich reductive materials enable us to communicate with each other with connection and intention, beyond stereotypes. I have developed supplemental content to describe racial identity/skin tone, queer identities, and a variety of disabilities. The latter category includes *le handicap, handicapé.e, personne à mobilité réduite, sourd.e/malentendant.e, aveugle/malvoyant.e, la surdité, la cécité, neurodivers(ité), des béquilles, un fauteuil roulant,* etc. Public transportation etiquette (and *places réservées* ... signage designating reserved and accessible seating) pair well with this lexicon; more advanced students enjoy learning about Blind and Deaf history, which is so vital to understanding French history. Other strategies I use to cultivate a sense of agency and belonging include beginning each class (after meditation), with a single slide introducing a diverse Francophone cultural figure—writers, artists, activists, dancers, musicians, etc. many of whom are American expats who spent significant time in France—accompanied by biographical notes (in French or English) and a quote. I produce the first ten or so and then pair students to produce this content. Another idea from Saran Stewart, this brief encounter with diversity increases the likelihood that all students will see themselves in course material and, even more importantly, as part of *la Francophonie*.

I also regularly engage students in developing the rubric by which their work will be assessed and reinventing an assignment or an entire segment of a course to better resonate with their interests and desired skill development.

## "You Get Proud by Practicing"

Laura Hershey, a writer and disability rights activist from Denver, was an alumnus at the college I attended. In my second year, campus administration sponsored a visit by Hershey, and she and I met over lunch. For a long time, I had been the only person "like me" on campus, and I recall feeling inspired and relieved by that simple lunch—a time to share disabled experiences and to learn from Laura's struggles and successes. Here is the first stanza of her poem:

> If you are not proud
> For who you are, for what you say, for how you look;
> If every time you stop
> To think of yourself, you do not see yourself glowing
> With golden light; do not, therefore, give up on yourself.
> You can get proud.
> *(www.thenthdegree.com/proudpoem.asp)*

I regularly use two strategies to foster pride, or self-acceptance: 1) asking regularly, as a way of awakening their own investment in what they have decided to do "What do *you* think of your work?"; 2) using the phrase, "your best work" and extending the time students have to develop it. Years ago, a talented student who struggled with "time management" helped me understand how important it is to give students the opportunity to meet their best work and to encounter their most engaged intellectual selves. This resulted in the spanned due dates that I describe above.

Most of the materials and strategies I have developed emerged on the fly. Never has flexibility unleashed the kind of unmitigated chaos that my own normative pedagogy training conditioned me to imagine, and I have yet to realize what I have lost in allowing these practices to take hold as cultural norms. Time and again, I am surprised to realize how much students appreciate the values and practices I describe here, and how few actually need them in order to prioritize wellbeing and personal investment over an external sense of achievement. Recentering the vulnerability of learning and doing as process, these strategies thwart perfectionism and eliminate exceptions altogether, making way for deeper learning and self-awareness, sustainable life rhythms, and an enriched, interactional present. Like Jollien's, may a simple "ça va?" ("How are you?") serve to remind us that our classroom holds the opportunity to practice the art and skill of bringing into being the communities and worlds we want to inhabit.

## Notes

1 Kristeva's 2002 appeal to President Chirac is entitled *Lettre au Président de la République sur les citoyens en situation de handicap à l'usage de ceux qui le sont et de ceux qui ne le sont pas* [Letter to the President of the Republic about People with Disabilities, for Disabled and non-Disabled People]. To date, this text remains untranslated.
2 Nationwide, only 15 percent of disabled people complete a four-year degree, compared with 35 percent of non-disabled people. In 2018 the poverty rate among working-age, disabled adults was 26 percent compared with 10 percent among non-disabled adults.
3 Although use of the term "mentally retarded" remains a norm in special education literature, disability studies scholars and activists reject it as a slur. Latinx, American Indian, Alaska Native, and English-language-learners are also over-represented in K-12 special education.
4 The principles of universal design are: (1) equitable use; (2) flexibility in use; (3) simple and intuitive use; (4) perceptible information; (5) tolerance for error; (6) low physical effort; (7) size and space for approach and use; (8) a community of learners; and (9) positive instructional climate (13–14).
5 The extent of my training is an online course in Mindfulness-Based Stress Reduction, a couple of intensive retreats, and a daily meditation practice.

## References

Broderick, Alicia and Zeus Leonardo. "'What a Good Boy': The Deployment and Distribution of Goodness as Ideological Property in Schools." *DisCrit: Disability Studies and Critical Race Theory in Education*, edited by David J. Connor et al. Teachers College P, 2016.

*Disability Status Report*. Disability Statistics. Cornell University, 2018. www.disabilitystatistics.org.

Gabriel, Katherine S. *Creating the Path to Success in the Classroom: Teaching to Close the Graduation Gap for Minority, First-Generation, and Academically Unprepared Students*. Stylus, 2018.

Hershey, Laura. "You Get Proud by Practicing." *The Nth Degree*, 1991. www.thenthdegree.com/proudpoem.asp.

Jollien, Alexandre. *Eloge de la faiblesse*. Marabout, 1999.

—. *In Praise of Weakness*. Translated by Michael Eskin. Upper West Side Philosophers, Inc., 2017.
Kafer, Alison. *Feminist, Queer, Crip*. Indiana UP, 2013.
Kristeva, Julia. *Lettre au Président de la République sur les citoyens en situation de handicap à l'usage de ceux qui le sont et de ceux qui ne le sont pas*. Fayard, 2002.
—. *La Haine et le pardon. Pouvoirs et limites de la psychanalyse III*. Fayard, 2005.
—. *Hatred and Forgiveness*. Translated by Jeanine Herman. Columbia UP, 2010.
Roksa, Josipa and Peter Kinsley. "The Role of Family Support in Facilitating Family Success." *Research in Higher Education*, vol. 60, no. 4, June 2019, pp. 415–436.
Scott, Sally S. and Wade A. Edwards. *Disability and World Language Learning: Inclusive Teaching for Diverse Learners*. Rowman & Littlefield, 2019.
Stewart, Abigail J. and Virginia Valian. *An Inclusive Academy: Achieving Diversity and Excellence*. The MIT P, 2018.
Stiker, Henri-Jacques. *Les Métamorphoses du handicap de 1970 à nos jours*. PU de Grenoble, 2009.
Tuitt, Frank *et al. Race, Equity, and the Learning Environment: The Global Relevance of Critical and Inclusive Pedagogies in Higher Education*. Stylus, 2016.

# 4

# WHY WE NEED TO TALK ABOUT RACE

## Improving Racial Inclusivity in the French Language Classroom

*Kate Nelson*

French instructors need to talk about race. French classrooms are well suited to unpack race, as Francophone materials often deal with problems pervasive in 21st-century America. Francophone texts provide a unique opportunity for American students to look at the legacies of racism sanctioned through colonialism, which I argue can help improve racial inclusivity in the classroom. While it is true that non-white Francophone authors are now standard in most French programs, some language-learning curricula still focus on a Eurocentric experience, lacking complex discussions of diversity and race (Glynn, 41).[1] This chapter intends to give instructors tools to create a more racially inclusive French-language classroom, where students of color and white students alike feel valued and invited to deconstruct race and racism.

A racially inclusive classroom welcomes diverse points of view, values students' personal experiences, and encourages all to participate in discussions in order to promote mutual understanding. In *Engaging the "Race Question": Accountability and Equity in U.S. Higher Education*, Alicia C. Dowd and Estela Mara Bensimon compare studies on race in higher education. They find that dialogues that encourage students to express their unique identity, including their race or ethnicity, promote more racially inclusive classrooms. For students who are not of the majority race or ethnicity, these dialogues can enhance students' sense of worth and belonging at the university, which can lead to greater student success (12–14). In this chapter, I will suggest strategies that aid French instructors in promoting a more racially inclusive classroom, with a focus on Francophone African materials. The chapter is divided into three sections: first, "Why We Have to Talk About Race," which focuses on how race functions in American society and proposes useful vocabulary to reframe classroom discussions of race; second, "Choosing Materials," which considers how to select and incorporate

DOI: 10.4324/9781003126461-5

texts from authors of color, as well as how to discuss these materials through a non-European cultural lens to avoid tokenism and racial capitalism; and third, "Guidelines and Practices," which proposes specific teaching practices to promote racial inclusivity in the French-speaking classroom.

## Why We Have to Talk about Race: Key Terms and Theories

Avoiding the topic of race has a three-fold impact: students of color may not feel invited to contribute to the discussion; all students miss an opportunity to disprove "colorblindness"; and instructors do not question how racism presents itself in their pedagogy (Dowd and Bensimon, 12–14, 18–19). Colorblindness is defined as the belief that ignoring race will combat the ills of systemic racism (Lewis and Diamond, 8; Garces and da Cruz, 12). Colorblindness prevents efforts to dismantle legalized and socialized racial inequities and perpetuates racist practices (Garces and da Cruz, 1–2). If instructors do not engage in discussions of racial inequities, they are perpetuating racist practices that hurt their students, according to Lewis and Diamond (7–12). Ibram X. Kendi's groundbreaking work, *How to Be an Antiracist* provides a wonderful place to begin understanding the concepts of racist and antiracist action and might help instructors better comprehend the lived realities of students of color. Kendi asserts that any action that reinforces systemic racism or engages in colorblind practices is passively racist and that everyone takes part in racist practices. According to Kendi, the goal is to recognize racist practices and disengage from them by supporting antiracist action. He asserts that "the movement from racist to antiracist is always ongoing—it requires understanding and snubbing racism based on biology, ethnicity, body, culture, behavior, color, space, and class" (13). Dismantling racism involves deconstructing the way race functions in our society to identify the foundations of racist practices. For French instructors, texts on French colonialism showcase overt racist practices, which are easier for students to identify and break down. Instructors can then transition to demonstrating how overt racism can turn into systemic racism. Antiracist praxis in the French-speaking classroom requires assessing how colonialism and postcolonial French-speaking societies have used race to subjugate others.

By deconstructing race in colonial and postcolonial settings, instructors can help students understand racism in our society, a goal that can help non-majority students feel more invested in their university experience, which might lead to "fuller participation." In literature on equity in higher education, full participation has been defined as the goal of "creating institutions that enable people, whatever their identity, background, or institutional position, to thrive, realize their capabilities, engage meaningfully in institutional life, and contribute to the flourishing of others" (Sturm *et al.*, 4). In Liliana M. Garces and Cynthia Gordon da Cruz's article outlining necessary measures for achieving racial equity in higher education, they argue that classroom discussions that break down structural racism are integral to achieving full participation for minority students. It is only by "accepting that racism is real and operates in different ways at different points in history, can we slowly work toward a different future that challenges racism" (3). French-language classrooms, which study texts from a variety of places and times, are well suited to deconstruct the dynamic manifestations of racism.

Discussions of systemic racism combined with antiracist strategies, which validate and perhaps empower students of color, create opportunities for students to share their unique knowledge while contributing to the goal of full participation. Dowd and Bensimon argue that efforts toward inclusion increase satisfaction for students of color and lower attrition rates (12–18). They also assert that what students gain from their university experience depends heavily on personal relationships with university authority figures. This is especially true for students—such as non-white students at a majority-white institution—who might have encountered "cultural imperialism" (13). A key to this relationship, according to Dowd and Bensimon, is valuing individual student experiences (13–14). Instructors should pull from students' "funds of knowledge," or the distinctive history and cultural identities of each student, to enhance the lesson by allowing them to contribute in a unique way (Vélez-Ibáñez and Greenberg). To allow students to fully share their funds of knowledge, the classroom environment should invite them to discuss what might be difficult parts of their identities, such as race or experiences with racism. By leading discussions about race, instructors can establish an environment conducive to addressing difficult subjects, which encourages students to share whatever they choose from their funds of knowledge.

In addition to valuing students' funds of knowledge, instructors can practice racial literacy to create a more racially inclusive classroom. Racial literacy "probe[s] the existence of racism and examine[s] the effects of race and institutionalized systems on their experiences and representation in US society" (Sealey-Ruiz, 386). Simply put, racial literacy is an attempt to understand how race and racism function in the subject material. For a discussion of a text to be racially literate, it should "simultaneously not lose sight of race and not only focus on race" (Garces and da Cruz, 10). Race is one of many factors that affect a person's life, and instructors should understand how race and racial structures influenced the text. For Francophone texts, concepts of race are intricately tied to the history of colonialism. Instructors should provide relevant colonial timelines to help students understand the position of the text in terms of legal, social, and historical change. Even if the author does not directly address the structural racism of colonialism and its postcolonial legacy, these factors influenced the creation and production of the text.

Deconstructing race and systemic racism in a text can lead to a more racially inclusive classroom, an important goal for French-speaking instructors who teach a language spoken by many different kinds of people across the globe. The aforementioned concepts aim to increase understanding of the importance of addressing race and providing useful vocabulary to do so. These terms and ideas should reframe instructors' perceptions of race and provide them with additional material to be explored.

## Choosing Materials: How to Avoid Tokenism and Racial Capitalism

This section will provide suggestions for racially inclusive syllabi and ideas for sourcing texts. First, one author should not represent an entire race or region. This is an example of tokenism, where texts or authors are included to check boxes rather than to represent valuable voices to be heard. Students might recognize tokenist practices, and as a result, students of color might see themselves as tokens in the classroom, especially in majority-white settings (Coté et al., 41). This leads them to feel marginalized, valued only for being non-white (Leong, 2155–56). A syllabus highlights the instructor's values, one of which must be valuing each student.

Second, instructors should make sure they are not including non-white texts for personal or departmental gain. Nancy Leong coined the terms *racial capital* and *racial capitalism* to describe this practice, which she defines as "the process of deriving social and economic value from the racial identity of another person" (2152). With many departments and instructors interested in reworking their syllabi to include non-white Francophone authors, instructors could unintentionally be using authors as racial capital. Racial capitalism could occur if one includes more non-white authors to make a course fit a diversity requirement or department goal, but then spends less time on those authors. Or, instructors could engage in racial capitalism by including non-white authors but then discussing the texts from a Eurocentric, white cultural standpoint, which fails to take into perspective the lived experiences of the author. The students should understand that these works are to be considered from a different cultural, racial, and historical viewpoint. Techniques for accomplishing this will be discussed in the third section.

Francophone manuals and anthologies are great resources for diversifying a syllabus, as the selections are generally shorter and include a variety of topics. From *Manuel de littérature africaine (classe de 1ère)* by Papa Guèye Ndiaye, I have successfully taught "Un étrange exil" by Cheikh Hamidou Kane, about a young African's difficulties after moving to France; "Pour une synthèse nouvelle…" by Aimé Césaire, which analyses the tensions between old and new in Black culture, then in humanity at large; and "Nuit de Sine," a poem by Léopold Sédar Senghor about the connections between ancestors, the earth, and the body. These works address topics familiar to many young adults while also incorporating race. Beginning with discussions on how race appears in the text can be a gateway to deconstructing the systemic racism the authors are pushing back against.

As a starting point for anthologies and manuals, the publishing house Présence Africaine offers solid resources. They print several books that provide instructors with great models for questions that amplify the author's voice. For example,

Ousmane Sembène's "Lettre de France," found in Ndiaye's collection, is about a young woman led to France on false promises and now imprisoned in her room. The short story is followed by questions that explore the larger cultural points expressed by the protagonist Nafi's experiences: 1) consider Nafi's homesickness and apply it to African-European cultural relationships; 2) compare Nafi's imagined experiences with her lived ones; and 3) study the relationships between colonial history and the motivations for Africans to immigrate to Europe (Ndiaye, 45–47). These questions approach the material from an African context by not asking students to draw from their personal experiences but instead to understand how the realities of others differ from their own. Students will still have to use their funds of knowledge to complete this exercise, but will expand their cultural and racial knowledge by imagining a different reality.

In addition to anthologies and manuals, graphic novels are an approachable medium that facilitates racial inclusion. The benefit of having images to guide discussions about race is another aid in stepping away from a Eurocentric viewpoint. L'Harmattan, a publisher that specializes in sub-Saharan Africa, has a *bande dessinée* (graphic novel) wing with selections from North and West Africa. *Lamsari et le trésor des Oudayas,* [*Lamsari and the Treasure of the Oudayas*] a graphic novel from L'Harmattan, is a fairly easy text that showcases Morocco's ethnic diversity and Rabat's history as an international port city. It also counters misconceptions of Muslim women by including a female detective as a protagonist. This book elicits dialogues about preconceptions of other cultures by showing students a more diverse, nuanced African society than they may have seen in other media. I have found this book to be a strong entry point for conversations on race because it allows students to see the diversity of a place that they might have previously believed to be homogenous.

For instructors who teach pre-20th-century courses, it becomes more difficult to create a racially inclusive syllabus. The topic of race should not be avoided nevertheless: even in Medieval times, the Crusades open the subject. Probing questions on conceptions of holy land, the white savior complex, Muslims as other, and false religious and cultural hierarchies can help students break down the pernicious and ongoing effects of orientalism and colonialism. Though written in 1984, Amin Maalouf's *Les Croisades vues par les Arabes* [*The Crusades Seen Through Arab Eyes*] counters the traditional European narrative of the Crusades and introduces students to a well-known Francophone author.

In an 18th-century course, instructors could include Voltaire's *L'ingénu; or The Sincere Huron* or Montesquieu's *Lettres persanes* [*Persian Letters*]. These texts could prompt discussions about the myth of the noble savage, fear of unexperienced cultural practices, anti-Blackness, and the role of racial labels in the perception of the other. These broad discussions, still tied to the texts, contribute to racial inclusivity and allow students of color to use their funds of knowledge. Even if there are not authors of color available for a particular century, students of color have greater academic success in classrooms that discuss questions of race, culture, and identity (Nieto, xiv).

## Guidelines and Practices: Praxis for Talking about Race

Before broaching the subject of race in the classroom, it helps to consider one's own race. I am a white, cisgender, heterosexual female. Before I write discussion questions for any text, especially one where the author or the characters do not share aspects of my identity, I think about how these factors influence my reading of the text and try to identify any racial biases. I have found it helpful to let my students know that I consider these influences before and while teaching the text.

In conjunction with recognizing racial biases, instructors will benefit from interrogating their own cultural biases. To identify cultural biases, it helps to consider what cultural knowledge one expects students to bring to the classroom, and what one does to include viewpoints other than one's own. It is especially beneficial to consider what funds of knowledge your students have previously shared that could contribute to the discussion. When students are asked to expand on the ideas proposed in the text, they should look for answers from the position of the characters or author. This way, students can try to understand experiences that are not their own or share their funds of knowledge if they align with the text. For instance, when analyzing a poem about African landscapes like "Souffles" by Birago Diop, instructors should avoid questions that exoticize the landscape. For Diop, the landscape is enchanting, not exotic, and represents a connection to his ancestors. Students should be asked to identify the sensations the author feels when seeing the landscape, as opposed to asking the students what sensations or images they see when reading the poem. By asking the students to see things from the author's perspective, students can challenge their cultural beliefs and encounter the author's humanity.

This practice also helps students realize that one's personal perspective might be influenced by racialized structures. The latter are defined as "the totality of the social relations and practices that reinforce white privilege" (Bonilla-Silva, 9). In other words, racism is built into our society, and it has shaped how we see the world. I have found that it helps open the dialogue by acknowledging that we are all part of racialized structures, instructors included, and that they have influenced our perspectives. This helps validate each student's lived experience and does not blame them for blind spots in their worldview. It is also a step toward deconstructing racialized structures. In the French-language classroom, instructors can unpack these issues by addressing current structures of privilege that stem from colonialism. This can help students realize that race is a construction, thus not real, and that racialized structures are based on falsely created categories (Lewis and Diamond, 4; Delgado and Stefancic, 9).

During the initial discussions that touch on race and racism, remember that it might be the first time they have heard an instructor talk about race. Some students might be excited about this; others might be intimidated. Students can identify the way systemic racism works in a Francophone context before applying it to their own reality, which allows a level of dissociation that might lessen concerns about broaching an uncomfortable topic. Additionally, students are often more likely to be honest or critical about overtly racist practices if they are not part of them. This critical thinking about race will easily map onto the complex history of American racism.

Ideally, race should be part of classroom discussions throughout the semester, so establishing a positive classroom climate from the beginning is crucial. Icebreakers that acknowledge race can be helpful. EdChange.org offers a "Critical Multicultural Pavilion" that proposes activities that can help students ease into discussions of race. Multiculturalism, though not "explicitly focused on race and racial realities," helps create a "foundation for race works to become part of the educational discourse" (Howard and Navarro, 257). Before choosing an activity, be sure to consider it from each student's perspective, especially students who might not have a country with which they identify culturally.

After discussions on multiculturalism, the next step is to introduce race into your textual analysis. In *What, Why and How Do We Do What We Do? Antiracism Education at the University*, Aminkeng A. Alemanji and Minna Siekkula suggest taking the following into consideration before designing a lesson that discusses race:

1. When writing questions and answering students, remember that you do not fully understand how race and racism function.
2. Find examples of structural racism in the text and think about how it affects the characters.
3. Talking about race is very personal and can force students to confront difficult realities.
4. Consider opening the discussion with this line: "I am here to discuss issues of race and racism with [you] from a learner's perspective."
5. Try to create an atmosphere of mutual respect, where students can ask questions that may expose their ignorance about race.
6. Remind students that you are talking about structural racism and racial power, not racists.
7. If you are encountering push back from your white students, help them work through their initial discomforts with talking about race, which Robin DiAngelo names as "white fragility."

*(Alemanji and Siekkula, 180–89; DiAngelo, 113)*

These guidelines can help structure a successful textual analysis that includes race. If the first discussion seems overwhelming, remember that deconstructing race and racism is an emotional task that requires ongoing efforts. If there is a difficult situation and you would like some guidance on best practices, reach out to your university's Diversity and Inclusion Office, if available. If not, the American Council on the Teaching of Foreign Languages has compiled a list of "Resources that Address Race, Diversity and Social Justice" that is specific to language teachers. Since the racial justice movements that began in early summer 2020, there have been a growing number of educators interested in antiracist teaching, and the resources for guidance and support are increasing as well.

## Conclusion

French departments around the nation suffered from their disinclination to embrace Francophonie during the 1990s. In "A Certain Idea of French: Cultural Studies, Literature and Theory," Lawrence Kritzman asserts that "eurocentrism and elitist attitudes … and the perception that … the good fight was now being played out in the politically hip universe of English-speaking literatures" led to a decline in enrollment and funding for French departments (146–47). Today, many French departments have already made the shift away from teaching uniquely European canonical authors to including women and Francophone authors.[2] We can continue this work by pushing beyond diversity toward the goal of racial inclusivity. Francophone literature and culture offer a plethora of "politically hip" materials that foster antiracist dialogue. There are classic books that discuss race forthrightly, such as Tahar Ben Jelloun's *Le racisme expliqué à ma fille* [*Racism Explained to My Daughter*] and Frantz Fanon's *Peau noire, masques blancs* [*Black Skin, White Masks*]. The works mentioned in the second section of this article are more subtle when decrying racism: they might show the violence of racism through the actions of the protagonist ("Un étrange exil"), address the cultural crises caused by structural racism and slavery ("Pour une synthèse nouvelle"), or ask the reader to consider the soul from an African perspective ("Nuit de sine"). The richness of Francophone literature provides nearly endless possibilities for antiracist teaching. It is our job to bridge the gap for our students between the racial reality of our world and the lessons to be drawn from the texts we teach. By creating a racially inclusive syllabus and classroom environment, instructors can work towards a more equitable society while also fostering student success and greater enrollment.

My goal is for this chapter to serve as a springboard for ideas and future learning. French instructors have unique tools to answer the calls for social and racial justice: we teach authors from all over the world who have experienced race in myriad ways; we can show students new angles to examine structural racism via the lens of colonialism; we can discuss racist practices in other countries before aligning them with racism in our society; we can foster a greater understanding of people around the world that students might not encounter in their other courses. The opportunities for implementation of these ideas are endless, with more resources and texts becoming available all the time.

We are teaching in a time of change. While change might sometimes seem overwhelming, it allows us to bring new methods to our classroom and to invent better ways to welcome our students. This chapter is just the beginning of the many ways we can improve racial inclusivity in the classroom.

## Notes

1 This may be because most educators in the United States are white: in 2017, 78% of all university faculty were white, while 80% of K-12 instructors were white ("Race/Ethnicity," Geiger). In a setting with overwhelmingly white teachers, students of color might struggle, as instructors might not be aware of how to best engage diverse cultures and identities (Glynn, 42, 45–46).
2 The first volume in this series, *Rethinking the French Classroom* (Meyer and Johnston), is a great resource for exploring female Francophone authors not found in the traditional canon.

## References

Alemanji, Aminkeng A. and Minna Siekkula. "What, Why and How Do We Do What We Do? Antiracism Education at the University." *Antiracism Education In and Out of Schools*, edited by Aminkeng A. Alemanji. Palgrave Macmillan, 2018, pp. 171–193.

Ben Jelloun, Tahar. *Le racisme expliqué à ma fille*. Éditions du Seuil, 2009.

Bonilla-Silva, Eduardo. *Racism without Racists: Color-Blind Racism and the Persistence of Racial Inequality in the United States*. Rowman & Littlefield, 2010.

Chanson, Jean-François. *Lamsari et le trésor des Oudayas*. L'Harmattan, 2015.

Coté, Brandon et al. "From Silence and Resistance to Tongues Untied: Talking About Race in the College Classroom." *Challenges of Multicultural Education: Teaching and Taking Diversity Courses*, edited by Norah Peters-Davis and Jeffrey Shultz. Routledge, 2005, pp. 47–61. doi:10.4324/9781315635644-8.

Critical Multicultural Pavilion. *Edchange*, www.edchange.org/multicultural.

Delgado, Richard and Jean Stefancic. *Critical Race Theory: An Introduction*. New York UP, 2017.

DiAngelo, Robin. *White Fragility: Why It's So Hard to Talk About Racism*. Beacon, 2018.

Diop, Birago. "Souffles." *Présence africaine*, no. 12, January 1951, pp. 187–189.

Dowd, Alicia C. and Estela Mara Bensimon. *Engaging the "Race Question": Accountability and Equity in U.S. Higher Education*. Teachers College Press, 2015.

Fanon, Frantz. *Peau noire, masques blancs*. Éditions du Seuil, 1966.

Garces, Liliana M. and Cynthia Gordon da Cruz. "A Strategic Racial Equity Framework." *Peabody Journal of Education*, May 2017, pp. 322–342. doi:10.1080/0161956X.2017.1325592.

Geiger, A.W. "Public School Teachers Much Less Racially Diverse than Students in US." *Pew Research Center*, 21 August 2020, www.pewresearch.org/fact-tank/2018/08/27/americas-public-school-teachers-are-far-less-racially-and-ethnically-diverse-than-their-students.

Glynn, Cassandra Lea. *The Role of Ethnicity in the Foreign Language Classroom: Perspectives on African-American Students' Enrollment, Experiences, and Identity*. U of Minnesota P, 2012.

Howard, Tyrone C. and Oscar Navarro. "Critical Race Theory 20 Years Later." *Urban Education*, vol. 51, no. 3, 2016, pp. 253–273. doi:10.1177/0042085915622541.

Kendi, Ibram X. *How to Be an Antiracist*. Vintage, 2019.

Kritzman, Lawrence D. "A Certain Idea of French: Cultural Studies, Literature and Theory." *Yale French Studies*, no. 103, 2003, pp. 146–147. doi:10.2307/3182542.

Leong, Nancy. "Racial Capitalism." *Harvard Law Review*, vol. 126, no. 8, 2013, pp. 2131–2226. www.jstor.org/stable/23415098.

Lewis, Amanda E. and John B. Diamond. *Despite the Best Intentions: How Racial Inequality Thrives in Good Schools*. Oxford UP, 2015.

Maalouf, Amin. *Les Croisades vues par les Arabes*. J'ai Lu, 1999.

Meyer, E. Nicole and Joyce Johnston. *Rethinking the French Classroom: New Approaches to Teaching Contemporary French and Francophone Women*. Routledge, 2019.

Montesquieu, Charles de Secondat. *Lettres persanes*. Flammarion, [1721] 2019.

Ndiaye, Papa Guèye, editor. *Manuel de littérature africaine (classe de 1ère)*. Présence Africaine, 1978.

Nieto, Sonia. *Language, Culture, and Teaching: Critical Perspectives*. Routledge, 2018.

"Race/Ethnicity of College Faculty." National Center for Education Statistics (NCES), 2019, nces.ed.gov/fastfacts/display.asp?id=61.

"Resources that Address Race, Diversity and Social Justice." American Council on the Teaching of Foreign Languages, www.actfl.org/resources/resources-language-educators-address-issues-race-diversity-and-social-justice.

Sealey-Ruiz, Yolanda. "Building Racial Literacy in First-Year Composition." *Teaching English in the Two Year College*, vol. 40, no. 4, 2013, pp. 384–398.

Sturm, Susan et al. "Full Participation: Building the Architecture for Diversity and Community Engagement in Higher Education." Imagining America: Artists and Scholars in Public Life Conference. Minneapolis-St Paul, MN, September 2011.

Vélez-Ibáñez, Carlos G. and James B. Greenberg. "Formation and Transformation of Funds of Knowledge among U.S.-Mexican Households." *Anthropology & Education Quarterly*, vol. 23, no. 4, 1992, pp. 313–335. www.jstor.org/stable/3195869.

Voltaire. *L'ingénu*. Ligaran, [1767] 2014.

# SECTION II
# Inclusively Speaking

# 5
# INCLUSIVE LANGUAGE PEDAGOGY FOR (UN)TEACHING GENDER IN FRENCH

*Kiki Kosnick*

From the first French class that I taught, I prompted my students not to assume that every hypothetical *je* (I) and *tu* (you) was masculine; I encouraged them to conjugate verbs in the form of *nous sommes arrivé(e)s*.[1] As a queer person, providing examples of same-gender couples and non-traditional families came naturally to me. I would beam when my students' understanding of grammatical agreement was evidenced through their attention to gender equality or their disruption of the heteronormative defaults so pervasive in our textbooks. Simultaneously, as I grew my connections and allyship within the LGBTQ+ community, some of my dearest friends came out as non-binary.[2] And I realized that I had no idea how to describe them in French nor how to share with my students a story involving one of them. Today, I identify as non-binary and thus negotiate the constraints and possibilities of French every day in my teaching.

The United Nations' website dedicated to gender-inclusive language (*langage inclusif*) explains: "Using gender-inclusive language means speaking and writing in a way that does not discriminate against a particular sex, social gender or gender identity, and does not perpetuate gender stereotypes." One might understand the UN's position as supportive of all genders. However, by failing to mention that gender-neutral forms are often used to express non-binary genders, not simply to make gender invisible, the UN reminds us that avoiding gender is not necessarily the same as affirming it. What is more, by simultaneously underscoring the usage of feminine and masculine forms, the UN's approach to gender inclusivity stands out as an example of how the possibility of non-binary gender expression easily—and, in my view, dangerously—risks collapsing into a feminist cause.

This essay makes a case for queer and feminist coalition building through a methodology for teaching French that creates multiple access points for the expression and validation of non-binary genders in ways that mutually reinforce interconnected linguistic and sociocultural struggles related to gender for women and non-binary people. First, I present an overview of the public debate surrounding gender inclusivity in French and outline the principles of *écriture inclusive* (inclusive writing). I then delineate a toolkit for gender-inclusive French that combines elements of *écriture inclusive* with neologisms for essential non-binary grammatical forms. Finally, I interweave these concepts in a gender-inclusive approach to French language pedagogy.

## The Failures and Imperatives of *Langage Inclusif*

In the Francophone context, *langage inclusif* overwhelmingly signifies linguistic salience of women and girls. Even from this extremely limited perspective on gender, gender-inclusive French continues to be fraught with polemics, particularly in the implementation of aspects of *écriture inclusive*. While promoting parity for people who use feminine pronouns by working against the concept of generic masculine and the rule that the masculine prevails over the feminine (*le masculin l'emporte sur le féminin*) codified in standard French, the *Manuel d'écriture inclusive* [*Gender-Inclusive Language in France: A Manual*] reifies gender binarism by defining *écriture inclusive* as: "the set of graphical and syntactical marks that ensure an equality of representation for *both* sexes" (Haddad, 4; my emphasis). The *Manuel* outlines the following three conventions of inclusive writing: "Usage of feminine forms for functions, jobs, ranks and titles; Usage of both masculine and feminine forms by enumeration in alphabetical order, by adding sparingly a [middot] (·), or by the use of gender-neutral [epicene] terms; Avoidance of capital letters in gender-specific terms such as 'Men' or 'Mankind'" (7). Although characteristics of *écriture inclusive* are valuable in expressing non-binary genders, the *Manuel* consistently refers exclusively to women and men.

Longstanding debates surrounding gender inclusivity in the French language intensified in fall 2017 when Éditions Hatier published the first textbook written in *écriture inclusive* (ÉH). International public controversy ensued. On October 26 the Académie Française released a formal declaration against "l'écriture dite (said to be) 'inclusive'" that disparages both the middot and double flexions ("[l]a multiplication des marques orthographiques et syntaxiques"), infamously arguing that they place the French language in mortal danger (péril mortel) by rendering it illegible and unpronounceable ("Déclaration"). What is perhaps most disappointing about the Académie's critique is that it fails even to acknowledge why *écriture inclusive* has been gaining traction in the first place. In response, 314 Francophone educators signed a manifesto published November 7 on Slate.fr that outlines their reasons for no longer teaching that the masculine prevails. They argue: "repeating this catchphrase to children … incites mental representations that load women and men to accept the superiority of one sex [male] over the other [female]" (my translation). Two weeks later, French Prime Minister Édouard Philippe chimed in with a statement regarding the "rules of feminization" in official government documents. Philippe begins by underscoring a commitment to "equality between women and men" while asserting that "the masculine is a generic form" (my translation). Citing studies conducted in 2017, the *Manuel d'écriture inclusive* succinctly responds to this common misconception: "use of the masculine form is not perceived as neutral despite its apparent intention. It actually generates fewer feminine mental representations among survey respondents [than] a generic epicene word" (19). Although the Prime Minister's statement requests usage of feminine forms of jobs and titles as well as double flexions—two conventions of *écriture inclusive*—paradoxically, it calls on concerned parties not to use "l'écriture dite inclusive." Philippe refers readers to Cerquiglini's 1999 *Femme, j'écris ton nom…* [*Woman, I Write Your Name…*] instead. In short, Philippe's rhetoric coopts conventions of *écriture inclusive*, distances *la République* from *écriture inclusive*, and reduces it to its most polemic characteristic: the middot.

Given that the middot is a valuable tool not only for women but also for non-binary people, it would be reasonable to critique this abundance of heated opposition as both misogynistic and queerphobic. One need only observe the reiteration of "écriture *dite* inclusive" (my emphasis) in the formal statements by the Académie Française and the Prime Minister alongside the quotation marks inserted around *inclusive* in the Académie's to recognize an attempt by these governing bodies to police the efforts of organizations and educators working towards progressive linguistic and social reform by categorizing their work as a failed performative—by dubbing *écriture inclusive* a misnomer while selectively appropriating it. Whereas the Académie's opposition to the middot is unwavering, on February 28, 2019 les immortel·les finally endorsed "féminisation" of jobs and functions after several years of opposition ("Féminisation"). That both the Académie and the Prime Minister refer to the usage of feminine forms as "féminisation" demonstrates that they continue to view the masculine as the default, privileged form and the feminine as a mere derivative. Éliane Viennot's work convincingly turns the notion of *féminisation* on its head by underscoring the *masculinisation* of the French language. Viennot highlights the existence of feminine forms throughout history while recounting how sexist grammarians eradicated egalitarian practices such as proximity agreements in favor of linguistic dominance of the masculine.[3]

We activist-educators might envision an Académie intent on working with language users to expand possibilities for communication that is intelligible and affirming of all genders. As the visibility of non-binary gender identities continues to increase both in global media and in our academic institutions, we must respond with open minds, caring hearts, and practical solutions. It goes without saying that as teachers of French we are tasked with negotiating the limitations of standard French not only in available textbooks but also in the vast bulk of literary, cinematographic, and journalistic materials currently at our disposal. Moreover, in some French programs, language purists maintain a majority. That we support our students' growth in standard French remains imperative in order to prepare them for engagement with Francophone cultural products, both contemporary and historical, in addition to target-language interactions in their day-to-day lives. At the same time, it is our responsibility to establish learning communities in which our students have access to vital tools of authentic self-expression—even, and especially, when the Académie fails to provide these tools. Such is certainly the case for non-binary students and users of French. The method described here aims to address this deep, complex, and ever-evolving need.

This pedagogic approach to French for all genders adopts and adapts conventions systematized in the 2019 *Manuel d'écriture inclusive* and infuses them with options for navigating the unique linguistic challenges of expressing non-binary gender. I delineate four key strategies—epicene words, rewordings, middots, and neologisms—and I demonstrate how to interweave them intentionally to promote gender inclusivity. While useful individually, I advocate for incorporating this toolkit of queer and feminist linguistic strategies in renewed and nuanced configurations as appropriate for the needs of each unique learning community, level of proficiency, and instructional objective. Building from the features of standard French that are inherently gender-inclusive (or least problematic), this combinatorial approach prioritizes clarity. It reinforces aspects of *écriture inclusive* while simultaneously centering and normalizing new and contested forms that are most indispensable to non-binary expression. In other words, this system encourages the life-giving and lifelong work—indeed, the political act—of learning to use language differently. By claiming agency over our grammar, we nurture greater language proficiency—both in ourselves and in our students. Such reflexivity and adaptability might also help to bridge the gap (read: strengthen the overlap) between language acquisition and the critical analysis of literary and cultural documents that all too often poses a challenge to students as they advance in our programs.

Going forward, I flesh out a framework for navigating the complexities of fundamental grammar topics while noting points of tension including relevant distinctions between writing and speech and the intelligibility of neologisms. I also offer insight on how to respond when conflicts arise between clarity, proficiency, and the necessity of gender-affirming linguistic expression. Although the proposed method focuses on the introductory level, the concepts are easily translatable. The beginning of any course or module is a great time to integrate and reinforce gender-inclusive practices while reviewing and expanding on foundational concepts. Such attention can be especially meaningful to students whose previous French classes failed to address gender inclusivity.

## Gender-Inclusive French Grammar Toolkit

### *Epicene words*

Epicene words including adjectives (e.g., *agréable, calme, timide*) and substantives (e.g., *bénévole, journaliste, psychologue*) are unmarked by gender. The unique singular form agrees with all genders; the plural bypasses *le masculin l'emporte sur le féminin* in its capacity to signify women, non-binary individuals, men, or two or more people of any gender without one prevailing over the other(s).

## Rewordings

This strategy encompasses morphological and syntactic adjustments such as synonyms and circumlocutions. Consider gender-inclusive model sentences like *je suis quelqu'un de curieux* or *je suis une personne joyeuse*. Here, adjectives qualify *quelqu'un* and *personne*, making the gender of the subject *je* inconsequential. For professions, highlight structures like *je suis spécialiste de l'informatique* (I am a computer specialist) and *je travaille dans l'informatique* (I work in computers) in lieu of *je suis informaticien·ne*. Regarding descriptions of people, when multiple options could express the same meaning, prioritize word choice in this order:

1. invariable expressions (e.g., *avoir hâte, être de bonne humeur*) and epicene adjectives (e.g., replace *gentil·le* with *sympathique*, replace *malheureuse* and *malheureux* with *triste*, etc.);
2. words for which a middot does not affect pronunciation (e.g., *fatigué·e, joli·e, nul·le, ravi·e*);
3. words with a middot which, although unpronounceable, are viable for written activities (e.g., *débrouillard·e, intelligent·e, patient·e*).

## Middots[4]

Mindful usage of the middot offers possibilities for increased non-binary inclusion, but because the middot is commonly considered an economical abbreviation of the double flexion of masculine and feminine forms—it is justifiably critiqued for reinscribing the gender binary. *Écriture inclusive* stipulates that a word written with a middot should be expanded alphabetically in oral communication. Accordingly, *les étudiant·es* in writing translates in speech as an utterance that precludes non-binary genders: *les étudiantes et les étudiants*. Florence Ashley makes the same point about "binary inclusive French" —calling out French feminists like Viennot for promoting binarism while crediting Quebecois feminists with efforts towards non-binary inclusion (2). Ashley clarifies that Viennot's brand of *français inclusif*, which disregards non-binary gender, is not the same as *français neutre* in which non-binary expression is attainable.

In writing, however, the plural form *étudiant·es* denotes: 1) two or more non-binary students; 2) the double flexion *les étudiantes et les étudiants*; or 3) the triple flexion *les étudiantes, les étudiant·es, et les étudiants*. It follows then that a non-binary person could write but not speak *je suis étudiant·e en français*. In such instances of oral communication, we rely on rewording: *je suis élève en français* or *j'étudie le français*. It is worth noting that whereas double flexions and feminine forms of jobs and titles are important for visibility of women, perhaps ironically, they create additional complications for non-binary people in that the Académie's "neutral" usage of the masculine acts as an umbrella under which both women and non-binary people remain obscured. Although the middot shores up aspects of gender-inclusive written representation, non-binary French necessitates additional strategies.

## Neologisms

These indispensable yet non-codified words and new word endings allow for written and oral linguistic expression that is unequivocally non-binary (i.e., not ambiguous through avoidance of gendered markers). Many French-language sources refer to *genre neutre* and *langage neutre*. I prefer the designation *non-binaire* over *neutre* because it resonates with my students while maintaining semantic distance from the linguistic concept of grammatical neuter (which risks reading as impersonal, inanimate, or indistinct). Despite many proposed non-binary terms and graphemes, there is minimal consensus and scant mainstream awareness. As educators committed to gender inclusivity, we must seek out, honor, and amplify the voices and linguistic practices of non-binary Francophones while also curating available options to meet the unique needs of our language-learning communities. My pedagogic practice regarding non-binary neologisms and word endings is shaped by several key sources.[5]

As primary grammar authorities in our classrooms, we must remember that the options we endorse constrain the possibility of our students' authentic self-expression. We should take care never to prescribe the limits of their gender while also supporting them to develop linguistic agency over it. I introduce my students to this shifting linguistic landscape, call on them to help to shape our shared practice, and encourage their autonomy in negotiating these nuances and tensions as their proficiency develops. Below, I present a synthesis of my current treatment of non-binary neologisms and word endings for each of the five classes of words marked by gender in French:

## Past Participles

Past participles in writing are rendered non-binary in the singular with a middot: *arrivé·e, attendu·e, parti·e*. For reasons already discussed in relation to the middot, some activist-scholars suggest alternate endings: *arrivæ, attendux, partix*. In the system developed by the linguist Alpheratz, a "z" is added to a past participle for plural agreement if needed ("Genre neutre"). Thus *arrivæ, attendux, partix* in the singular become *arrivæs, attenduz, partiz* in the plural. *Arrivæ* defaults to the standard addition of an "s" since the "æ" already differentiates it from *arrivé* and *arrivée* in writing. Similarly, since feminine and masculine past participles are phonetically identical, there is no need to distinguish non-binary forms in speech. In writing, whereas *je suis parti·e* connotes positions between masculine and feminine, *je suis partix* conveys disidentification from an innately binary gender spectrum while providing an option that is irrevocably non-binary.

## *Pronouns and Determiners*

The palpable need for third-person non-binary pronouns and determiners in French is evidenced in the proliferation of academic inquiry, journalistic coverage, and social media content devoted to the topic in recent years. Signaling this cultural shift, researchers published online "Le Chantier linguistique: éléments pour une grammaire non-binaire" ["The Linguistic Work Zone: Components for Non-Binary Grammar"] during the 2015 Atelier Queer Week (Coutant *et al.*). Notably since then, Vassar College responded by hosting the 2018 symposium "Legitimizing 'iel'" (Swamy and Mackenzie). My usage of non-binary pronouns has crystalized around forms referenced—and sometimes criticized—because they combine elements of traditional feminine and masculine pronouns to create portmanteaus that have the advantage of being readily intelligible given their similarity to standard forms, e.g., the third-person subject pronoun *iel* (pronounced [jɛl]) blends the phonemes of *il* and *elle*. For transparency, I present *iel* and associated pronouns and determiners in bold alongside feminine and masculine forms:

> subject pronouns : *elle,* **iel,** *il* & *elles,* **iels,** *ils*
> demonstrative pronouns : *celle,* **cellui,** *celui* & *celles,* **celleux,** *ceux*
> disjunctive pronouns : *elle,* **ellui,** *lui* & *elles,* **elleux,** *eux*
> direct object pronouns: *la,* **læ,** *le*
> definite articles: *la,* **læ,** *le*
> indefinite articles : *une,* **un·e,** *un*
> possessive determiners : ma, **maon**, mon; ta,**taon**, ton; sa,**saon**, son

An increasingly well-known alternative to *iel* is *al*, a pronoun first established by Alpheratz in the 2015 novel *Requiem*. In Alpheratz's lexicon, *al* also replaces the *il* of impersonal expressions like *il pleut*. *Al* resists the /i/ and /ɛ/ phonemes that distinguish *il* from *elle* while reading as a third-person pronoun. Similarly, *al*'s definite article *lu* and indefinite article *an* escape criticism directed at the merged forms *læ* and *un·e* commonly employed with *iel*. In addition, *an* (pronounced [ɑn]) works in oral communication whereas *un·e* does not. Conversely, for Anglophones learning French, it is advantageous that *læ* and *les* are homophones because usage of *them* as both a non-binary singular pronoun (*læ*) and a plural pronoun (*les*) is already a conditioned sensibility. Taking *al* and *iel* as examples, either pronoun could be used to affirm an individual's non-binary gender or to refer to an individual of any gender whose pronouns are unknown. By extension, *als* and *iels* are non-binary plural pronouns analogous to the exclusively feminine *elles* and exclusively masculine *ils*. Proposing *als* or *iels* as *neutre pluriel*, as Alpheratz does for *als*, resolves the problem of *le masculin l'emporte sur le féminin*—and, might I add, *sur le non-binaire*. Nevertheless, this strategy creates a different, interconnected problem: unequal linguistic representation of non-binary people.

Whereas *elles* and *ils* would maintain distinct pronouns—and *elles* would finally take up space as materialized by Monique Wittig in *Les Guérillères* over fifty years ago—non-binary people would share their pronouns with: 1) impersonal expressions; 2) people whose pronouns are unknown; and 3) groups of two or more people of incongruent genders when referenced collectively. This problem is paralleled in English with: 1) plural *they*; 2) non-binary singular *they* (e.g., They are my best friend.); and 3) *they* in reference to a person whose pronouns are unknown (e.g., Someone called and they said…). The difference in French is that adopting *als* in the fashion of *they (plural)* withholds from *ells*—and, here again, also from *als* (the collective non-binary *als* or *iels, et al.*, etc.) who are just now becoming linguistically possible—the opportunity to be uniquely marked and affirmed in language after centuries spent eclipsed by *ils*. Moreover, compulsory avoidance of gendered language results in denying transgender women and men who use binary pronouns the experience of having their gender acknowledged. Notably in the classroom, we must not overlook the significance of pronouns and their relationship to gender, especially for students who face marginalization.

## Adjectives and Substantives

Many nouns and their qualifiers are unsurprisingly complex given the multitude of endings and agreement rules already codified in standard French. Systematizations of gender-neutral adjectival and nominal inflections have been proposed similar to those for past participles.[6] In order to prioritize clarity in my facilitation of language acquisition—including attention to pronunciation and orthography—I reference newly developed adjectival and nominal endings but I do not teach them (yet). Because the combined usage of epicene words, rewordings, and middots addresses adjectives and nouns to some extent, I prefer to leverage these strategies. I do, however, teach non-binary options for family terms including *adelphe* and *frœur* (sibling) and *tancle* (parent's sibling).

## French for All Genders: An Instructional Manifesto

1. Begin with unfussy structures that activate broad communicative potential and are inherently gender-flexible. This approach conditions learners to express meaning, not morphemes, which helps to disrupt the exact-translation impulse that often interferes with accuracy. Prepare to adapt your pedagogical materials by centering, emphasizing, minimizing, and supplementing in ways that attend to inclusivity, proficiency, and learning objectives.
2. Introduce first-person and second-person subject pronouns at the outset. When you progress to third-person pronouns, include at least one non-binary

option such that standard pronouns and neopronoun(s) are given equal attention: *Al/Elle/Iel//Il/On étudie le français*. Reconsider activities that require students to gender themselves and never put them on the spot in class without their consent. Focus instead on practicing forms using pictures of celebrities and their pronouns. For example, non-binary singer Sam Smith's pronoun is *they*. This doesn't necessarily mean Sam would use *iel* in French, but they might. Simply noting this creates an instructive moment in which we are reminded to check our assumptions about gender and pronouns.

3. Avoid dreadful textbook exercises that emphasize gender binarism such as *Il est français et elle est française*. When approaching *être*, foreground structures like *Al/Elle/Iel//Il/On est de Montréal* and nous sommes en ville/à la bibliothèque/au cinéma. Teach articles and adjectives with objects first. *Qu'est-ce que c'est? C'est une chaise? Mais non, c'est un livre. C'est le livre de Kiki. C'est un bon livre. C'est une histoire intéressante.* Introduce nationalities and reinforce agreement by focusing on preferences. *Voilà un petit restaurant japonais. J'adore la cuisine japonaise. Je n'aime pas le cinéma américain mais j'aime la musique américaine.* For descriptions of people, leverage epicene words, rewordings, and (silent) middots.

4. Give lots of energy to verbs; they are quite egalitarian. Start with *aimer* and *détester*. Conjugate for all genders. Showcase dynamic irregular verbs like *faire* and expressions with *avoir*. Progressively incorporate more complex forms.

5. Work towards equitable instruction and assessment. Consider who is centered in your examples and whether all students have appropriate tools to express their lived experiences. Investigate and correct bias in your grading practices. Remember that language production in the first-person requires additional work for students who use feminine and non-binary pronouns. Take care not to disproportionately advantage students who use masculine pronouns.

6. Practice anti-racism, anti-classism, and anti-ableism in addition to queer and feminist allyship. In our classrooms, we have the opportunity to create the most affirming environment possible for our students. In order to initiate the conversations we most desperately need, we must be willing to speak, make mistakes, and learn how to correct these mistakes. This requires transparency, vulnerability, autonomy, and a sense of belonging—which makes the language classroom an ideal place to grow this work.

7. Be empowered that when we teach language, we teach a framework for being in the world, making meaning, and encountering difference. In the French-language classroom, this work requires us not only to teach gender in renewed and ever-evolving ways but also, inextricably, to unteach everyday linguistic and psychic assumptions related to gender. Let our pedagogies give life to the world we envision as we coalesce (not standardize) the possibilities of authentic expression for all genders.

## Notes

1 Aligned with the conventions of écriture inclusive, I now generally denote such forms with a middot as in nous sommes arrivé·es.
2 For clarity, I use non-binary (in French, non-binaire) as an umbrella term for gender identities outside or in-between the gender binary (e.g., genderqueer, genderfluid, pangender) as well as those that disidentify with the concept of gender (e.g., agender, genderless). Although non-binary is an increasingly popular and readily embraced term, individuals under this conceptual umbrella might or might not identify as non-binary. A non-binary person might or might not also identify as transgender. It is important to note that gender identity does not necessarily determine pronoun usage. For example, someone who is non-binary might use masculine or feminine pronouns exclusively or in conjunction with non-binary pronouns.
3 See Viennot. Notably, "Françaises, Français: le langage inclusif n'est pas une nouveauté!" provides a tidy synopsis.
4 A notable update in the 2019 edition of the Manuel d'écriture inclusive is the deletion of the second middot from plural forms. For example, ami·e·s per the 2017 convention is now written ami·es. To type the middot on Windows, press Alt+0183; on a Mac with QWERTY keyboard, press shift+option+9. For more information, see page 26 of the English *Manual* or page 27 of the French Manuel available at www.motscles.net/ecriture-inclusive.
5 For further context, including analysis of innovative usage of standard French in Garréta's novel *Sphinx*, see Kosnick. For a history of linguistic innovations related to gender in French, see Greco. For a small case study centering the experiences of my French 101 students, see Garbe. See Knisely for forms in use by non-binary Francophones with attention to frequency and comprehensibility. For helpful infographics, see blogger *alexentousgenres*. For an overview including additional forms not discussed here and a proposed systematization of *français neutre* that emphasizes Alpheratz's *Grammaire du français inclusif*, see Ashley.
6 Ashley surveys modular forms (e.g., middot forms like *radical·e* and portmanteaus like *rêveureuse*) and Alpheratz's systematized forms (e.g., *radicalx* and *rêvaire*) on page 12.

## References

Académie Française. "Déclaration de l'Académie française sur l'écriture dite 'inclusive.'" 26 October, 2017, www.academie-francaise.fr/actualites/declaration-de-lacademie-francaise-sur-lecriture-dite-inclusive.
Académie Française. "*La Féminisation des noms de métiers et de fonctions.*" March 1, 2019, www.academie-.francaise.fr/actualites/la-feminisation-des-noms-de-metiers-et-de-fonctions.
Alexentousgenres. "*Le Langage neutre en français.*" April 19, 2017, www.entousgenresblog.wordpress.com/2017/04/19/quels-pronoms-neutres-en-francais-et-comment-les-utiliser.
Alpheratz. "Genre neutre." *Alpheratz*, 2018, www.alpheratz.fr/linguistique/genre-neutre.
—. *Grammaire du français inclusif.* Vents solar, 2018.
—. *Requiem.* CreateSpace, 2015.
Ashley, Florence. "Les personnes non-binaires en français: une perspective concernée et militante." *H-France Salon*, vol. 11, no. 14, 2019, www.h-france.net/Salon/Salon Vol11no14.5.Ashley.pdf.
Cerquiglini, Bernard. "Femme, j'écris ton nom…Guide d'aide à la féminisation des noms de métiers, titres, grades et fonctions." *Vie Publique*, 1999, www.vie-publique.fr/rapport/25339-guide-daide-la-feminisation-des-noms-de-metiers.
Coutant, Alice *et al.* "Le Chantier linguistique: éléments pour une grammaire non-binaire." Slideshare, March 8, 2015, www.slideshare.net/noemiemarignier/queer-week.

@Éditions Hatier. "Très fier.ère.s d'avoir publié le premier manuel scolaire en écriture inclusive! Magellan Questionner le Monde CE2." Twitter, September 23,2017, www.twitter.com/editionshatier/status/911553296313327616?lang=en.

Garbe, Rebecca. "Embracing *écriture inclusive*: Students Respond to Gender Inclusivity in the French-Language Classroom." *Augustana Digital Commons*, May 2020, https://digitalcommons.augustana.edu/honrstudent/11.

Garréta, Anne. *Sphinx*. Grasset, 1986.

Greco, Luca. "Linguistic Uprisings: Towards a Grammar of Emancipation." *H-France Salon*, vol. 11, no. 14, 2019, www.h-france.net/Salon/SalonVol11no14.3.Greco.pdf.

Haddad, Raphaël. *Gender-Inclusive Language in France: A Manual*. Translated by Elsa Stéphan. Mots-Clés, 2019. www.motscles.net/ecriture-inclusive.

Knisely, Kris Aric. "Le français non-binaire: Linguistic Forms Used by Non-Binary Speakers of French." *Foreign Language Annals*, vol. 53, no. 4, Winter 2020, pp. 850–876.

Kosnick, Kiki. "The Everyday Poetics of Gender-Inclusive French: Strategies for Navigating the Linguistic Landscape." *Modern & Contemporary France*, vol. 27, no. 2, 2019, pp. 147–161. www.tandfonline.com/doi/full/10.1080/09639489.2019.1588869.

Philippe, Édouard. "Circulaire du 21 novembre 2017 relative aux règles de féminisation et de rédaction des textes publiés au Journal officiel de la République française." November 21, 2017, www.legifrance.gouv.fr/jo_pdf.do?id=JORFTEXT000036068906.

*Slate.fr*. "Nous n'enseignerons plus que 'le masculin l'emporte sur le féminin.'" November 7, 2017, www.slate.fr/story/153492/manifeste-professeurs-professeures-enseignerons-plus-masculin-emporte-sur-le-feminin.

Swamy, Vinay and Louisa Mackenzie, eds. "Legitimizing 'iel'? Language and Trans Communities in Francophone and Anglophone Spaces." *H-France Salon*, vol. 11, no. 14, 2019, https://h-france.net/h-france-salon-volume-11-2019/#1114.

United Nations. "Gender-Inclusive Language." www.un.org/en/gender-inclusive-language.

Viennot, Éliane. "Françaises, Français: le langage inclusif n'est pas une nouveauté!" *The Conversation*, 15 Oct. 2018, www.theconversation.com/francaises-francais-le-langage-inclusif-nest-pas-une-nouveaute-104622.

—. *Le langage inclusif: Pourquoi, comment?* Éditions iXe, 2018.

—. *Non, le masculin ne l'emporte pas sur le féminin*. Éditions iXe, 2017.

Wittig, Monique. *Les Guérillères*. Paris: Les Éditions de Minuit, 1969.

# 6

# HOW CAN WE TEACH FRENCH INCLUSIVELY?

## Challenges and Resistance

*Dominique Carlini Versini*

Inclusive language has been at the center of heated debates in France over the past forty years. These debates took a new turn in 2016 when the *Manuel d'écriture inclusive* [*Inclusive Writing Manual*] was published. The *Manuel* makes a series of recommendations to be more inclusive of the feminine in writing. These include: the feminization of names of professions, the use of both the feminine and the masculine rather than employing the "neutral" masculine, and the rejection of antonomasia (such as Woman or Man) (Baric and Haddad, 6). Researchers have also noted the potential of inclusive writing to make room for queer and non-binary expression in French, notably through the use of the middot to include both the feminine and masculine endings of a noun when it is referring to people (i.e. *auteur·rice*; writer) or through gender-neutral words (Lessard and Zaccour, 22).[1] The publication of the manual has placed inclusive language under the spotlight again and generated a new outburst of attacks from its opponents. Most notably there was animosity towards the feminization of titles and professions and the use of the middot, commonly referred to in French as *écriture inclusive* (inclusive writing). The case of the feminization of titles and professions is particularly relevant to this paper, as I will discuss teaching grammatical gender to students.

As I will argue in this chapter, understanding inclusive language practices requires a reflection on the history of the French language. Indeed, Éliane Viennot notes that numerous names of professions existed in both the feminine and the masculine forms, but from the seventeenth century onward, the predominantly male and masculinist grammarians erased the use of the former (45–62) and asserted the now infamous rule according to which: "*Le masculin est plus noble que le féminin*" (The masculine form is nobler than the feminine) (61).[2] The debates gained new vigor since the 1980's in France (Viennot et al., 65). French feminists and other supporters of feminization were repeatedly attacked by their opponents, and most notably by

DOI: 10.4324/9781003126461-7

members of the ultra-conservative Académie Française, who proved to be extremely reluctant to introduce the feminine into the professional lexis. Their reaction revealed a rigid understanding of language and a resistance to progress when it comes to women's emancipation and gender equality in France.[3] At a time when universities and Modern Language departments all over the UK and the global North are struggling to respond to the need for engaging in equality, diversity, and inclusion practices, it is of great importance to think about these issues in the French language classroom.[4]

In this chapter, I examine the challenges that teaching inclusive language creates in the French grammar class as well as in literary classes and in interactions outside the classroom. I discuss my experience introducing the feminization of French names of professions, titles, and other forms of inclusive writing to first, second, and final year French BA students in the UK and in Ireland. I acknowledge various forms of resistance encountered from students as well as my own difficulty as a native French speaker de-masculinizing French when speaking and writing. For me, teaching language inclusively is a destabilizing practice that makes the classroom a space of negotiation where numerous voices can be heard. Ultimately, I demonstrate the importance of grammar as a point of entry into the complexity of language and culture and as an inclusive tool of learning.

## Teaching French Inclusively: An Empirical Account

Over the course of the last two years, I have taught French language to BA students at an Irish and a British institution.[5] My profile is a hybrid one, as I have experience in teaching French language since my graduate studies, which has been the core of my teaching, and I have also been teaching cultural modules to undergraduate and graduate students. I currently teach written skills modules to students at all levels of the French undergraduate curriculum. These modules combine a mix of grammar, translation, and essay writing on societal issues. My research interrogating women's words and their place in society informs my teaching, which takes root in a belief in the classroom as a space of diversity and inclusion.[6]

Research shows that grammar is one of the most important linguistic components in the language classroom both from the perspective of teachers, who devote extra time to it during the class, and for learners (Fougerouse, 166–67) even before phonetics or vocabulary. Grammar is perceived as a stable and safe base by learners to build language acquisition (167). However, it is my contention that language teaching and learning should be understood as more than the acquisition of a set of rules, but also as a point of entry to the culture studied. Grammar teaching then reveals the tight intertwining of language and culture and becomes a negotiating position for the teacher to convey to students a clear understanding of how the language works, while embracing its cultural potential. For the purpose of this article, I see grammar as a tool to understand the historical erasure of the feminine in language and to undo that erasure through inclusive strategies. This tension is especially difficult to maneuver in the case of French grammar teaching, which is traditionally perceived by English native learners as difficult (Abu-Laila, 13). This difficulty lays notably in the centrality of gender in the French language and the complexity of some of the agreement rules. In addition, French inanimate nouns also have a grammatical gender, adding an extra layer of confusion for learners. This is notably observed by Alison Rice, when she comments on her students' identification with a character of one of Chahdortt Djavann's *Comment peut-on être Français?* [*How can one be French?*], Roxane:

> In discussions focusing on *How Can One Be French?*, students like to rehearse Roxane's struggle to learn the gender of all nouns, and they tell similar stories of their own battles with the notion of assigning a gender to inanimate objects or ideas when nothing similar exists in their native tongue.
>
> (29)

In this context, it is not easy for the teacher to include what could be perceived as extra difficulties by learners.

Over the past academic year, I have discussed forming the feminine of nouns as part of a grammar lesson in the core module French Language 2 for second-year undergraduate students. This is an important topic when acquiring French, and even more so for English native speakers, as it differs drastically from most of my students' native language. The lesson is based on a worksheet that students completed at home. Exercises consist for instance in finding the correct gender of a noun and making the relevant agreements or in transforming a text from the masculine to the feminine. In addition to the more typical exercise/correction-based approach, the seminar was also an opportunity to introduce current debates taking place around inclusive writing in France.[7] The introduction of these debates was followed by a discussion with students. The teaching team, comprised of myself and three other colleagues, also uploaded resources online for students to reflect on during their own time. The resources we provided include the *Manuel d'écriture inclusive* mentioned above, a *France Culture* podcast, an article in *Le Monde*, a video on *France TV* on the topic, and an article on inclusive writing in French written in the student journal by an undergraduate student at the School of Modern Languages and Cultures. These resources were chosen to encourage students to think about these debates out of the classroom, as well as to offer them the opportunity to work on their linguistic skills by engaging with a variety of written and audio-visual content. The assignment also provided an opportunity to promote students' achievements by sharing a piece written by a fellow student. Thus, the seminar offers both a base to consolidate their knowledge of French grammar and to make them think more critically about grammar and more broadly about language and the way we use it. Language acquisition goes hand in hand with problematizing societal issues and their impact on the way that we speak.

These resources were also a way to make students reflect on French as "une langue vivante" (a living language), evolving throughout history and open to change. Indeed, looking back at the history of French helps us to understand how it was shaped by ideological forces. Maria Candea and Laélia Véron note that the conception of the masculine as "neutral" is a recent linguistic construct, meant to replace the sometimes-criticized notion of the superiority of the masculine over the feminine (127). The erasure of the feminine in language originated in the 17th century, notably coinciding with the foundation of the Académie Française by Richelieu (1634) and took mainly two forms. First, the dismissal of the proximity agreement, widely used at the time (Viennot, 64–9), according to which the adjective or past participle agree with the closest noun. Thus, it was the place of the noun in the sentence that determined the agreement, rather than the notion of superiority or the one of nobility mentioned in the introduction to this chapter. Secondly, it is through lexical erasure that masculinist grammarians sought to impose the dominance of the masculine in language. As noted above, they rejected the use of the feminine to refer to certain professions or titles, including writer, doctor, poet, philosopher, and many others (Candea and Véron, 123–30). Language historians speak of a true war waged against some of these feminine nouns (Evain; Candéa and Véron, 124; Viennot, 52). This erasure was rooted in the belief that these nouns could and should only exist in the masculine form, as the cultural domain, and notably the writing sphere "est le propre de l'homme seul" (is a peculiarity of men only), as observed by a French legislator in 1801 (Candea and Véron, 128).

Women and feminists have played and continue to hold a central role in revaluating the place of the feminine in the French language. This was a long battle, as women's struggle for emancipation took other forms, and what is traditionally considered the first wave of feminism in the 19th century focused mainly on the right to vote and to education. It is only with the second wave that linguistic questions were brought to the fore again by feminists (Candea and Véron, 132). As a result, in the 1980s the representation of the feminine in language gained political momentum in Francophone countries, including in France under the Mitterrand government (133). The Académie Française appeared in the last decades just as opposed to the inclusion of the feminine in language as it was centuries ago. In fact, it still referred to the feminization of professions and titles as "*véritables barbarismes*" (true barbarisms) in 2014, and just like in the past, its opposition was the strongest when it came to prestigious professions, as observed by Viennot.[8] However, real progress has been made in recent years in France, with for instance the creation of the Haut Conseil à l'égalité entre les femmes et les hommes (High Council for Equality Between Women and Men) by the French government in 2013, which published a guide for inclusive communication. Recent calls for inclusive writing have continued the work of feminists of the second wave, as well as suggesting new strategies to further inclusion in language. Knowing the long and rich historical context that led to these inclusive strategies and introducing it in the French language classroom allows us teachers, as well as our students, to improve our understanding of French and to fight the conception of grammar and indeed, language, as natural phenomena, happening outside of the social order and its norms.

The use of inclusive language is not limited to the content of the class; it extends to inclusive practices in the classroom and more broadly to interactions with students. Most of my teaching is done in French, which requires a constant attempt to bring the feminine in language both orally and in writing. This involves using the middot or epicene language when referring to people in PowerPoint presentations, or via emails. This also involves introducing words with which students are not necessarily familiar. With this in mind, I started using the term "autrice" (writer in the feminine form) instead of "auteure" (writer in a feminine form closer to the masculine *auteur*) or "femme auteur" (woman writer) at the time of the publication of the *Manuel d'écriture inclusive* in my own writing and speaking practice as well as in my language and literary classes. *Autrice* is not a neologism, but the correct feminine form of the noun, that fell into oblivion for centuries due to the active campaign led against its use discussed above.[9] When introducing it to students, I made sure to refer to the Latin origins of the word as well as the circumstances that led to its subsequent erasure. At the time, mine was an act of linguistic resistance, as the Académie refused to sanction the use of the word *autrice*, as well as other names of prestigious professions up until February 2019.[10]

## Response and Resistance

These various inclusive practices were met overall with positive engagement from students. As noted above, in my second-year grammar class, the introduction of the topic was followed by discussion. Some tension arose during the debate in class. Most students thought inclusive writing was a positive and useful move towards equality, diversity, and inclusion. Some (female) students considered it a comparatively unimportant step toward greater equality, leaving more important battles to be fought. I asked other groups of students—namely fourth year grammar students and third year students on their year abroad—whether they thought learning inclusive language practice made grammar more difficult to learn. Students in both of these groups replied that they felt they were more flexible in their use of grammar rules than native speakers of French. These various discussions with my students, about inclusive language and about their learning, helped to shape my teaching and my understanding of inclusion. In the French Language Culture and Society module in which I introduced Marie Darrieussecq's *Truismes* [*Pig Tales*] to first year students at the University of Limerick, some of my students started using the term "autrice" in their essays when referring to Darrieussecq, which, as a teacher and advocate of the term, was a true pleasure to read.

Consistently using inclusive language can be a real challenge. As astutely acknowledged by my students, as a French native speaker from France, moving to a more inclusive speaking and writing practice involves un-learning grammatical structures that have shaped my everyday use of French. This is particularly difficult with the use of the plural. When writing to students, as mentioned above, it is easy to use the middots to be inclusive of both the masculine and the feminine. However, when speaking, I find it more difficult to refer to the plural in an inclusive way. This often leads to cumbersome sentences, particularly when the adjective takes a different form in the feminine and the masculine, which it often does (i.e. *les étudiants et les étudiantes sont contents et contentes;* students are happy). To use the plural in an inclusive way more effectively, I make sure to use epicene words (i.e. *les élèves sont ravi.e.s;* pupils are happy); or bend the official grammatical rule and go back to the proximity agreement (i.e. *les étudiants et les étudiantes sont contentes*).[11] This is part of a reflexive process which is not easily adaptable to the flow of speaking. As a pedagogue, I am also afraid of making language learning more confusing to my students, especially as there are few tools available to help teachers teach language more inclusively.

## *Fighting Set Hierarchies in the French Language Class*

Indeed, teaching French grammar and other linguistic components inclusively can constitute a real challenge for the language teacher because of some of the resistance noted above, but also because of the relative absence of resources to promote inclusive language in the classroom. Recently in France, the *Manuel d'écriture inclusive* and the work of Viennot have been essential in promoting inclusive language. The challenges that an inclusive practice of oral French poses are to my knowledge unexplored by research on the question, and although this work is welcome, I suppose that some of these resistances get resolved through habits. However, when it comes to teaching French inclusively in the foreign language classroom, there is a real need for more research and discussion on good practice, a discussion this chapter hopes to foster. Although there is some variety in the treatment of inclusive language in French grammar textbooks, the resources are limited, and there is currently no systematic approach on how to teach inclusive grammar in French departments in the UK. In the absence of resources and of institutional standards on the issue, teaching French grammar inclusively becomes a negotiation between tradition and innovation. For instance, I encourage my students to use feminine and epicene nouns as much as possible, as well as the middot if they feel comfortable with it, but I choose to not promote the use of the proximity agreement so far, as students are assessed on what is considered to be the "correct" grammatical rule in their exams. This is an ongoing reflection in my teaching practice, and it increases the importance of giving students space to express themselves. Hence, the classroom is more than a place where the teacher imparts knowledge to the students; rather, it is an inclusive space where students are invited to reflect on the language and voice their opinions and potential concerns.

As a conclusion, these debates should be thought of as part of equality, diversity, and inclusion strategies in French departments, and in other romance languages, as these questions are central to understanding issues of inequalities among genders. Indeed, "l'invisibilisation linguistique des femmes" (the linguistic erasure of women) (Houbedine-Gravaud, 31) echoes the broader issue of the role of women in contemporary society and of the prolonged discrimination they have been facing in the workplace and beyond. Teaching inclusive language is then a positive force in the French classroom. It is a way of introducing students to the history of the language they learn, inviting them to reflect on gender dynamics in society at large, and encouraging them to think of language as a social phenomenon caught in these dynamics. It is also an opportunity to tell our female students that they too can become *une professeure* (a professor), *une Secrétaire d'État,* or *une autrice*, as they can think of and name themselves as such in French.

## Notes

1 See also Kiki Kosnick's article "The Everyday Poetics of Gender-Inclusive French: Strategies for Navigating the Linguistic Landscape" for more specific development of these strategies.
2 Translations here and elsewhere are my own. See, on that topic, the recent manifesto signed by 314 French teachers "Nous n'enseignerons plus que 'le masculin l'emporte sur le féminin'" (We will no longer teach the rule that "the masculine form takes precedence over the feminine").
3 Other Francophone parts of the world, and notably Québec, have been much more forward-thinking about this issue. See for instance the recommendations of the *Office québécois de la langue française*. For a full account of the Académie Française's opposition to the feminization of names of professions see Viennot *et al.*
4 As also shown by the current discussion about BAME students and staff in British universities and all over the global North.
5 I thank my colleagues from the University of Limerick in Ireland and Durham University in the UK for their help and support of my reflections on this topic.
6 I am currently engaging with inclusive writing in my research, thinking about it in Marie Darrieussecq's translation practice in my article "Translating Woolf: Marie Darrieussecq's *Un lieu à soi*."
7 The program of the module is based on the module convenor's work, Vasanti Piette.
8 See "La Féminisation des noms de métiers, fonctions, grades ou titres—Mise au point de l'Académie française. For instance, the Académie Française was not opposed to using the term *secrétaire* (secretary) in the feminine form when referring to an assistant, but the word had to be used in the masculine for a State Secretary (Viennot *et al.*, 94).
9 For the history of the word, see Aurore Evain's article: "Histoire d'autrice, de l'époque latine à nos jours," as well as my article on inclusive translation mentioned above.
10 See the most recent Académie Française's report on the topic "La féminisation des noms de métiers et de fonctions."
11 Another possibility suggested by the supporters of inclusive language is to agree with the highest number (i.e. *Cent femmes et un chien sont contentes* as opposed to the currently correct form *cent femmes et un chien sont contents*; [One hundred women and a male dog are happy]).

## References

Abu-Laila, Zaki Mohammad-Adel. "Enseigner la grammaire française en classe de FLE : Quelles méthodes faut-il adopter?" *Journal of Arts and Humanities*, vol. 8, no. 3, March 2019, pp. 12-24. www.theartsjournal.org. doi:10.18533/journal.v8i3.1595.

Académie Française. "La féminisation des noms de métiers, fonctions, grades ou titres - Mise au point de l'Académie française." October 10, 2014. www.academie-francaise.fr/actualites/la-feminisation-des-noms-de-metiers-fonctions-grades-ou-titres-mise-au-point-de-lacademie.

—. "Déclaration de l'Académie française sur l'écriture dite 'inclusive.'" October 26, 2017, www.academie-francaise.fr/actualites/declaration-de-lacademie-francaise-sur-lecriture-dite-inclusive.

—. "La féminisation des noms de métiers et fonctions." March 1, 2019. www.academie-francaise.fr/actualites/la-feminisation-des-noms-de-metiers-et-de-fonctions.

Baric, Carline and Raphaël Haddad. *Manuel d'écriture inclusive*. Mots clés, 2016.

Bouanchaud, Cécile. "Cinq idées reçues sur l'écriture inclusive." *Le Monde*, November 23, 2017. www.lemonde.fr/les-decodeurs/article/2017/11/23/cinq-idees-recues-sur-l-ecriture-inclusive_5219224_4355770.html.

Candea, Maria and Laélia Véron. *Le français est à nous!* La Découverte, 2019.

Carlini Versini, Dominique. "Translating Woolf: Marie Darrieussecq's *Un lieu à soi*." *L'Esprit Créateur*, vol. 60, no. 3, Fall 2020, pp. 34–45.

Darrieussecq, Marie. *Pig Tales*. Translated by Linda Coverdale, New Press, 1997. [*Truismes*. P.O.L, 1996].

Djavann, Chahdortt. *Comment peut-on être français?* Flammarion, 2006.

Evain, Aurore. "Histoire d'autrice, de l'époque latine à nos jours." *Sêméion. Travaux de sémiologie*, no. 6, 2008. siefar.org/wp-content/uploads/2009/01/Histoire-d-autrice-AEvain.pdf.

Fougerouse, Marie-Christine. "L'enseignement de la grammaire en classe de français langue étrangère." *Éla. Études de linguistique appliquée*, no. 122, 2001/2, pp. 165–178.

France TV. "C'est quoi l'écriture inclusive?" November 22, 2017, www.lumni.fr/video/c-est-quoi-l-ecriture-inclusive.

Haut Conseil à l'égalité entre les femmes et les hommes. "Pour une communication sans stéréotype de sexe: le Guide pratique du Haut Conseil à l'Egalité," www.haut-conseil-egalite.gouv.fr/stereotypes-et-roles-sociaux/zoom-sur-article/pour-une-communication-sans-stereotype-de-sexe-le-guide-pratique-du-haut.

Houdebine-Gravaud, Anne-Marie. "Femmes / langue / féminisation: Une expérience de politique linguistique en France." *Nouvelles Questions Féministes*, vol. 20, no. 1, 1999, pp. 23–52.

Joubin, Valentine and Tara Schlegel. "Écriture inclusive: un point ce n'est pas tout." *France culture*, 22 December 2017, www.franceculture.fr/emissions/le-magazine-de-la-redaction/ecriture-inclusive-un-point-ce-nest-pas-tout.

Kosnick, Kiki. "The Everyday Poetics of Gender-Inclusive French: Strategies for Navigating the Linguistic Landscape." *Modern & Contemporary France*, vol. 27, no. 2, April 2019, pp. 147–161. doi:10.1080/09639489.2019.1588869.

Lessard, Michaël and Suzanne Zaccour. *Manuel de grammaire non sexiste et inclusive. Le masculin ne l'emporte plus!* Syllepse, 2018.

Office québécois de la langue française. "Principes généraux de la rédaction épicène," bdl. oqlf.gouv.qc.ca/bdl/gabarit_bdl.asp?id=3912.

Rice, Alison. "Worldwide Women Writers and the Web: Diversity and Digital Pedagogy." *Rethinking the French Classroom. New Approaches to Teaching Contemporary French and Francophone Women*. Edited by E. Nicole Meyer and Joyce Johnston, Routledge, 2019, pp. 27–34.

Shearwood, Eleanor. "Feminisé.e: To What Extent Does Gendered Language Affect Our Attitudes Towards Gender?" *The Definite Article*, Durham University, January 29, 2019, www.thedefinitearticle.org/linguistics/category/feminiseacutee-to-what-extent-does-gendered-language-affect-our-attitudes-towards-gender.

*Slate.fr*. "Nous n'enseignerons plus que 'le masculin l'emporte sur le féminin.'" November 7, 2017, www.slate.fr/story/153492/manifeste-professeurs-professeures-enseignerons-plus-masculin-emporte-sur-le-feminin.

Viennot, Éliane *et al. L'Académie contre la langue française*. Éditions iXe, 2016.

—. *Non, masculin ne l'emporte pas sur le féminin! Petite histoire des résistances de la langue française*. 2nd ed., Éditions iXe, 2017.

# 7

# A CLASSROOM FOR EVERYONE

## Creating French Courses that Embrace Learning Differences

*Kathryn A. Dettmer and Brenda A. Dyer*

Walking into a classroom, French teachers, experienced and novice, share certain goals. They desire to get everyone speaking French, to have students fall in love with French, to continue taking courses, and perhaps even to declare a major or a minor. Everyone means everyone. They can win over the students in their classes who are there only to fulfill a requirement. They can create lessons to suit their students' different learning styles. Most importantly, if they believe in equity, they must find a way to teach the students with language-oriented learning disabilities, such as dyslexia[1] and audio processing disorders,[2] for whom traditional language classes can really be a struggle. Nevertheless, we can all create learner centered differentiated instruction for everyone by designing classes that build in clarity and scaffolding for the students, with the goal of creating community and equity. Progressively, we become more confident teaching in this way and by remembering that teaching is also a learning process and that practice and experimentation are not just required, but one of teaching's greatest joys.

Now, imagine things from the perspective of a student with language-oriented learning disabilities. You enter a classroom already believing you are going to fail, anxious because you know how much harder you have to study than other students, feeling the same dread in the pit of your stomach that you remember from elementary school reading instruction. When class starts, you are immediately feeling overwhelmed, lost, and afraid to ask for help because if you do, someone will notice that you do not belong. You are embarrassed to work with classmates who seem so much smarter than you because they understand what to do. By the end of class, a little of your dream of graduation and career has been eroded and you are sure that you will disappoint not just yourself, but your family too. Students who are diagnosed with a learning disorder often feel this way (Sparks, "Foreign Language" 42) entering our French classrooms.

DOI: 10.4324/9781003126461-8

Students with language learning-oriented disabilities, such as dyslexia or audio processing disorder, share certain difficulties when learning French. These students all have deficits in their native language abilities (Sparks, "Foreign Language" 15) that impact second language acquisition. These students often lack phonetic coding ability (Carroll, 17). Carroll notes that they have trouble hearing and connecting the sounds that make up words to the letters written on the page, making it difficult for them to reproduce the sounds that they are hearing. He adds that they frequently lack grammatical sensitivity allowing them to understand patterns of meaning created by grammatical structures, and they lack the vocabulary to discuss grammar (19). Rote memorization can be problematic for certain students, making it difficult to learn verb patterns or vocabulary (20). These students might also struggle with inductive learning that would help them to make educated guesses based on their received language input (22).[3]

This chapter is the result of a nearly twenty-year conversation that we have had with each other and with other language instructors about how to reach and keep students who struggle with language-oriented learning differences. Our explorations brought us to the competencies detailed by Carroll in the Modern Language Aptitude Test (MLAT) and to Universal Design of Learning (UDL), a framework, based on the science of how humans learn, that has become a touchstone for rethinking our French classes and how to make them accessible and challenging for all students. UDL stresses the importance of affective networks (the *why* of learning), recognition networks (the *what* of learning) and strategic networks (the *how* of learning) and provides specific guidelines on how to provide multiple means of student engagement, representation of material and opportunities for expression of learning that are invaluable to both novice and experienced teachers who strive to teach inclusively ("The UDL Guidelines").

Students with dyslexia or audio processing disorder are often exempted from the language requirement at the university level or granted accommodations that might or might not prove effective for them. In our experience, students with a diagnosis do not always take advantage of the accommodations, such as extended quiet time for testing, in-class note takers, test and text readers, or extended deadlines. Perhaps they do not want to call attention to themselves, perhaps these accommodations have not helped in the past, or perhaps they think that they can rely on coping mechanisms that they developed in elementary school, when learning to read the first time, but that might prove inadequate in a university environment. Using the principles of UDL and keeping in mind the four competencies suggested by Carroll, instructors should design their classes to reduce the need for individual accommodations and provide multiple paths to learning French making it more equitable for all students.

In this chapter, we will discuss designing and teaching French 101 in a way that supports students with language-oriented learning disorders. These are not just our suggestions for the best way to include "othered" students. These are our recommendations for creating a truly equitable classroom where all students become more inductive learners and find their voices in French.

## Setting the Tone

Before classes start, there are techniques based on the Universal Design guidelines instructors can use to explicitly set students up for success. We send an email to our students outlining our pedagogical and practical expectations for the course and how to prepare for the first class. We attach a survey asking about their language experiences and learning preferences that shows them our interest in them as individual learners, as it helps us to anticipate how we might need to adapt our lessons. This first, personal connection with them sets the tone and begins to shape our future learning community by showing that we acknowledge different paths to learning French, welcome diverse learners, and are committed to creating an environment where everyone's learning needs can be addressed.

Students with dyslexia and auditory processing disorder often lack organizational skills (Konyndyk, 35). An explanation of how information is structured in class, on the Learning Management System (LMS) and in the syllabus, models organization for them, providing them with a vocabulary and framework that they can apply to the organization of their own materials. We take care to create an LMS page that is clear and in effect reduces barriers to student learning. The course calendar includes a day-by-day breakdown of material covered and assignments due. The use of color and sans serif fonts make materials easier for students with dyslexia to read.[4] The colors focus the eye for all students and point out what is important or when the subject has changed.[5] Digital course material is posted in flexible formats, such as PDFs that allow for changes in size of text, labeled images, color, contrast, and font, but can also be read aloud to the students by a reader program. We include audio and video clips that allow modifications of the volume or speed. We also provide links to additional helpful information such as online dictionaries or PDF readers to support learning and encourage student autonomy.

When class begins, we explore the LMS together, modeling the flexibility of materials, the applications needed to use them properly, and where to locate them to ensure that students use them without feeling singled out. This transforms what might be an accommodation for one student into a tool for everyone. It is also important to manage the physical classroom to optimize student learning. A poor sound system, either with static or low volume, can hinder a student's ability to associate the letters with sounds. Chairs that do not move will not allow students to work with their classmates and to move around when needed, that can make building community more problematic. These basic procedures are not difficult, but if not done properly can create significant barriers to students with language-oriented learning disorders.

## First Week of French Class

Sometimes people need proof that they can learn. Proving to students who struggle with language issues that they can learn French on their first day can be a very powerful experience, particularly for learners who have not had a great deal of success in other classes. We have designed two activities to prove to our students they can do it from the very beginning. "Tell Me about Me" is the first activity that we do. This activity focuses on modeling some of the metacognitive tools needed to learn French and helps to build community in the classroom. We tell students we will introduce ourselves in French twice and ask student to speculate about what they will hear. This allows students to activate their prior knowledge of this particular social situation and prepares them to be more receptive to what they will hear. After the introductions, we ask the students to share what they have heard. This gives all the students a chance to check their understanding and contribute to a discussion. Students also get to know something about us, making us more human and approachable, fostering the development of a classroom community that will support student learning. This activity, especially because we pantomime certain things and include cognates in our introductions, provides immediate success to optimize motivation, which can be lacking in students with learning difficulties. The discussion of listening strategies and the use of prior knowledge give students a process to follow throughout their time in French class. Modeling this kind of metacognitive approach to students with learning disorders helps them to internalize the logic of what is taught and provides a strategy for learning that can be transferred to other disciplines.

To build on this success, we conduct our next activity, "First Day: First Conversation," which sets the expectation that all students will speak French in class and builds community between students who are working together as they learn about each other. We introduce the vocabulary that students will need to meet someone for the first time, using slides and choral repetition. The slides, which remain posted throughout the activity, give visual support to the students as they work, which is particularly helpful for students with auditory processing or memory difficulties. Choral repetition optimizes the amount of low-stakes practice that each student is asked to do before they must produce language on their own. Many students with dyslexia and audio-processing disorders have difficulty attaching sounds to letters, so we follow up our choral repetitions by asking students to make observations about sound-letter correlations in French. When students look for patterns and hypothesize about what letters make which sounds and which are silent, they engage in an active discovery of the phonetic rules of French, which provides them a metacognitive strategy that they can apply to future learning. We then ask our students to move around the room and meet at least five other students. This type of pair work not only helps build community in the class, it allows for short blocks of repeated practice in different iterations that students with learning difficulties need to better internalize materials (Schneider and Crombie, 17–18). With these short, structured bursts of the type of conversation that are relevant to everyday life, the students learn their classmates' names, collaborate with other students, and prove to themselves that they can speak French. To follow up, students write short dialogues for homework that they read aloud with partners in the next class. Planning activities that use and review the same material in different modalities makes the information easier to retain for students with dyslexia and audio-processing difficulties as it reinforces the association of sounds with written representation.

These early activities give the students confidence and enable them to increase their tolerance for the ambiguity inherent to language learning. The activities also start to work on deficits that students might have when they have dyslexia and audio-processing disorder. Activating a student's prior knowledge makes receiving and internalizing new information, like vocabulary or grammar, easier (Lang, 43). The visual reinforcement of the vocabulary on the slide enables students to check when they are unsure, but also allows them to attach sounds to letters. Being told to let language flow over them, or that they know what to expect in a situation, lowers anxiety making students more comfortable and open to learning.[6] Practical vocabulary that can be used to communicate in real-life situations sparks interest and helps students to retain the information. Being transparent about our goals and methodology concerning these activities supports students' development of the metacognitive skills that they need to become more autonomous learners.

## Using Direct Instruction to Guide Student Learning

Direct instruction of rules and learning strategies from the start can help students with language-oriented learning disorders immediately find their footing in the French classroom, giving them confidence that they can use this knowledge to make progress that sets them up for learning other grammar, spelling, or phonetic information in the future (Konyndyk, 92). Direct instruction is not a traditional grammar lecture filled with technical jargon or memorization of rules, but rather an interactive lesson designed to elicit student input as they explore how the French language works. Before class, we ask students to prepare by either reading about the new structure in their textbook or watching a grammar tutorial online, which provides alternative ways to access information. We then assess their understanding and guide their learning by having them fill in charts, answer questions, and make connections with previously learned knowledge as we model the language-learning competencies we hope to foster. This technique also encourages a collaborative learning environment because we use it to create understanding together.

As an example, we will examine our method of teaching the use of definite and indefinite articles with nouns in French, an early structure taught in most beginning French courses. We begin by activating the students' prior knowledge with a review of previously learned vocabulary, asking students to identify classroom objects. Giving learners the option to reply individually or as a group varies the performative requirements of language learning that can be stressful for some students. Choral repetition gives them a less-threatening space to practice, allowing them to gain confidence in pronunciation while further creating a collaborative, supportive classroom climate for all. Furthermore, by asking students to retrieve this vocabulary, we are reinforcing their ability to recall and providing them with the necessary practice that leads to long-term learning (Lang, 91–111).

We then help students to develop grammatical sensitivity by making an explicit connection between this vocabulary and the syntactical logic of French, often comparing it with English to highlight the differences (Konyndyk, 100). For beginners, we find that the judicious use of English to discuss grammar is the most efficient way to support students who lack inductive language learning ability.[7] We make no assumptions that our students understand grammatical terminology, but instead have the class define terms together. Once all students have a common understanding of what nouns and articles are, we can begin to examine how these structures are used to create meaning in French.

Novice learners often have difficulty discerning between what is critical and what is less relevant, so it is important to provide cues that help them focus on the aspects of structures that matter most. As we explore how nouns and articles function in French, we elicit student input to fill in a chart that organizes the articles by gender, number, and whether they are definite or indefinite. This clear graphic organizer helps students visualize and process this information into useable knowledge. We draw their attention to the differences between definite and indefinite articles and point out that the literal meaning of these grammar terms are clues to their use: defined/specific vs. undefined/generic, further demystifying the jargon of grammar. Students see that the choice of article has significance and that grammar is linked to meaning.

We then ask students how English and French articles differ. Students immediately recognize that French articles indicate gender and invariably wonder how to tell if a noun is masculine or feminine. We ask them to look at their vocabulary list to see if they can discern any patterns. Together, the class generates two lists that compare which noun endings seem to be masculine and which seem to be feminine. We then provide them with a pre-prepared, color-coded "cheat sheet" that gives a more complete list of endings that usually indicate gender, with common exceptions. The color-coding can break up dense text for students with dyslexia and help them focus on the pertinent information. Students compare their list with this sheet, so that they can check their hypotheses and identify nouns that are counterintuitive, like *le musée*, (museum) whose double "e" might lead students to think it is feminine. When learners are asked to look for patterns, categorize information and verify their assumptions, they are developing metacognitive strategies that facilitate memorization and long-term learning that can also be applied to other contexts. We tell students to keep this sheet handy to use as a reference, but ultimately the gender of nouns must be memorized. We encourage them to practice each new noun along with its article, and to make connections between the endings on the list with new vocabulary whenever possible. This framework gives beginners critical insight into the logic of the French language and provides a strategy to counteract the difficulty with rote memorization that students with learning difficulties often have.

We continue our exploration of French articles by asking students to compare *la chaise* (the chair) and *les chaises* (the chairs)—orally and in writing—and how articles indicate number. Once again, we draw our students' attention to a critical feature of French that they might underestimate, particularly those who lack grammatical sensitivity and phonetic coding ability. We stress that the final "s" of a noun in French is a visual, written marker of plurality, but because it is silent, one must listen for the article to determine whether a noun is singular or plural in spoken French. Repeated pronunciation practice of singular noun-article pairs with their plural counterparts, along with visual supports to bolster sound-letter associations, highlights the differences and models for students how French works. Students with dyslexia and audio processing disorders particularly benefit from repeated and explicit focus on how sounds and letters correspond in the French language (Konyndyk, 95), but this direct instruction of how grammar, phonology, and meaning function together in French prepares the entire class, filling in gaps in their understanding, so that they can optimize their learning as they practice the structures and vocabulary in follow-up classroom activities.

This step-by-step examination of articles in French provides students with a model of how to think about language, search for patterns, and infer rules from language input that they can apply as they learn new structures. When students realize that they can develop language-learning abilities, they shift from an assumption that some students are inherently "good at French" towards a growth mindset, stressing learning as a process that can improve with effort, good strategies, and guidance.

## Assessment and Feedback

Assessment is essential to student success and should be done in ways that foster growth in their knowledge and confidence, provide options for self-reflection, and encourage students to continue their French studies. High frequency, low stakes formative assessments provide students with timely feedback that helps to shape their attitudes about learning, as well as gauge their progress towards meeting the learning outcomes for the course. Feedback should be specific and non-judgmental and give clear recommendations on how learners can improve. Formative assessments should be scaffolded and can be as varied as weekly quizzes, homework assignments, and in-class activities that provide multiple means to express learned knowledge with various levels of support for practice and performance to meet differing student needs. For example, to assess any group activity where students mingle, we listen carefully to their speech and make corrections to individual students by modeling correct pronunciation and giving them opportunities to repeat it back to us. We also notice common errors and practice corrections with the whole class as a follow-up activity. Both approaches relieve the embarrassment of being corrected in front of the whole group and reinforce the idea that everyone is having similar problems whether they have a language-oriented learning disorder or not. Homework assignments provide an opportunity for written practice and feedback. We point out both the positive and those areas in need of improvement, linking our comments to what was discussed in class. Students see that we are involved in their learning, aware of where they might be struggling, and ready to respond to their patterns of learning. We use the information gleaned from these low-stakes assessments to review material that has not been mastered as a warm-up in the next class, further emphasizing that language learning is a process that takes time and practice.

By the time that the students take the weekly low-stakes quiz, they are generally well prepared to show us what they have learned. Frequent short quizzes that divide material into manageable chunks support student learning and can reduce test anxiety. Recognizing that students work at different paces, they are all given the time that they need to finish the quiz. We stress that we are interested in what they can do in French, and the quiz is a tool that will help to evaluate what they might still need to learn.

We return to previously learned vocabulary at midterm, where it is included in a listening comprehension exercise and an individual oral exam, in which students are asked to introduce themselves and start a conversation with us in one-on-one meetings outside of class time. Requiring students to recycle material from the first week of class reinforces the importance of recall and spaced practice in long-term learning. During these meetings, after the exam, we provide students verbal feedback about their progress in French, but also discuss learning strategies and ways to overcome challenges that they might be having. We also take this opportunity to discuss realistic goal setting for learning French and encourage them to enroll in the next course.

The final summative assessment is a video in which students introduce themselves, using information learned over the course of the term and mirroring activities from the first day. A draft is posted on a discussion board, so students can give and receive feedback from their classmates. Students have the time to think about what they will say and to practice before they present and focus how they will use their voice to show what they have learned in French 101.

When we explicitly teach the hows and whys of grammar, phonetic coding, and inductive learning to support students with dyslexia and audio processing disorders, we are teaching more than the French language itself. As they make strides on their different paths to learning French, our students acquire the skills for how to learn. Purposeful modeling of metacognitive tools and discussions of language learning strategies lead students to reflect on their personal learning processes in general. Teaching students how to set individualized learning goals, how to study in ways that play to their strengths and support their weaknesses, and how to cope with the ambiguities inherent to language learning will make them more effective in all their classes. This ability to generalize and transfer knowledge and skills to new contexts lies at the heart of lifelong learning.

As we developed these teaching practices over time to better meet the needs of students with dyslexia or audio processing disorder, we found that each new alteration improved the learning of not only those students but of all our students. What works best to include and support students with language-oriented learning disabilities includes and supports all students. When all students benefit from a method or an intervention, deeper learning and greater equity can be achieved.

## Notes

1 Dyslexia is a neurobiological disorder "characterized by difficulties with accurate and/or fluent word recognition and by poor spelling and decoding abilities." Students with dyslexia generally exhibit deficits "in the phonological component of language" unrelated to cognitive abilities and the effectiveness of classroom instruction. Students might have reading comprehension deficits that in turn "can impede growth of vocabulary and background knowledge" (International Dyslexia Association).
2 Audio processing disorder "refers to deficits in the neural processing of auditory information not due to higher language or cognition" and "is not due to hearing loss." This disorder can affect "higher order language, learning and communication functions" (American Speech Language and Hearing Association).
3 Carroll's competencies are the basis of the MLAT exam. He believed that these competencies are innate. We disagree.
4 This issue is discussed in detail in Konyndyk, Schneider, and Combie and in UDL.
5 Text color can be important for other students, as well. Low vision students have difficulty with light color fonts and students with colorblindness can struggle with slides that combine green and red.
6 Lowering anxiety to allow students to learn better and more efficiently is a core UDL principle.
7 As student French proficiency increases, we phase out the use of English and lead these guided grammar explorations in French.

## References

American Speech Language and Hearing Association. "Central Auditory Processing Disorder." *Overview*, 2020, www.asha.org/practice-portal/clinical-topics/central-auditory-processing-disorder.
Carroll, J. "Cognitive Abilities in Foreign Language Aptitude: Then and Now." *Language Aptitude Reconsidered*, edited by T. Parry and C. Stansfield. Prentice Hall, 1990.
CAST. The UDL Guidelines, August 31, 2018, udlguidelines.cast.org.
International Dyslexia Association. "Definition of Dyslexia." July 16, 2018, dyslexiaida.org/definition-of-dyslexia.
Konyndyk, Irene Brouwer. *Foreign Languages for Everyone: How I Learned to Teach Second Languages to Students with Learning Disabilities*. Edenridge Press, 2011.

Lang, James M. *Small Teaching: Everyday Lessons from the Science of Learning*. Jossey-Bass, 2016.

Schneider, Elke and Margaret Crombie. *Dyslexia and Foreign Languages*. David Fulton, 2003.

Skinner, Michael E. and Allison T. Smith. "Creating Success for Students with Learning Disabilities in Postsecondary Foreign Language Courses." *International Journal of Special Education*, vol. 26, no. 2, 2011, pp. 42–57.

Sparks, Richard L. "Foreign Language Learning Problems of Students Classified as Learning Disabled and Non-Learning Disabled." *Topics in Language Disorders*, vol. 21, no. 2, 2001, pp. 38–54. doi:10.1097/00011363-200121020-00006.

—. "Myths About Foreign Language Learning and Learning Disabilities." *Foreign Language Annals*, vol. 49, no. 2, 2016, pp. 252–270. doi:10.1111/flan.12196.

Veal, Peggy. "Differentiation and Accommodations: Buffet Style Learning." *Tflmag.com*, March 9, 2016.

# 8
# DIVERSIFYING THE CURRICULUM
## From Structural Changes to Classroom Lessons

*Jessica S. Miller*

### Isolated but United

This essay describes the process of reshaping a college-level French curriculum in a small Wisconsin state system campus along one guiding principle: to build a curriculum that reflects the diverse identities of French speakers around the world while affirming those of our learners at the same time. This was done by 1) aligning the program with the standards and guidelines created by the American Council on the Teaching of Foreign Languages (ACTFL) for proficiency and cultural competence; and 2) designing new courses and updating lessons to pique interest and help learners to understand the relevance of learning a second language today as it pertains to their personal interests, social priorities, and professional needs. I will first discuss my motivations for this long-term, ongoing endeavor; then describe student learning outcomes and program assessment protocols; continue with ideas for courses, units, and lessons; and conclude with preliminary observations on the impact of those changes.

In these pages, readers will find tools to help them wherever they are in their journey to transform their French courses or programs. Because French sections tend to be comprised of one or two teachers in most K-12 programs and many universities, collaborative work resources are thinning, time and responsibility constraints are growing. Volumes such as this one enable French educators to pool common experiences so we can build solid and complex material that will increase our teaching effectiveness. The suggestions in this essay may not be right for everyone, as they reflect solutions that I have found valuable in my context. Everyone reading this is at a different stage of their career, having forged their own path at their own pace, built, perhaps multiple times, their unique identities and world vision. Nevertheless, I hope that the scope and variety of my ideas will give readers momentum to implement positive change of any shape and size, even though they might be the only French teacher at their school.

## Possible Selves

I started teaching at the University of Wisconsin-Eau Claire (UW-Eau Claire), a predominantly white institution, in 2006. Being a French woman in my late twenties, I felt that I should teach the culture that I had experienced firsthand for authenticity's sake. For the first few years of my career, I mostly echoed what textbooks presented as the default French-speaking culture, catering to the expectations of my Eiffel Tower-loving students, leaving us in our comfort zone, and failing to show the complexity of Francophones. My inaction was an affirmation of the French colonial view: metropolitan France is the nucleus around which smaller, less important electrons gravitate. In my classes just as in textbooks, Black, Indigenous, and People of Color (BIPOC) were pushed to the margins. Fear of unfamiliar cultural perspectives, avoidance of contentious debates, desire to assert my place of authority in the classroom, pressure to perform at a high level of student satisfaction, implicit gender bias disadvantaging women (MacNell, 298; Peterson, 1), are all factors that validated my complacency and lack of courage. Now, my identity as a teacher has itself changed. I have since equipped myself with phrases like "I don't know but I will look into it" and have committed to step outside my comfort zone in order to provide multiple narratives to better serve all my students and learn along with them.

My long-term goal now is to make structural changes to the curriculum that can transform the way UW-Eau Claire students view the French-speaking world from a singular entity to a complex amalgam. A more truthful representation of the diverse reality will at the same time create opportunities for all students to relate to some of the voices presented in my courses. I believe that identifying with people who speak French makes its study more engaging, increases relevance and empathy, and contributes to deeper learning. Second language (L2) learners develop "possible selves" (Dörnyei, 104), i.e., a second identity that may or may not coincide with a speaker of the target language. Increased motivation to acquire an L2 would derive from the ideal alter ego seeing itself as potentially realizable. I posit that building that new identity is easier for white people, for example, in the United States, because whiteness is the default identity at home as well as in the target culture (France) in most textbooks. In other words, their actual selves are converging with their "possible selves" as soon as they start learning French.

Whiteness, in this context, might facilitate learning French because it bridges the "ego-related affective gap," which successful language learners must cross (Brown, 65). Similarly, if the target culture is presented as a trove of historic architecture without consideration to accessibility (e.g., the romanticizing of steps in Montmartre and other Parisian monuments in cinema), a learner with a physical disability might not be able to project themselves visiting France. Schumann referred to that gap as "social distance" to be reduced to facilitate L2 acquisition. Today's coronavirus (COVID-19) pandemic restrictions give that term a whole new meaning, but Schumann also called it "social solidarity" (135) and defined it as congruency between two groups "[in] terms of political, cultural, technical or economic status, in a language contact situation" that could lead to a positive attitude and encourage L2 development. The goal of this curricular redesign is to reduce the aforementioned "social distance" in order to promote equitable L2 acquisition.

## Backward and Transparent Design

I followed the broad principles of backward design (Wiggins and McTighe) to ensure that the curricular restructuring would be well conceived, effective, coherent, and sustainable. The rest of the essay is organized according to the three-step process of backward design: first the outcomes, then acceptable evidence (e.g., assessments), and finally instructional activities in alignment with the other two elements, described through thematic units and possible lesson topics. Backward design brings articulation to the curriculum by clarifying and centralizing the destination and by providing a map with the roads to reach it. Although it requires upfront investment, this effort is worthwhile. For example, assessments built prior to learning events are more likely to hit the targets with precision and therefore be effective instruments to measure learning. Other works worth consulting first are Glynn *et al.*, Clementi and Terrill, and online ACTFL resources.

I also applied Winkelmes's Transparency Framework, whose goal is to enhance student success equitably by consistently providing information on the purpose of an assignment, the tasks involved, the steps to successfully complete the assignment, and the scoring criteria. Many students, especially those who do not have acquaintances able to help them navigate the expectations of higher education, benefit from seeing assignments broken down into step-by-step instructions. Teachers can also discover that the assignments they create are not as simple as they think, requiring prior groundwork that may not be obvious to all students, or doable for those with less access to certain resources.

## Student Learning Outcomes

In 2014 enrollment numbers in French were decreasing at my institution. Without data, I could not identify what needed improving, nor could I convincingly advocate for French programs. That year, our department formed an ad-hoc committee to draft cross-language program-level outcomes requested by our administration. That push coincided with my desire for a more structured French program that would better serve students. Lack of logical articulation within and across courses probably led to confusion, and was likely erecting barriers keeping some students from pursuing language studies. Seeing the administration value program outcomes was encouraging. Our committee eventually adapted ACTFL guidelines into six outcomes compatible with our mission for all modes of communication (see Miller and Lindseth for a detailed description).

The phrase "a variety of topics of a personal, public, and professional nature" is used in three of our Student Learning Outcomes (SLO). Those words emphasize the importance of understanding several aspects of one's identity, as well as being familiar with matters beyond oneself that are of public interest, in addition to discipline-specific topics that would help L2 speakers function in a professional setting. Although the UW-Eau Claire's student body continues to be somewhat homogeneous, diverse backgrounds and identities must be acknowledged and given representation if we want all students to meet the stated SLOs. If we do not equip everyone with tools to talk about themselves, to describe their personal and professional interests according to their own viewpoints, to be free to approach any topic of public interest through their own lens, we will fail our mission and our students.

Other key words in our SLOs relate to society, intercultural competence, and critical thinking. Sonia Nieto lists the development of critical thinking as an "essential component of social justice" (46), which strengthens the argument that intentionally and visibly diversifying the curriculum will support student success in programs that adopt those outcomes. She describes a real multicultural education as "pervasive," "comprehensive," with "pluralistic perspectives" in which "students would be encouraged to become critical thinkers" (76). Because these SLOs do not mandate the study of pre-determined topics, each language program is free to determine appropriate course content. Given the richness and ever-changing nature of practices, products, and perspectives in any given language section, the topics educators could select are virtually limitless and certain to keep our creative sparks lit, as well as students engaged in meaningful reflection.

## Program Assessment Protocol

In 2017 our College of Arts and Sciences allotted resources to develop Equity Diversity and Inclusion-based "Strategic Initiatives," i.e., administrative or curricular projects promoting diversity. Together with Dr. Martina Lindseth, a colleague in the German section, we designed a program-level assessment protocol so we could 1) create a built-in sustainable way to collect data and determine if our students were meeting the program outcomes; and 2) ensure that EDI topics are part of the evaluation process and have a centralized place in our curriculum and a determiner of success (see Miller and Lindseth). Keeping workload in mind, we aimed at creating a solid outcome-based assessment protocol that would enable us to easily track data on all modes of communication, interpret them, and use them to improve our students' learning experience. We collapsed our six outcomes into three pairs, each connecting one mode of communication to cultural EDI-related content.

Below are excerpts of the prompts given according to this protocol in an advanced French course in Spring 2020 (FREN 401: Contemporary Societal

Issues). The presentation task yielded a variety of student-selected topics such as generational roles in Hmong communities, inclusive language, accessibility regulation, Romani traditions, and environmental problems as social justice issues.

**Interpersonal task:** In a five-minute individual oral interview, discuss current challenges related to disabilities in a French-speaking area. 1) Describe at least one measure taken to include people with disabilities; 2) explain what two major obstacles might still exist; and 3) talk about your personal experience with inclusion (or lack of inclusion) of people with visible or invisible disabilities.

**Interpretive task:** (1) Summarize in a precise and concise way the video in which ski champion Marie Bochet shares a message: what is the takeaway, and what are some important details? And 2) How is Marie Bochet's perspective on disabilities similar to and different from Nantenin Keïta's, in your opinion? Similar to and different from someone in your culture? Compare and contrast European, African, and North American cultures by referring to situations involving disabilities.

**Presentational task:** In a video presentation, debate a social question relevant to a French-language culture: 1) choose a topic of public interest that shows diverse cultural perspectives; 2) develop three arguments for and three arguments against; and 3) create a narrated PowerPoint to be exported in video format.

## Curricular Map

Creating diverse lessons to encourage reflection on EDI issues is a good starting point but cannot be the end goal if one wants to inflect change. Doing the latter without considering structural modifications down the road might even have the opposite of the intended effect. Just like corporate EDI training that addresses surface-level issues assigned to employees who can check it off their to-do list, proposing lessons and courses without further coherence within the curriculum can marginalize those teaching events, anchoring experiences that center around able-bodied, white, heterosexual, and/or gender-conforming people's view of the French-speaking world as the accepted canon. Kris Knisely outlines five strategies to uphold the principles of queer inquiry-based pedagogies that are pertinent to take in consideration before and during a curricular reshape. They include, but are not limited to, co-constructing and reflecting with your learners, avoiding presenting discussion of marginalized groups as special days, and keeping in mind that inclusion of trans, non-binary, and gender non-conforming groups should not be the sole responsibility of community insiders.

The curricular plan of UW-Eau Claire French continues to evolve, however, much work remains. The guiding force is the desire to portray the French-speaking world as rich and multifaceted, without denying the colonial history that created *la Francophonie*, while calling out stereotypical representations. So far, I have reworked the content of the courses I teach (i.e., two courses that make up the Intermediate sequence, Pronunciation, Societal Issues) and created a brand-new course (Environmental and Linguistic Diversity). The next step will be to re-evaluate the content of other courses and replace some with new ones that can fill remaining gaps.

In addition, non-binary language is modeled throughout all redesigned courses. Example sentences, songs, or films frequently showcase work by LGBTQ+ members, people with disabilities, and BIPOC without drawing attention to them. Gender-neutral subject pronouns such as *iel* (third person singular) and *iels* (third person plural) are used in conjugation templates and at random in examples; strategies to avoid assigning gender forms are taught as valuable tools. For instance, we can use *l'élève* for "student" (as opposed to *l'étudiant* or *l'étudiante*, which requires marking the gender), *une personne qui fait...* (someone who does...) to talk about occupations (as opposed to using occupation names that require to mark the gender), *les droits humains* (human rights) instead of the default *les droits de l'homme* (men's rights). That is possible because I am generally able to develop the material myself and make it available to students via course packs. On top of distancing myself from the single narratives perpetuated by many textbook publishers (e.g., vocabulary and model conversations often refer to a stereotypical French way of life), course packs provide flexibility as authentic material gleaned from websites can be interchanged rapidly. I recognize that the ability and freedom to design content that is tailored to my teaching style, my students' needs, and aligned with my long-term goal is a luxury. Glynn *et al.* (45) provide different models to adapt existing curricular material for those wanting to teach languages for social justice.

Laying out a curricular map facilitates checks that topics do not repeat and that learners are exposed to a variety of cultures. Detailed visuals for all the five courses that I teach are available on my website. They include all the outcomes, unit themes, weekly lesson topics, targeted structures, and Francophone regions studied. Tables 8.1 and 8.2 below show some ways in which FREN 201 and FREN 202,

**TABLE 8.1** Themes, Essential Questions, and Cultures Explored in FREN 201, Intermediate 1, with the subtopic "History" and the Target Proficiency of Intermediate Low.

| *Essential questions* | *Authentic videos and texts from:* |
|---|---|
| Module 1: Identities | Canada |
| How does history influence who we are today? | New Caledonia |
| | French Antilles |
| Module 2: Urbanism | France |
| How does architecture reflect perspectives and practices? | Morocco |
| | Réunion |
| Module 3: Art | Rwanda |
| How is art similar and different across cultures? | Belgium |
| | Louisiana |
| Module 4: Sports | Senegal |
| How do we compete? | World |

**TABLE 8.2** Themes, Essential Questions, and Cultures Explored in FREN 202, Intermediate 2, with the subtopic "Cultural Perspectives" and the Target Proficiency of Intermediate Mid.

| Essential questions | Authentic videos and texts from: |
|---|---|
| Module 1: Public vs. private<br>How do we share who we are? | Guinea<br>Vanuatu<br>Republic of the Congo |
| Module 2: Our objects<br>How do we make our choices? | Canada<br>Mayotte<br>Togo |
| Module 3: Beauty<br>How do we define beauty? | France<br>Cameroon<br>Morocco |
| Module 4: Community needs<br>How do individuals affect groups? | New Caledonia<br>Polynesia |

the feeder courses to all our French programs, are articulated together through a consistent structure, and strive to provide multiple cultural perspectives. However, over-representation of certain French-speaking communities is also apparent. I therefore need to continue looking for material from cultures not yet featured in my courses to replace some that appear multiple times. Table 8.3 shows the basic articulation of FREN 401, a course on Contemporary Societal Issues focused on social justice.

## Lessons

The courses that I teach are now structured around the flipped classroom format (Kim et al.), and each week includes practice in all modes of communication

**TABLE 8.3** Themes, Essential Questions, and Topics Explored in FREN 401, Contemporary Societal Issue, with the subtopic "Social Justice" and the Target Proficiency of Advanced Low.

| Essential questions | Authentic videos and texts on: |
|---|---|
| Module 1: Sexism<br>How do languages reflect gender? | Inclusive writing<br>Women's rights<br>Political discourse |
| Module 2: Racism<br>How is racism similar and different across cultures? | History<br>Religion<br>Film |
| Module 3: Ageism<br>Why do cultures assign different values to life stages? | Names<br>Rights and duties<br>Communication |
| Module 4: Ableism<br>What policies help or hinder individuals? | Sports<br>Workplace |

(interpretive, presentational, interpersonal, intercultural) on a topic seen through the lens of a different culture presented via authentic videos and texts. Within a week, students learn targeted structures related to the course and are assessed on that week's outcome. A module is comprised of three weeks and asks an "essential question" that is discussed in class at the end of each Module (see Tables 8.1 and 8.2 above). Changing to a flipped format a few years ago and adapting that structure to all my classes required extensive work but provided the opportunity to simultaneously rethink the French curriculum. With an average of 12 credits per semester, a research agenda to pursue, and advising and service to fulfill, I had to make incremental changes for this process to be manageable. What I was learning along the way was rewarding and encouraged me to continue.

One such example dates back to when I started making changes to the introductory French sequence, though I later switched to intermediate courses and did not fully complete that redesign. Back then, two of my students were Hmong American, which was more than usual despite the fact that nearby Minnesota and Wisconsin are respectively the second and third US States with the largest Hmong population ("Hmong in the U.S. Fact Sheet"). I wondered how to make French studies more relevant to them and learned that refugees had not only been relocated to the United States, but also to France and French Guiana. I subsequently created a lesson about Hmong history for FREN 102 (Beginner 2), with a video explaining how Hmong people settled the town of Cacao in French Guiana, comparing their past and current challenges and including short interviews. Students made vocabulary lists to describe the town in 1977 and in 2017, helping them to make comparisons in French. In English, we discussed the facts in more depth, and I pointed out the multiple perspectives needed to understand such a complex issue. Local relevance warrants an increased representation of Hmong communities in French classes in Wisconsin, in my opinion. I plan to include more Hmong material this year in the Intermediate sequence.

Other local cultural connections should be made, such as incorporating indigenous stories. The Ojibwe culture is an important part of Wisconsin's identity, and contact between indigenous groups and French traders is obvious in the toponomy: city names like *Lac Courte Oreilles, La Crosse*, and even *Eau Claire* may be segues into researching local folklore, sorting real stories from legends (e.g., there is likely no relation between *Eau Claire* and French-speaking explorers), and comparing practices, products, and perspectives related to Ojibwe people in Wisconsin with those in French-speaking Canada, for instance. Such future possibilities for lesson development are exciting for their potential to spur meaningful conversations with both local and global relevance while affirming the diverse cultural identities in our student body.

## Impact

Anecdotal evidence suggests that the changes implemented have had a positive effect on student satisfaction and enrollment. In course evaluations, my rating as "excellent" instructor went from 56% for the 2011–16 period to 88% since then. Enrollment data show a sharp increase starting in Fall 2015 with 52 students and culminating in Fall 2020 at 102, more than ever previously recorded and despite staffing constraints. Multiple factors undoubtedly explain this success. Among them, I hypothesize that my commitment to the material that I create and curate increases my enthusiasm, which makes my teaching more accessible and engaging. Students also consistently praise the multicultural aspects of my courses: it is noticed and valued.

Program assessment data became available at the end of Spring 2018. It is still too early to draw conclusions relating to student success as this evaluative instrument is fairly new and needs adjustments. The numbers indicate that 79% meet and 21% do not meet the benchmark for the Interpersonal mode, 86% meet and 14% do not meet the benchmark for the Interpretive mode, and 66% meet and 34% do not meet the benchmark for the Presentational mode. The latter, paired with the assessment of critical thinking, has the largest number of students not meeting the benchmark.

As mentioned earlier, Nieto stresses the importance of critical thinking to social justice (46). That makes me think that more students will be meeting the "Presentational mode and critical thinking" outcomes once all the courses have been redesigned and articulated in a coherent and consistent manner through the lens of social justice. Keeping equity and diversity in the "DNA" of language programs will create courses that all learners can navigate easily, in which they will recognize themselves, and through which they will understand the multidimensional nature of cultures and identities, and thus realize their "possible selves." The challenge is to demonstrate critical thinking in one's L2 that requires high-level proficiency skills and cannot be practiced fully until the Intermediate High level at least, even in a performative assessment. If we teachers can create scaffolded opportunities for students to think critically throughout the curriculum at various stages of their proficiency development while developing an awareness of EDI-related issues, we will have made a significant positive impact on our students as L2 learners and empathetic contributors to our society.

## Words of Encouragement

Creating and selecting L2 material that is effective that elevates our learners' linguistic and cultural skills, that aligns with national guidelines and standards, and that helps students to meet course and program outcomes while engaging them and guiding them to think of our societies with a critical eye, is extraordinarily complex. Luckily, L2 teaching suits itself to a wide range of content, and our profession gives us relative freedom of choice. Lang provides strategies to incrementally bring change to one's teaching, and his suggestions could be adapted by an L2 teacher wanting to promote diversity. I am also happy to share all my material upon request. Lastly, if you recognized your fears in my own hesitation to address unfamiliar cultures and tackle controversial topics, let my students' words further convince you to make the risky leap. Now more than ever, I feel as if I know so little. Yet my students disagree, describing me as "incredibly knowledgeable" in their evaluations. The irony is not lost on me, and I still doubt the accuracy of those statements, but this positive reinforcement has the merit of keeping me learning, teaching, and learning again.

## References

Brown, H. Douglas. *Principles of Language Learning and Teaching: A Course in Second Language Acquisition*. Pearson Education, 2014.

Dörnyei, Zoltán. *The Psychology of the Language Learner: Individual Differences in Second Language Acquisition*. Routledge, 2005.

Glynn, Cassandra et al. *Words and Actions: Teaching Languages through the Lens of Social Justice*. American Council on the Teaching of Foreign Languages, 2018.

Kim, Jeong-Eun et al. "Exploring Flipped Classroom Effects on Second Language Learners' Cognitive Processing." *Foreign Language Annals*, vol. 50, no. 2, 2017, pp. 260–284.

Knisely, Kris. "Teaching Trans: The Impetus for Trans, Non-Binary, and Gender Non-Conforming Inclusivity in L2 Classrooms." *How We Take Action: Social Justice in K-16 Language Classroom*, edited by K. Davidson et al., Information Age, Forthcoming.

MacNell, Lillian et al. "What's in a Name: Exposing Gender Bias in Student Ratings of Teaching." *Innovative Higher Education*, vol. 40, no. 4, 2015, pp. 291–303.

Miller, Jessica S. and Martina Lindseth. "Taking Ownership: Making Program Assessment Doable, Sustainable, and Rewarding." *The Language Educator*, vol. 14, no. 2, 2019, pp. 40–43.

Miller, Jessica S. "*Teaching*." 2020, people.uwec.edu/millerjs/teaching.html.

Nieto, Sonia. *Language, Culture, and Teaching: Critical Perspectives*. Abingdon: Routledge, 2010.

Peterson, David et al. "Mitigating Gender Bias in Student Evaluations of Teaching." *PLoS ONE*, vol. 14, no. 5, 2019. doi:10.1371/journal.pone.0216241.

Pew Research Center. "Hmong in the U.S. Fact Sheet." 2017, www.pewsocialtrends.org/fact-sheet/asian-americans-hmong-in-the-u-s.

Schumann, John. "Social Distance as a Factor in Second Language Acquisition." *Language Learning*, vol. 26, no. 1, 1976, pp. 135–143.

Wiggins, Grant and Jay McTighe. *Understanding by Design*. Association for Supervision and Curriculum Development, 2005.

Winkelmes, Mary-Ann, et al. *Transparent Design in Higher Education Teaching and Leadership: A Guide to Implementing the Transparency Framework Institution-Wide to Improve Learning and Retention*. Stylus, 2019.

# 9
# EMBRACING THE FRANCOPHONE WORLD ACROSS THE FRENCH CURRICULUM

*Stephanie Schechner*

Data from the most recent report by the Organisation Internationale de la Francophonie (OIF) indicated in 2018 that French has grown to be the fifth world language; it is spoken by 300 million people worldwide (up from 274 million just since 2014), and 48% of French speakers live in Africa, 6% in the Americas, 1% Asia and Oceania, and 45% in Europe. It is the second foreign language taught worldwide, after English. The OIF even predicts that in 2070, there will be some 747 million Francophones, mainly in North Africa and sub-Saharan Africa (Organisation Internationale de la Francophonie). These data from the OIF show that French is a vital and growing world language: not just—nor even primarily—a European language. This linguistic and cultural expansion creates both an opportunity and a responsibility to develop a curriculum that serves the entire French-speaking world.

If French Studies in the United States is to flourish,[1] faculty need to consider a variety of strategies to encompass the rich diversity of the Francophone world. Although our program is small and my university is not particularly diverse, we teach students who have emigrated from all over the French-speaking world (in addition to students whose families hail from French- and Spanish-speaking countries).[2] In order to meet the challenge of a diverse French-speaking world, we revised our curriculum; recruited and retained a mix of native, heritage, and second-language learners; and created classrooms that are welcoming to all. This chapter explores the research that supports our efforts as well as the specific strategies we have deployed to build a robust French program. First is a discussion of how a new curricular model displaces France as the center of inquiry. Following this is the issue of how to build a supportive, diverse learning community that serves the needs of native, heritage, and second-language learners. Finally, I consider how to frame difficult conversations around race, racism, and (neo-)colonialism in order to give

DOI: 10.4324/9781003126461-10

students the opportunity to explore their individual identities as French speakers within the wider context of the diverse Francophone world.

## Revising the Curriculum: Embracing the French-speaking World

In order to revise a curriculum, it is necessary to go beyond, adding some Francophone courses and a Francophone World course. A more thorough rethinking of our curriculum is necessary if we are to destabilize France as the "center" of our inquiry. In my course, Introduction to Francophone Culture and Civilization, our examination of the global phenomenon of migration points to a way to teach about France within a broader framework that has a leveling effect on the traditional tendency to prioritize metropolitan French culture as somehow superior to Francophone culture.

For this course, we use a traditional textbook *Héritages francophones: Enquêtes interculturelles* [*Francophone Heritage: Intercultural Studies*], which looks at Francophone communities in North America as a starting point to explore the countries of origin of these communities. This allows students to understand how French-speaking migrants from all over the world (France, Africa, the Caribbean, Asia, and the Middle East) ended up in North America. We study the early colonists/explorers who were sent by French kings to claim territories in what are now Canada and the United States, as well as the more recent immigrants who have come to the United States for religious, political, and economic freedoms as well as for refuge from conflicts worldwide. In addition, we explore the migration of people from the Caribbean who were enslaved by white Europeans and had come to speak French as a result of colonization.

Despite using a traditional text and classic approach, we go beyond a simple representation of migration to consider links between the past and the present. By drawing connections between early migrants like the Huguenots who fled religious persecution in 16th and 17th century France and more recent refugees like Rwandans fleeing the ethnic conflict between Hutus and Tutsis, I aim to show students that migration is a more universal phenomenon rather than one only to be associated with "third world countries" in the 20th and 21st centuries. Indeed, many students are unaware of the early history of French-speaking arrivals to North America, having previously connected the term "refugee" exclusively with people of color from around the world. As a result of our discussions, students develop an understanding of "Francophone culture" that spans multiple centuries as well as different races and ethnicities.

In this particular course, the concept of "ethnic cleansing," which the United Nations has defined as "rendering an area ethnically homogeneous by using force or intimidation to remove persons of given groups from the area" (United Nations Office on Genocide Prevention and the Responsibility to Protect), offers an opportunity for illuminating the connections between historically and culturally distant phenomena in the French-speaking world. Our study of the ethnic cleansing and subsequent socioeconomic oppression of French-speaking Canadians by English-speaking Canadians and Americans de-centers the metropole and shows students the historically negative perception of "Frenchness" in North America, thereby allowing students to connect "Frenchness" to ideas about other minority groups in the French-speaking world.

After studying "Le Grand dérangement" [The Great Expulsion] (a movement on the part of the Anglo-Canadians in the 1700s to purge Quebec and the Maritime provinces of French-speaking, Catholic inhabitants), we follow the later migration of French-speakers to New England for socio-economic reasons during the Industrial Revolution. Many students are stunned to learn of the living and working conditions in the "Little Quebec" sections of New England cities that included tenement-style housing, permanent indebtedness to employers, and child labor. "The Shuttle," a song in English by Chanterelle, a Franco-American band, is a particularly poignant illustration of this historical moment. We explore the song's description of the injuries and toil of those working in textile mills, and this often yields reactions of shock on the part of students. In conjunction with this song, we also view and discuss historical photographs that depict labor conditions in New England textile mills.[3]

Having identified origins of the socioeconomic oppression of French-speaking Canadians and Franco-American immigrants, students are now better prepared to analyze the poem "Speak White" by the Quebecois writer Michèle Lalonde. This text draws explicit parallels between the treatment of Canadian Francophones by Anglophones and the treatment of Blacks worldwide by whites. Our discussion of this poem over the years has yielded two critical insights. First, it demonstrates to students how "Frenchness" has been marked for oppression in North America (both by Anglo-Canadians who persecuted the French-speakers [by forced migration, forced conversion to Protestantism, or massacre] and by US businesspeople and community leaders who subsequently exploited this vulnerable community as it took root in New England and demanded cultural assimilation that resulted in loss of language and cultural traditions). Second, by drawing connections between the oppression of Franco-Canadians and the oppression of Blacks (both in the US and throughout the Francophone world), students begin to unpack the complex assumptions that often support the way history is taught in the US. In the same way that students need to be able to recognize internalized racism that can create hierarchies within communities of color, the study of hierarchies within white communities lends nuance to students' understanding of how inequalities are defined and systematically reinforced.

In addition to teaching about French heritage in Quebec and the United States, I, like many French teachers, have also worked to craft a more inclusive set of readings in courses on "French literature." The shift in emphasis toward inclusivity reflects not just the addition of literature of previously marginalized groups, but also the re-reading of texts from the traditional French canon. This effort has been articulated by Christie McDonald and Susan Rubin Suleiman who argue persuasively that:

> Transactions between and among cultures and peoples, both outside and inside France's national boundaries (which themselves have changed over time) have been present in every period of literature in French. The approach we are proposing places, paradoxically, negotiations with otherness and boundary crossings at the very center of French literary history.
>
> (x)

If we are to understand and explain French literature to our students, the authors in this volume suggest that we must do so within a resolutely global context, one that reveals rather than obscures the migrations, influences, and interconnectedness of the entire French-speaking world. Indeed, this is the central claim of the manifesto "Pour une littérature-monde en français" ("For a World-literature in French"), which preceded *French Global* by three years. The time has come to recognize "the center … is from now on everywhere, in the four corners of the earth. Death to Francophonie. And birth of a world-literature in French" (2; my translation). This manifesto, signed by 44 authors writing in French, signals challenges ahead for scholars and students alike who must "relearn to walk" (3) but simultaneously shines a light on "this creative effervescence" (3) that will heretofore characterize this literature, unchained from a national identity.

One example of how my students and I seek to re-read canonical texts is an upcoming project one of my French majors will be pursuing this year. For her senior project during the spring 2021 semester, one of my students who is from Algeria will be reading Albert Camus's *L'Étranger* alongside Kamel Daoud's *Meursault, contre-enquête* [*The Meursault Investigation*], which is a rewriting of the tale from the perspective of the murder victim's brother. In particular, we will be asking how the two texts dialogue with one another, how the more recent text destabilizes and questions the assumptions of the earlier text, and how both texts participate in the French canon as defined by scholars, prize committees, journalists, and the public at large. This project will allow my student not only to read against the assumptions of the traditional metropolitan, French canon, but also to inscribe her own identity, as a differently abled female who is a member of an ethnic minority in Algeria, into the conversation between the two texts.

## Native Speakers, Heritage Speakers, Second-Language Learners: Our Diversity is Our Strength

Adapting the French classroom to the realities of the 21st century world is not just a matter of curricular shifts. The profile of French language learners in the US is equally diverse and that diversity must be addressed in the inclusive French classroom. In this section, I will discuss balancing the linguistic needs of heritage, native, and second-language speakers. In addition, I will explore how to ensure that all students feel that their individual identity is respected and that no one is pressured to represent an entire culture or ethnic group.

Historically, the field of heritage language teaching has advocated for specialized courses and programs to suit the issues faced by heritage speakers.[4] However, more recently, scholars have begun to "... argue for the need to institutionalize HL education in language departments and to mainstream it in the larger educational system" (Carreira and Kagan, 153). Relatively little research has been conducted on French heritage speakers in the US higher education context. However, the US Census from 2010 says that there are about 3 million speakers of French/French Creole over the age of five living in the United States. As a population, French heritage speakers in the US are quite diverse, comprising the children and grandchildren of immigrants from Canada, Europe, Africa, and the Caribbean.

Native speakers of French now living in the US often have had their learning of French interrupted by their own immigration. In our classrooms, we have taught some native speakers who grew up speaking French in another country until they were eight years of age while others lived in French-speaking countries until they were fifteen years of age. Regardless of the duration of the break from full immersion in a French-speaking environment, these students typically have high levels of fluency when speaking, but much lower and more complicated levels of proficiency when writing. Those whose formal education in French was interrupted at a younger age have often developed strategies such as the phonetic spelling of words as an adaptation to their mixed fluency. In the classroom, we often highlight the ways in which all students have linguistic challenges before them. We emphasize that language learning is a life-long process and draw parallels between our native speakers who are taking French and the English speakers who continue to study English at the university level in order to fully perfect their usage.

Recruiting diverse students brings significant benefits for all learners: increased awareness of linguistic diversity among French speakers, development of cross-cultural proficiency, and a sense of self as a member of the Francophone world. Of course, given the diversity of our students, fostering a positive, supportive classroom environment takes work. We seek to guide students to develop a collaborative, respectful community. As in every language-learning classroom, we make extensive use of pair and small-group activities. Neomy Storch and Ali Aldosari argue in their study that benefits from pairing students of different proficiency levels accrue if the pair relationship is a collaborative one (33). As faculty teaching heterogeneous groups of students, we need to develop activity prompts and instructions that support students in the creation of collaborative relationships subsequently highlighting the benefits of working together across proficiency levels to communicate, to learn, and to problem-solve. To this end, we must seek to scaffold such interactions appropriately so that native and heritage speakers are not put into the role of "expert," but rather are asked to create meaning with second-language learners.

For example, if we revisit our study of "Speak White," a typical prompt for this discussion would ask students to work in groups to identify the various cultural references in the poem, a wide-ranging set of historical events and personages. This text references the US Civil Rights movement as well as colonialism and the liberation struggles throughout the French-speaking world, thus ensuring that both American-born and immigrant students will have the opportunity to bring their own cultural knowledge to the table. In this type of exercise, students analyze a text that helps them make connections between their very different lived experiences and cultures.

## Difficult Conversations: Racism, Immigration, and (Neo-)Colonialism

Now, more than ever before, we need to be able to address issues of racism, immigration, and (neo-)colonialism in our classrooms. A good starting point is to recognize the full diversity of everyone in the room. To begin such discussions I talk about my own, very mixed, heritage as an American. This opens the door to asking *all* students to be aware of and to discuss their own cultural, religious, ethnic, racial, and socioeconomic heritage. Rather than putting native and heritage speakers on the spot as the sole emissaries of "other" cultures, discussions should allow students to develop a conceptual understanding of how languages, literatures, and other cultural products and practices inform *everyone's* sense of identity. Each student's personal intersectional identity needs to be implicated in these discussions.[5]

To illustrate how identities of individual students inform the content of the Widener French curriculum (without burdening such students with the responsibility of "representing" an entire group), I would like to describe briefly one of my former students, whom I will refer to using the name "Ismael." A native of Guinea (Conakry) in West Africa, Ismael expressed and we subsequently discussed a number of interesting opinions over the years. During his first year studying with us, we were discussing the theme of marriage in the context of "La Montagne de feu" ["The Mountain of Fire"] written by the Martinican Suzanne Dracius. Ismael stated that he believed marriage was a way to liberate oneself, as one had the freedom to choose one's spouse in a way that one does not choose one's parents or siblings. Other students might characterize marriage as an oppressive structure that binds the couple in unequal partnership. However, Ismael's view of marriage as liberating disrupted both racial and gender stereotypes in this discussion.

Ismael's contributions to class discussions often led to new insights, but not always by comfortable paths. For example, several years later, in a class discussion that touched on tensions between recent African immigrants to the USA and African Americans who had descended from enslaved Africans, Ismael expressed views that were extremely judgmental and derogatory toward African Americans. Another African-born student challenged him regarding these stereotypes on the basis of knowledge firmly grounded in the historical realities of institutionalized racism as well as empathy for the generations of African Americans who have survived and thrived in the US. This was a fascinating exchange to witness for all involved. On the one hand, this was a profound moment of personal awakening for the student being challenged regarding his anti-African American prejudice. On the other hand, this exchange forced everyone in the room to recognize the diversity of opinion among the Black students. In both these classroom exchanges (on marriage and on African Americans), the professor in the room facilitated but did not "lead" the discussion. The students themselves were comfortable enough to express and challenge one another's opinions and cultural blind spots. "French Studies" can—indeed must—become the kind of cultural crossroads in which individual identities, in all their complexity, are recognized in addition to the beliefs, institutions, and structures that support racism and other forms of oppression.

As the above examples illustrate, one of the benefits that comes with studying in a program such as ours is the opportunity it gives to students to reflect critically on their individual identity. Research done on heritage speakers highlights the importance of language to identity formation. Montgomery *et al.* describe the complex ways in which heritage learners develop their individual identity through the study of language. While their findings are based on a study of heritage speakers, we would do well to realize that: "According to Hilliard, one's language 'is not simply a means of communicating in a narrow sense. Psychologically, it is a prime source of cultural identity ... linked to one's worldview, identity, self-concept and self-esteem'" (27, 18). For *all* our students, language study will clarify how they come to see themselves and the world around them. While native and heritage speakers have non-academic connections to the language prior to arriving in our classes, the impact of language study on the identity formation of second-language learners is no less profound. In particular, second-language learners encounter a diverse community in our French classrooms and come to understand their own place in it. As a result, their own worldview is affected by their participation in this diverse group. Although we discuss how cultures have interacted negatively in the past in the context of exploration and colonization, we are simultaneously offering students a new, collaborative model for cross-cultural contact in the classroom based on shared language and learning.

Students in our program have the opportunity to define their own identity in terms of their role as a Francophone when they choose the topic for their senior research project. Over the years, this learning activity has served as a chance for students to express their interests but also their sense of who they are as learners and as members of our community and the community beyond our program. Here are some illustrative topics students have pursued:

- A student from Guinea opted to study the works of Léopold Sédar Senghor (1906–2001) in an effort to develop a more pan-African consciousness of colonialism and post-colonial Africa.
- A student from the Democratic Republic of Congo studied the novel *African Psycho* by Alain Mabanckou, which led to illuminating discussions with her

mother about experiences from the student's childhood living in the DRC during the civil war.
- An American student with strong feminist and LGBTQ+ ally beliefs pursued a summer research project on the French lesbian author, Mireille Best (1943–2005) and created a *Wikipedia* page devoted to her life and work.
- A student from Egypt who felt undereducated about the Middle East explored the first three volumes of the graphic novel series *L'Arabe du futur* [*The Arab of the Future*] by the French-Syrian author Riad Sattouf.

These capstone projects represent the best that a program like ours has to offer students: cross-cultural opportunities to explore the diversity of the French-speaking world; chances to develop a sense of themselves as members of an international community; and a supportive learning environment for the intellectual development required to pursue complex research questions. In conclusion, our program is one that provides a model of inclusivity not only in terms of texts studied but also in terms of students welcomed. We aim to foster a truly diverse community of learners and to nurture them as they claim their individual place within the French-speaking world.

## Notes

1 In 1998, there were 199,064 students of French in the United States, by 2016 that number had fallen to 175,667 according to the Modern Language Association Language Enrollment Database. For a discussion of cost and accountability in higher education as well as a path forward, see "Searching for Accountability in Higher Education: A Balanced Framework of Goals and Metrics" a report by Spiros Protopsaltis supported by the New America Organization, a center-left think tank in Washington, DC. For a critique of language learning in general in the popular press, see Simon Kuper's article "Learning another language? Don't bother" in the *Financial Times*.
2 Many of these students at my institution had migrated to the US earlier in their lives with their families. Our university does not recruit a large international student population, but for those that do, offering a diverse French and Francophone curriculum could be a recruiting benefit.
3 The New England Historical Society website is one reliable source for such images: www.newenglandhistoricalsociety.com.
4 One example of such a program is the Heritage Language Program at the University of California San Diego created in 2001–02.
5 In addition, we discuss the distinct phenomenon of intersectionality, as defined by Kimberlé Crenshaw, who has developed this term to address interlocking systems of oppression that impact Black women in ways that are distinct from other power relationships.

## References

Camus, Albert. *L'Étranger*. Folio, [1942] 2005.
Carreira, Maria and Olga Kagan. "Heritage Language Education: A Proposal for the Next 50 Years." *Foreign Language Annals*, vol. 51, 2018, pp. 152–158. doi:10.1111/flan.12331.

Chanterelle. "The Shuttle." *Mademoiselle Voulez-vous Danser?* Franco-American Music from the New England Borderlands. Smithsonian Folkways Recordings, 1999.
Crenshaw, Kimberlé. "Mapping the Margins: Intersectionality, Identity Politics, and Violence against Women of Color. "*Stanford Law Review*, vol. 43, no. 6, 1991, pp. 1241–1299, www.jstor.org/stable/1229039.
Daoud, Kamel. *Meursault, contre-enquête*. Éditions barzakh, 2013.
Dracius, Suzanne. "La Montagne de feu." *Diversité: La Nouvelle francophone: An IntermediateReader and Francophone Anthology*. 2nd edition, Houghton Mifflin, 1999.
Forget, Robert and Michèle Lalonde. *Speak White*. Performance by Michèle Lalonde, NationalFilm Board of Canada, 1980, www.nfb.ca/film/speak_white.
Kirkby, Charlotte. "Mireille Best." *Wikipedia*, 25 April 2020, en.wikipedia.org/wiki/Mireille Best.
Kuper, Simon. "Learning Another Language? Don't Bother." *Financial Times*, www.ft.com/content/3da3335c-330d-11e4-93c6-00144feabdc0.
Mabanckou, Alain. *African Psycho*. Poche, 2006.
McDonald, Christie and Susan Rubin Suleiman, editors. *French Global: A New Approach to Literary History*. E-book, EBSCO eBook Collection, Columbia UP, 2010.
"Modern Language Association Language Enrollment Database, 1958–2016." Modern Language Association, apps.mla.org/flsurvey_search.
Montgomery, Zak K. et al. "'You're not Latino, You're American': Heritage Learners of Spanish Navigate Issues of Cultural Identity in Higher Education." *College Student Affairs Journal*, vol. 36, no. 1, pp. 17–31, 2018.
National Center for Education Statistics. "Status and Trends in the Education of Racial and Ethnic Groups." nces.ed.gov/programs/raceindicators/indicator_REB.asp.
New England Historical Society. www.newenglandhistoricalsociety.com.
Organisation mondiale de la francophonie. *La Langue française dans le monde: Édition 2019*.
—. www.francophonie.org/sites/default/files/2020-02/Edition%202019%20La%20langue%20francaise%20dans%20le%20monde_VF%202020%20.pdf.
Protopsaltis, Spiro. "Searching for Accountability in Higher Education: A Balanced Framework of Goals and Metrics." *New America*, www.newamerica.org/education-policy/reports/searching-accountability-higher-education-balanced-framework-goals-metrics/.
Redonnet, Jean-Claude et al. *Héritages francophones: Enquêtes interculturelles*. Yale UP, 2009.
Sattouf, Riad. *L'Arabe du futur: Coffret tomes 1, 2, et 3*. Allary, 2017.
Storch, Neomy and Ali Aldosari. "Pairing Learners in Pair Work Activity." *Language Teaching Research*, vol. 17, no. 1, pp. 31–48, 2012. doi:10.1177/1362168812457530.
United Nations Office on Genocide Prevention and the Responsibility to Protect. "Definitions." www.un.org/en/genocideprevention/ethnic-cleansing.shtml.
Widener University Office of Institutional Research & Effectiveness. *Widener University Fact Book 2015–2019*. www.widener.edu/sites/default/files/2019-10/Widener-Fact-Book-2019.pdf.

# 10
# UNLEARNING THE LANGUAGE OF DIVISIVENESS

*Eilene Hoft-March*

This essay was written in the midst of the events of spring 2020, namely George Floyd's murder, the re-blossoming of Black Lives Matter (BLM) protests, and, as a consequence, a very belated inkling in the minds of many white Americans that racism is deeply entrenched in our culture, its institutions, and us. The scale and persistence of protests make me hopeful that many communities are edging toward essential conversations about race in this country. *May it be so.* However, the story of one of my white students confirms me in the belief that equity-inspired resistance, while certainly not futile, is only an initial step in the direction of effecting social change. The student in question lent his active allyship to BLM demonstrations in his community. At one of these events, language devolved and violence erupted among groups (including police) in genuinely dangerous ways. Caught in this maelstrom, he began to reconsider his participation in an event that, from his vantage, seemed to dead-end if not turn counter-productive. The experience reified the fierce often unbridgeable division that we see in public spaces and in media. Sadly, it dampened his desire to participate in demands for long overdue social justice.

Reactions such as this one confirm me in a belief that educators in French and Francophone Studies (even white, cis-gender, heterosexual, female elders like myself) have an excellent opportunity to move our students along the spectrum from value-driven resistance in the direction of the kinds of thoughtful civil dialogue needed to mobilize individuals, communities, and even whole societies toward social change and redress of social inequities. Language and culture faculty are well positioned to teach the habits of attention, reasoning, and speech requisite for humane and civil discourse. The very components indispensable to successful interaction in another culture are also indispensable to engaged dialogue: the specific, connoted language we use; the cultural context(s) in which it is

DOI: 10.4324/9781003126461-11

deployed; the historical knowledge we learn and bring; the implicit and explicit institutional structures we recognize; and the ways in which we engage other speakers. Civil discourse should not be deemed a lofty ideal, although it can bespeak understanding, openness, generosity, compassion, and ethical drive. Effectively applied, civil discourse can be a highly useful practice bent toward the recognition and expression of diverse ideas, perspectives, and experiences; the search for common ground; and, at its most effective, the negotiation of mutually acceptable, inclusive, and fair solutions.

In making a claim for teaching civil dialogue in the French-speaking classroom, I will be using as my main example an advanced level course taught in the French and Francophone Studies program at my small private liberal arts institution. Like many institutions of its ilk, mine has a reputation for being progressive, socially and perhaps even politically. My home department (French and Francophone Studies) represents diversity through its departmental members, its curricular content, its strong connections to interdisciplinary programs, and its departmentally staffed program in Dakar, Senegal. Students representing many identities as well as students interested in issues of diversity tend to gravitate to our program. That said, it would be a mistake to assume that we have done our job merely with good intentions, diverse content, or even with a diverse audience. As John Palfrey and Alberto Ibargüen note: "campus environments can chill speech on both the left and the right—expression that is a long way from hate speech—in ways that are counterproductive" (ch. 12). Furthermore, even well-informed students might not have the opportunity—let alone the tools—to consider others' positions or to question their own. This might lead to a reflexive intolerance that entrenches them and prevents them from learning from or because of others and thus from evolving into the citizens we need, those who can work on negotiated, equitable changes to our communities.

To return to the description of this advanced course: its title, "La Chose franco-arabe" (The Franco-Arabic "Thing") was borrowed from historian Jacques Berque's very broad designation of France's fraught relationships to the Arab world over several centuries (Laurens, 9). My use of the term focuses more on the current and ever problematic crossed-culture issues (the unarticulated "thing") that still dog contemporary France. The catalogue description for the course emphasizes content, particularly diversity as it represents the experiences of non-dominant groups of people, mainly those of North African origins, living within the dominant, mostly white French culture. We quickly review France's colonial history, focus on learning about populations of Maghrebian origins living in France, and look at issues of identity, inequities, and access that are further complicated in the current populist climate. We approach these ideas through a variety of sources in French: novels, short stories, essays, excerpts, films, podcasts, and on-line and in-person interviews.

As essential as is its content, the course's general education requirement status as "speaking intensive" provides the perfect opportunity to emphasize the skills and reflexes foundational to democratic dialogue. Speaking intensive suggests that class activities and performance tasks focus on language production, although I consider speaking only half of the equation. I match each speaking assignment with varied and targeted listening tasks for the class audience. In this way, an essential aspect of foreign language pedagogy (e.g., focused attention on understanding spoken language) also serves the pedagogy of civil dialogue. After all, attentiveness to others is prerequisite to respectful engagement with them.

In what follows, I have organized more detailed discussion of my experience of this course into five sections: 1) language: an entry point into the experience of others; 2) contexts: an appreciation of how the culture(s) got to their current state; 3) identities: the dynamics, constructedness, and social costs of identity; 4) critical tools: analytical tools that help us to recognize our participation in other-excluding systems; and 5) speaking and listening: tasks that model the steps involved in genuine dialogue.

## Language

What is obvious to language pedagogues—that words do not always have absolute equivalents—is not always so for language students. In this class, we focus on language that is anything but neutral, harboring exclusionary histories, racist undertones, politicized judgment, partisanship, or dog whistles. For example, "harki" yields the technically accurate gloss: "Algerian soldier who fought with the French during the War of Independence" [Reverso] without mentioning the various and often severe consequences of that allegiance for the Harkis. A reading from Besnaci-Lancou's chapter, "1962: Summer of Blood" adds the connotation of an Algerian whose entire family was perceived by Algerian neighbors to be traitors. In addition, a France 24 video on the Harki camp at Rivesaltes has vintage footage of their internment in rudimentary camps by the French ("Billet"). The term accrues connotations of crossed loyalties, perceived betrayals, collateral damage, or colonial contempt, depending on one's experience.

Another term, "communautarisme," can cause students problems for its resemblance to some form of the neutral to positive concept of community. That the word can also express a fearfulness of cultural isolationism, sectarianism, or militant separatism makes students more alert to context and to speaker. In a similar vein, we watched a clip of a heated interview with Emmanuel Macron in which journalists challenged his expressed belief in "diversity" as opposed to "multiculturalism," words that students take to be synonymous. We discuss how Macron's was not a preference for a trending term, but that it bore political connotations. A neoliberal term, it appeared, though France's recent move to quotas for immigrant workers suggests a more overtly conservative concern about growing immigrant communities.

Somewhat differently, the term "Beur," offers the chance to observe shifting references over time from an originally depreciatory term, to an identity embraced around the time of the March of the Beurs (1983) and, in some contexts in the mouths of some speakers, back to a pejorative designation.[1] An inclusive practice (reaffirmed in our class) is to use similar terms with care and, in conversations, to cultivate the reflex to let people self-identify.

In sum, articulating the questions students should bear in mind as they acquire specific vocabulary promotes an initial awareness of how to negotiate diversity. Is the term inflected with historical, social, political, racial, gender, or cultural significance? Does it raise loaded questions? Does it signal the speaker's adherence to particular values or ideologies? Has it shifted connotations over time? Explicitness and accuracy can make a vital difference in avoiding misconceptions and miscommunications.

## Contexts

Having an opinion in the current climate of rapid response posts and instant messaging—ostensibly, a version of democratic speech—often encourages alliances based on buzzwords, superficial knowledge, and little in the way of knowledge or analysis. It behooves us to underscore with students that democratic speech environments presuppose knowledge and understanding of issues to be considered, their evolution, and their implications as a condition of responsible engagement.[2]

A relevant starting point for us is France's history with Algeria: France's colonial imposition, its usurpation of land and resources, its harnessing of an Algerian labor force, creation of a white European elite, and immigration policies post-Independence that powered France through its Thirty Glorious Years (1945 −75).[3] This history helps students grasp how the last sixty years of Maghrebian presence in France cannot be dropped into categories neatly marked "immigrant" or "assimilated," to use conservatively favored and highly problematic political terms. Living in a culture claiming to privilege individualism, students need reminders of how minority cultures—and the individuals identified with them—adapt, survive, or subsist within a dominant culture. Our reading of Leila Sebbar's *Mes Algéries en France* [*My Algerias in France*] helps to raise those complicated dynamics of cultures nested within cultures. Sebbar is uniquely situated for having origins in both Algerian and French cultures, a personal history in both countries, and a life spanning before and after Algerian independence. Although her book presents as an album of images and memories with personal significance, it reveals undervalued connections between the two cultures. Algerian maquisards resisted France in the same ways French resistance fighters foiled German occupants. French women ethnologists lived among Algerian women and revised the centuries-old orientalist image of dancing girls and odalisques. On French soil, Sebbar visits immigrant worker foyers, harki hamlets, chibani cafés, and Muslim cemeteries. The highly visual nature of this album (photographs, postcards, advertisements, etc.) models a position of observation and, less objectively but more compassionately, of appreciation of and gratitude for that first generation of Algerian immigrants that is all but forgotten by the dominant culture.

We also look at cultural manifestations that draw more of the dominant culture's attention, religion being a primary, often visible, example. American students tend to assume that religious freedom is an uncomplicated civil right, American experience notwithstanding. The course gives us an opportunity to evaluate the French concept of "laïcité" (secularity) and its ramifications. In talking about Islam under the rule of secularity, we discuss, for example, the social effects in France when Muslim communities must rely on Algeria, Morocco, Turkey, and Saudi Arabia to build mosques and train imams (70% of practicing imams are not French) (Daoud). I excerpt some of our information—doubling as listening practice—from a radio series on France Culture titled "Questions d'Islam." One discussion centered on the wearing of burqas and burkinis in public spaces, in contravention of France's 2010 "anti-burqa" law. Generally, even my non-Muslim students deem the ban on hijabs in public schools in France a violation of civil rights, but are more conflicted about the burqa. Does it function as an expression of religious freedom or as submission to gender inequality? On the other hand, a remark made by a French Muslim captured student attention: the burqa liberated her from objectification whereas, in her estimation, many French women embrace the "burqa-size 6" mentality, i.e., a willing subjection to objectification cultivated through their appearance ("Provocations"). This enlarged the discussion from religious patriarchy or cultural imperialism to a broader social issue of women's (self-)objectification, obliging us to "turn the analytical lens back on hegemonic knowledge forms to denaturalize the patterns that these forms portray as a just-natural standard" (Salter, 308).

## Identities

Nothing appears more indisputable than statistics, so I have students collect population breakdowns from the INSEE (National Institute of Statistics and Economic Studies) and Pew Research websites. Census statistics from 2018 indicate that 9.7% of the population was born outside of France, something close to 40% of that percentage in other European countries, with about 25% from North Africa. Categories start to blur when we look at the 11.2% second generation of "immigrants," half of whom have parentage of mixed national origins. We also note that, while France has the largest Muslim population in Europe, 10% are converts. Then we begin the business of interrogating these "facts," the flat and probably false categories they suggest, the misinterpretations and pseudo-knowledge they risk conveying. This exercise ushers in our discussions of identity.

Excerpts from Amin Maalouf's *Identités Meurtrières* [*In the Name of Identity*] give us a gentle entry into identity issues. Himself an example of hybridity and adaptation (a Christian, Lebanese-born, Arabophone, French-writing "Immortal"), Maalouf discusses context-based identifications with specific cultural, ethnic, gender, and religious groups. Most if not all students relate to his descriptions of constructed identities, fleeting or long-term allegiances, and even reductions or distortions of their identities by others. Certainly, Maalouf's humanist conviction of acknowledging what is profoundly human in every individual is precisely the platform on which social justice firmly stands. Moreover, his passages on responsible reciprocity where individuals of two cultures (e.g., Islamic and non-Islamic French) coexist suggest models for dialogue. However, his explanations of violence as the logical consequence of acute tribalism risk an ultimate shift of blame on "others," which we need to interrogate. This discussion of Maalouf thus helps us pivot to our critical tools.

## Critical Tools

I borrow and modify a critical toolkit from American theorists that helps students analyze oppression and racism as effects of the cultures in which we all participate. Although students often hear and even use the terms "intersectionality" and "systemic racism," an efficient tutorial in each ensures accurate use of these conceptual frameworks. In several versions of a classic article, Kimberlé Crenshaw maintains that the "isms" that might intersect in people's lives do not coincide with separate "anti-ism" practices. Her "focus on the intersections of race and gender only highlights the need to account for multiple grounds of identity when considering how the social world is constructed" (1245) and how that world does not serve individuals situated at certain intersections. After viewing Philippe Faucon's film *Fatima*, students discuss the multiple intersecting patterns of subordination of the main character, a Moroccan-born domestic worker with modest skills in the French language, financially fragile, self-sacrificingly maternal, divorced, and non-conforming to some of the socio-cultural expectations of her neighbors in low-income social housing. The class tries to imagine solutions socially or politically available to Fatima. The film hints that her self-affirming journal in Arabic and the successes of her daughters offer a modicum of self-valorization, but the students recognize that this is a narrative resolution rather than a socially practicable solution for those like Fatima who are multiply marginalized.

A second critical tool that gives an even more encompassing understanding is that of systemic oppression. Although the term is virtually ubiquitous at this time, I sense that students conflate "systemic" with "systematic," which not only dilutes its meaning, but also implies intentional behaviors. A useful document prepared by the Québécois Ligue des Droits et Libertés (The Quebec League of Rights and Freedoms) titled "Le Racisme Systémique... Parlons-en!" ("Systemic Racism... Let's Talk about it!") clearly presents intersectionality, sexism, white privilege, implicit bias, institutional racism, and Islamophobia as elements of systemic oppression. I use this material in concert with my French adaptation of the graphic "What Racism Looks Like" to give students a concise analytical framework to apply to course content. For example, we compare the films *The Secret of the Grain* (Abdellatif Kechiche) and *The Disintegration* (Philippe Faucon) in spite of differences in tenor. In the first film, a laid-off Tunisian dockworker undertakes to open a seaside couscous restaurant. The circumstances of his termination, the difficulties he encounters trying to initiate a small business, and the attitudes of the local politicians and bankers he must persuade can be traced to entrenched practices that profoundly disadvantage him without seeming to do so. The students recognize both the ostensibly objective rules and attitudes that are applied and the value of the work the man, his family, and his friends invest in the enterprise. The film makes abundantly clear that he is locked out of a system organized to facilitate wealth building for the advantaged white majority. Quite differently, *Disintegration* elicits from students an understandably negative response to a young Maghrebian's radicalization. Despite exceptional performance in his technical program, the young man cannot get an interview let alone employment. Deeply frustrated by his failure to enter into the workplace, thereby attaining economic success, independence, and recognition, he turns instead to his local Muslim community. Faucon is careful to separate the Islamic beliefs taught by the local imam and the radical, fundamentalist precepts that are foundational to the terrorist training run by a jihadist operative. Capitalizing on the young man's experience of racist exclusion and appealing to a sense of—tribal, Maalouf would say—superiority, the jihadist enlists the young man in a terrorist attack. Comparing the films helps to clarify that both protagonists seek to contribute to their culturally mixed communities but that accepted, intrinsic discriminatory practices effectively guarantee their personal failures. While the films capture everything from subtle to overtly racist, Islamophobic, classist, privileged behaviors of individuals, the latter are only one aspect of a closed and insidious system advantageous to and reinforced by dominant white culture. With this more encompassing and explicit understanding of the dynamics of oppression, students appreciate that democratic solutions to these inveterate problems need to come from addressing institutional policies and practices as much as individual attitudes and behaviors.

## Speaking and *Listening*

I scaffold speaking/listening exercises according to length and sophistication with an overall goal of reinforcing the skills of thoughtful, mutual engagement. For all oral presentations, students must give special attention to making their work accessible and garnering audience response (no verbatim PowerPoints). The audience participates by generating questions in explicit categories: clarification, extension, solicitation of opinion, and respectful challenge. For longer exposés with analysis, I require speakers to draw from a bank of phrases (indicating order, contrast, amplification, disagreement, doubt, emphasis, etc.) that helps them to organize the movement of their developing thought, flag their position, offer illustrative examples and metaphors, etc. Moreover, in fine-tuning their presentations, they need to articulate other points of view, using language for exceptions, concessions, and acknowledgment of counterarguments (for these last, instructors should discourage fallacious argument pre-emptively). A primary goal of this assignment is to make students alert to how they present information, how they position themselves in interpreting what they have researched, and how they might sound to an audience.

Debate,[4] the next level of oral assignment, can allow students to enter into a controversy without personalizing their engagement. Debate's format also compels students to shift from the security of prepared remarks to the unexpected requirements of extemporaneous responses and rebuttals based on close listening. Moreover, debates require thought about the implications of one's own position and critical and strategic engagement with the countering point of view. Especially to our purposes here is the consideration of a community's or a culture's ideology and its ramifications. (Examples: should the French state collect data on race, ethnicity, and religion in its censuses [it currently does not]? Should the French state be able to refuse naturalization to an immigrant for reasons of incompatibility with French values [it currently does]?) This anticipation of other possible perspectives needs to occur both in preparing for the debate and in listening in real time to opposing arguments. In post-debate sessions, the class spends time discussing "debate" as often practiced in our classrooms, our cultures, our news media, and our social networking. We acknowledge that the agonistic argumentation of debate makes it seem incumbent to prevail over opponents rather than to find a reasonable compromise worked toward from opposing positions.[5] Understanding conflict as part of an illuminating and potentially productive process helps us to move into the next major class activity.

The ultimate speaking exercise for my students is to conduct live interviews, remotely or in person, with native-speaking informants. Within my contacts, I have sought a variety of experiences, identities, and views: a pied-noir who experienced the exodus from Algeria as a child, an ideologically conservative Frenchman, a second-generation Franco-Algerian, and an Egyptian Muslim woman from the community. In preparation, students collaborate on a list of courteously formulated but sometimes direct interview questions. They also review a Website (Kerbrat-Orecchioni) describing a range of communicative behaviors signaling everything from hostility to receptiveness. Particularly useful for non-native speakers is the continuum of modes of positive engagement both linguistic and extra-linguistic with a compendium of possible responses, including demurring and politely challenging.

For one particular class, students were a model of courtesy during the live interviews, but understandably cautious about pursuing difficult lines of inquiry. For instance, they asked a (non-Muslim) guest to opine about "prayer in the street," a reference to Muslims praying on public sidewalks for lack of neighborhood mosques. Students had already listened to an interview on this very issue with Eric Lejoindre, Mayor of the 18$^{th}$ arrondissement. Lejoindre reported that the overwhelming majority of complaints his office received about prayer in public space had come from people who did not live or work in Paris. Thus, when our guest talked about the many complaints that had come from the residents of the 18th, the students realized, without confronting him, that he believed what might have been reported in some media but was flatly denied by a first-hand source.

In our post-interview debriefings, the class discussed ways in which we might have continued the dialogue. In the future, I plan follow-up interviews as a way of continuing engagement. In the case cited above, we agreed that an outright challenge to someone's opinion, perceived as objectively supported, might stoke a standoff. We discussed reformulating the issue as a possible problem for the worshipers in the community, rather than a situation perceived as problematic only to outsiders. We also considered other entry points to the issue, noting that the guest had concluded the interview by maintaining that he was French to the core and would always defend the purity of his culture. Minimally, we could have returned to those assertions to understand better what he meant and how he thought French culture might be imperiled (our inference from his comments). Further, we might have drawn parallels to his sentiments with those of the Muslim community: that its desire for cultural cohesion, religious traditions, and social alliances are a source of cultural pride and of fear of losing identity. These might be common grounds from which to open the next dialogue to productive parallels. Finally, we had the opportunity to apply the most serious critique of all to ourselves: that the voices that also needed to be heard in any genuine discussion of the problem, let alone of viable solutions, would need to come from members of the communities in question.

## Conclusion

I began this essay with the anecdote of a student who felt disheartened by a perceived lack of impact of efforts at redressing a deep and enduring history of racism. But what he and millions of others in more than 4,000 cities worldwide have helped to initiate is an acute awareness of the need for serious and sustained discussions that can bring a majority together in the shared understanding of social injustices and shared construction of effective, corrective actions. For our part, we band of French and Francophone colleagues have distinct opportunities to train the next generation in the difficult democratic practice that is civil dialogue. However, we must be deliberate, explicit, and unrelenting about what that practice entails and then teach it: informed engagement; acute sensitivity to language and its varying values; a respectful, attentive, empathic demeanor to what and whom we cannot know; and the will to concede just enough but demand much to address the interests of the marginalized. A better and fairer collective future will—as it probably always has—depend on such dialogues.

I gratefully acknowledge support for the creation of this course from Lawrence University's Inclusive Pedagogy initiative funded by the Andrew W. Mellon Foundation.

## Notes

1 The term "beurette" has definitely come under fire as racist, sexist, and colonialist (www.lesinrocks.com/2020/06/04/actualite/societe/pourquoi-il-faut-arreter-demployer-le-mot-beurette).
2 Christopher Tinson and Javiera Benavente set out four sine qua non for Democratic Speech Environments, two of which are the requirement to become educated about an issue and the commitment to share an understanding of history.
3 Importantly, this invites some parallels with US history and lays groundwork for later discussions of sustained, systemic racism.
4 I use Steven Johnson's "Debate as a Pedagogical Tool" for its invaluable guidance in preparing students, formulating the essential components, and designing debate assignments and expectations. Most compelling is his insistence that the exercise be "audience centered…the focus of persuasive effort is the audience, not the opposition" (54).
5 Kerri Morris urges teaching students the basics of an ethical practice of rhetoric. Following Aristotelian rhetorical practice and Henry Johnstone's ethical imperative, she lays out a matrix for speakers that encourages resoluteness against intimidation, fairness and openness to opponents' arguments, and gentleness and compassion in refraining from crushing an opponent for the sake of winning (46). Democracies depend on such conduct.

## References

Besnaci-Lancou, Fatima. *Fille de harki [Daughter of a Harki]*. Atelier, 2005.
"Billet Retour Rives-Altes" ["Return Trip Rives-Altes"]. www.youtube.com/watch?v=okoZiLd0wZo.
Cassendo, D. "Le Racisme systémique… Parlons-en!" [Systemic Racism… Let's Talk about it!]. https://coco-net.org/wp-content/uploads/2018/05/ldl_brochure_racisme_final.pdf.
Crenshaw, Kimberlé. "Mapping the Margins: Intersectionality, Identity Politics, and Violence against Women of Color." *Stanford Law Review*, vol. 43, no. 6, 1991, pp. 1241–1299.
Daoud, Kamel. "France Has Millions of Muslims. Why Does It Import Imams?" *New York Times*, January 28, 2019, www.nytimes.com/20a19/01/28/opinion/france-islam-imams-import-algeria.html.
Faucon, Philippe, director. *The Disintegration*. Pyramide, 2011.
—. *Fatima*. Pyramide, 2015.
"Five Facts about the Muslim Population in Europe." www.pewresearch.org/fact-tank/2017/11/29/5-facts-about-the-muslim-population-in-europe.
"Immigrés, Étrangers | Insee." www.Insee.Fr,www.insee.fr/fr/statistiques/3633212.
Johnson, Steven L. "Debate as a Pedagogical Tool." *Start Talking: A Handbook for Engaging Difficult Dialogues in Higher Education*, edited by Kay Landis, U of Alaska and Alaska Pacific U, 2008, https://cdn.vanderbilt.edu/vu-wp0/wp-content/uploads/sites/59/2017/03/01130311/Start_Talking_full_book_pdf.
Kechiche, Abdellatif, director. *The Secret of the Grain*. Criterion Collection, 2007.
Kerbrat-Orecchioni, Catherine. "La conversation." http://users.skynet.be/fralica/refer/theorie/theocom/oral/dialoral.html.

Laurens, Henry. *Français et Arabes depuis deux siècles: la Chose franco-arabe* [Two Centuries of French and Arabs: The Franco-Arabic Thing]. Tallandier, 2012.

"Les provocations de la burqa et du burkini." www.franceculture.fr/emissions/questions-dislam/visibilite-de-la-pratique-islamique-en-france.

Maalouf, Amin. *Les Identités meurtrières* [*In the Name of Identity*]. Grasset, 1998.

Morris, Kerri. "Rhetoric and the Method of Democracy." *Start Talking: A Handbook for Engaging Difficult Dialogues in Higher Education*, edited by Kay Landis, U of Alaska and Alaska Pacific U, 2008, https://cdn.vanderbilt.edu/vu-wp0/wp-content/uploads/sites/59/2017/03/01130311/Start_Talking_full_book_pdf.

Palfrey, John and Alberto Ibargüen. *Safe Spaces, Brave Spaces: Diversity and Free Expression in Education*. Boston, MA: MIT Press, 2017, Project MUSE, muse.jhu.edu/book/60818.

"Qui sont les Harkis?" ["Who are the Harkis?"]. www.youtube.com/watch?v=vNgDIxOYQXo.

Salter, Phia S. and Glenn Adams. "Provisional Strategies for Decolonizing Consciousness." In *Antiracism Inc.: Why the Way We Talk about Social Justice Matters*, edited by Felice Blake *et al*. Punctum Books, 2019.

Sebbar, Leila. *Mes Algéries en France: Carnet de voyages*. [*My Algerias in France: Travel Notebook*]. Bleu autour, 2004.

Tinson, Christopher and Javiera Benavente. "Toward a Democratic Speech Environment." www.aacu.org/diversitydemocracy/2017/spring-summer/tinson.

"What Racism Looks Like." https://fpg.unc.edu/sites/fpg.unc.edu/files/resources/other-resources/What%20Racism%20Looks%20Like.pdf.

# SECTION III
# Embracing Cultures/Extending Contexts

# 11
# STRATEGIES FOR TEACHING DIVERSITY AND INCLUSION IN INTRODUCTORY LITERATURE COURSES

*Dominique Licops*

In this chapter, I share the principles of course design and teaching strategies that I developed for undergraduate introductory literature courses while participating in fora about diversity, equity, inequality, and inclusion in our classrooms. These principles and strategies are founded on a commitment to a student-centered pedagogy of active learning transposed from the foreign language classroom to the foreign literature classroom.[1] One of the central questions in these times of increasing violence and inequalities and heightened awareness of our global history of colonialism, racism, and hetero/sexism becomes: how can we harness this pedagogy to transform our classrooms into inclusive learning environments where diverse students explore questions of identity, difference, diversity, power, exclusion, and inclusion in French language literatures? How can we create a community where that exploration leads to self-reflection and better understanding of our positions in this complex world through the identities represented in the texts we study? One answer lies in developing a pedagogy grounded in intercultural competence and foreign literature pedagogy, and in selecting texts that model complex dynamics relating to diversity, exclusion, and inclusion.

In their model of Intercultural Teaching Competence (ITC), Nanda Dimitrov and Aisha Haque explain that "knowledge of the existence of cultural differences … and an awareness of the *limits* of [our] cultural knowledge" and "[t]he ability to analyse events, social phenomena, and motivation from multiple perspectives" are "fundamental [… to] intercultural competence" (442, 444; my emphasis). A pedagogy that centers on diversity and inclusion fosters awareness of our cultural blind spots and openness to diverse ways of knowing. A focus on marginalized characters and their intercultural journeys leads to defining intercultural learning in terms of an informed, evolving, respectful conversation among our own cultures and worldviews and those represented in the texts. As students analyze the dynamic of

DOI: 10.4324/9781003126461-12

blindness and vision inherent in the characters' navigation of several cultures and how this dynamic affects the characters' personal development and their relationships with others, they learn to navigate diverse environments and how diversity shapes identity. Discussion of the characters' learning of a new language and culture also reflects students' learning of the language and literature, and by comparison, reveals to them their preconceptions and biases.

The ITC model provides a blueprint for inclusive teaching that "nurture[s] diversity" more effectively (437). Three sets of competencies are central to inclusive teaching: foundational competencies that "focus on an instructor's own intercultural awareness and ability to model intercultural competencies for their students" (443), "facilitation competencies [that] encompass the instructional skills necessary to recognize learners' needs, build community in the classroom, create shared academic expectations, as well as the ability to facilitate active learning with diverse audiences" (445), and curriculum design competencies that "include the ability to ... create learning materials that transcend the limitations of monocultural disciplinary paradigms [and] scaffold student learning so students [can] master intercultural skills relevant to their discipline" (448).

Selection of a diverse corpus is key to providing opportunities to study diverse identities in various contexts.[2] Scaffolding texts with images, paratexts, interviews and designing sequences of varied activities and assignments helps students explore the complex relationships between history, culture, identities, biography, and genres. We explore how texts present the social production of identities and differences, how characters deal with social dynamics of inclusion and exclusion, how they negotiate and critique social systems that exclude them, and in what conditions they imagine alternative models that value diversity and inclusiveness. Activities focusing on dis/identification with characters engage diverse students by validating their multiple positionalities vis-à-vis the characters. Students develop their intercultural and interpretive skills and build their cultural self-awareness as they go from analyzing the work of cultural critic in the texts to performing that role in the final project.

Integrating ITC competencies with foreign literature pedagogy makes teaching more inclusive. In fact, the rubrics of human learning that Elizabeth Bernhardt applies to literature teaching—time on task, appropriate feedback, prior knowledge, situated learning, task difficulty, multiple solutions, and release of control (201)—are also central in ITC. Combining the following features of both approaches is key to creating an inclusive learning community: designing classroom activities and assessment so students spend time practicing intercultural and interpretive skills, scaffolding and sequencing activities according to risk level and task difficulty, and giving students opportunities to "demonstrate learning in a variety of ways" for "real-life contexts" (Dimitrov and Haque, 448, 450). In addition, principles for effective group dynamics emphasize trust building, complementarity, and respectful collaboration to lead to production.

In Mme de Graffigny's *Lettres d'une Péruvienne* [*Letters from a Peruvian Woman*], Zilia, the Peruvian princess who is abducted and brought to France, exemplifies the challenges of cross-cultural understanding. When her experiences contradict her culturally situated reason, she suspends her judgment, observes more, and asks questions. Zilia also reflects on her blind spots, e.g., her blindness regarding her fiancé, Aza (letter 38). She questions the limits of reason, since it cannot comfort a desperate soul, but remarks on the similarity of souls in contrast to the differences in Peruvian and French dress. Zilia refuses to marry the French aristocrat Déterville, offering him a friendship based on the exchange of knowledge and virtue, which she promises to take as a guide for judgment (letter 40). We analyze how Zilia engages with foreigners and the linguistic and cultural learning that is a condition and result of this engagement. We gather that rationality is insufficient, that intercultural relationships require an ethical and spiritual stance. Suspension of judgment and the recognition of a shared humanity enable a cross-cultural relationship based on reciprocity. In this sense, Zilia is an intercultural teacher who "model[s] and encourage[s] non-judgmental approaches to exploring ... difference" (Dimitrov and Haque, 445). Graffigny's model is an early variation of the "Describe-Analyze-Evaluate model, an intercultural training strategy used to model the skill of withholding judgment until one has had a chance to explore alternative explanations ... of individuals' behaviour" (445). We also reflect on the conditions of Zilia's inclusion in Enlightenment society, since it depends on her moral and emotional strengths grounded in Peruvian culture and her means as a princess, which enable her to resist assimilation to the period's gender norms.

This sequence of activities considers students' diverse linguistic and interpretative skills and identities. We start with understanding Zilia's journey by collectively reconstructing the narrative based on the illustrations of the 1752 edition. Pedagogical editions provide students the necessary cultural and literary knowledge to practice their interpretive and intercultural skills. Students work on the 2005 introduction in complementary and collaborative group work. With an understanding of the novel as love story and philosophical novel, and how these genres express gender and cultural differences in Enlightenment colonialism, students engage in close reading. Groups each outline a letter focusing on Zilia's responses to cultural differences and analyze expressions of cultural analysis and comparisons. The assignment builds on the class's discoveries: students 1) endorse Zilia's stance as a cultural critic and imitate Graffigny's style to write a letter where Zilia critiques an aspect of their home country; and 2) reflect on what they learned about the novel by endorsing an outsider perspective on their society. Students' choice of the aspect they critique minimizes the risk of self-disclosure (Dimitrov and Haque, 447). This exercise values students' diverse perspectives.

Claire de Duras's *Ourika* is the first novel to present a Black heroine living in Europe, suffering from the alienation resulting from the interiorization of racism, sexism, and classism (Little xi). We study the mechanisms by which a society justifies its domination, e.g. by accusing the marginalized of transgressing the social order it presents as "natural." We discuss how this racist trope persists today in the stereotyping of marginalized people. We explore Ourika's limited agency, her ability to critique racism and inability to question the hetero/sexism and classism that limit her notion of happiness to an aristocratic marriage. Ourika's pain at rejection by the society that raised her in its image contrasts with Zilia's ability to define her relationship with the dominant culture. This contrast leads to discussing access to cultural resources and community and its impact on inclusion. Ourika only knows about Black people through the dominant dehumanizing portrayal, which compounds her solitude. We compare Zilia's understanding of "nation" with Ourika's experience of "race" and study the historicity of paradigms of individuality, community, race, and class.[3] Students learn how exclusionary discourses and counter-discourses of inclusion evolve historically, while certain of their characteristics persist over time. Students then use these conceptual tools to reflect on their experiences.

After reading *Ourika*, students explore "various disciplinary approaches" to the novel by comparing editions. This task "matches the real world" (Dimitrov and Haque, 449–50; Bernhardt, 203–04), allowing diverse students to relate to the material. Each group studies an edition's paratext and writes a description for a timeline of the novel's iconographic history. Students decide which edition they would buy based on these blurbs. We discuss the editors' agendas and politics by analyzing the paratexts, focusing on the representation of Ourika and Black women in the texts' iconography.[4] This activity familiarizes students with multiple perspectives and the editor's role as a cultural critic whose presentation of the text frames the reading. Students discuss their positionality in relation to the editions based on understanding the editors' positionality as mediators between text and readership.

While in the first novels we explore the representation of the "Other" by writers who are privileged as aristocrats yet marginalized as women, Maupassant's *Le Horla* [*The Horla*] brings us into the psyche of the white man of privilege.[5] A text where a privileged protagonist faces an inexplicable, *foreign* phenomenon counterbalances the previous readings' focus on outsiders navigating a dominant culture. The contrast strengthens student understanding of the intersectionality of identities and the impact of power in relation to difference. Moreover, the fantastic genre dramatizes the confrontation of two methodologies "we use to make sense of the world" (Dimitrov and Haque, 444), as protagonist and reader decide between the scientific or the supernatural explanation. We discuss 19th-century positivism, its definition of European Man as rational being, and its association of irrationality with the "Other." The first-person journal where the protagonist grapples with his unfamiliar experiences provides a counter/model of how to approach difference. It also illustrates Sidonie Smith's and Julia Watson's point about white male subjectivity:

> Where Western eyes see Man as a unique individual rather than a member of a collectivity, of race or nation [or class], of sex or sexual preference, Western eyes see the colonized [or the Other] as an amorphous, generalized collectivity.
>
> *(xvii; my additions)*

Indeed, the protagonist defines himself in relation to his property and servants' obedience, but cannot see them as individuals, nor as fellow sufferers, instead forgetting them in the fire meant to kill the Horla.

Students write an analytical essay on *Ourika* or *Le Horla*. Previous exercises of close reading and analyzing various editions, as well as the creative-reflexive assignment, have familiarized them with the work of literary and intercultural analysis and interpretation. Peer-reviewing essay outlines based on a rubric further builds on this scaffolded and sequenced approach to learning literary and intercultural interpretation to create shared academic expectations, since peer activities allow diverse learners "to learn from each other and share the ... cultural [and linguistic] knowledge they bring to the classroom" (Dimitrov and Haque, 447; my addition).

After these novels representing "the Other" from a European perspective, we turn to texts written after decolonization by those perceived in the Western tradition as "Other" because it is essential to "incorporate content ... that represent[s] diverse perspectives" and "validates cultural differences" (Dimitrov and Haque, 449). Including diverse voices opens up a space where students can identify the materials with their living conditions and reflect on the mechanism of dis/identification. The classroom thereby becomes relevant to our social environment, contributing to solve a perceived disconnect between academic culture and students' experiences.[6]

An interview of the Beur writer, sociologist, and politician and the film adaptation of his first autobiographical novel, *Shantytown Kid*, provide context for Azouz Begag's *Béni ou le paradis privé* [*Béni or the Private Paradise*].[7] With Béni, the protagonist of the second volume, we encounter the smart adolescent-*cum*-cultural critic, who negotiates his family's Algerian culture and French culture. His candid and humoristic "verbal photographs" (Rogers, 3) provide, as Alec Hargreaves explains, "an antidote to [the racial tensions ... present in the 1980s], inviting majority ethnic readers to enjoy the company of engaging ... characters grappling with serious problems that are ... best tackled with good rather than ill will" (xvi). We explore Béni's tactics to counter racism, especially acting. His thoughts on the performativity of identity create the utopian vision of a society in which ethnicity isn't a factor of exclusion. However, Béni's meanness toward his siblings is the dark side of his privilege thanks to his school success—revealing that gender and lack of education compound racism. Because theatrical techniques diversify students' engagement with the material by including diverse learning styles,[8] I build on Béni's insights about identity and performance, and have students role-play characters who navigate scenes fraught with racism and sexism. By playing characters, students practice perspective-taking, then discuss identification and intersectionality. The discussion becomes a dialog between students and text as they bring their experiences to bear on the text and reflect on how it sheds new light on them.

The ending provides food for thought as Béni's rejection (an instance of racial profiling) from the nightclub, the private paradise of the title, topples into a magic realist flight toward the paradise of light, where he does not need to hide his identity. It is an opportunity to practice our responses to uncertainty, another shared concern in foreign literature pedagogy and ITC. Negotiating multiple meanings is a hallmark of literary interpretation while teaching strategies that "model tolerance for ambiguity and help learners deal with the uncertainty of exploring difference" is a foundational competency of ITC. Texts that do not have "clear, single" interpretations or present "open-ended situation[s and] complex problem[s …] promote tolerance for ambiguity" (Dimitrov and Haque, 445). *Ourika* and *Le Horla* similarly have ambiguous endings. We ponder whether Ourika finds acceptance in religion, or still pines for unrequited love. Whereas the equivocal haven she finds is brief, we discuss the meaning of Béni's flight given the integration he desires. *Le Horla*'s ending adds to its central ambiguity, as it leaves us wondering if the Horla is destroyed or the protagonist will commit suicide.

With Chinese Canadian Ying Chen's *Les Lettres chinoises* [*Chinese Letters*], we shift from Francophone literature implicated in French colonial history toward the history of globalization. This novel dramatizes a further point of congruence between foreign literature pedagogy and ITC: understanding how students' prior knowledge affects their learning (Dimitrov and Haque, 444; Bernhardt, 202–203). In this novel, Sassa, who lives in Shanghai and Yuan, her *fiancé*, who emigrates to Montreal, exchange letters about migration. Their friend Da Li joins Yuan, and also exchanges letters with Sassa. Chen explores the dynamics of intercultural learning in this triangular relationship. Each character is in the outsider position, with partial knowledge and partial blindness. They read between the lines of the other's letters, as they navigate their new Canadian reality and engage in a Francophone concept-oriented discourse and a Chinese rhetoric of the implicit. In negotiating two cultural codes, they become models for students who learn to decode what Chantal Zabus calls the palimpsistic text, in which the migrant's language transforms the host society's language. American students see their realities refracted through a doubly foreign perspective since North America is the cultural "Other" in this story. Chinese students discuss their similarities and differences with the characters and author; and students from other backgrounds bring yet other perspectives—leading to a kind of global learning that engages multiple cultural and linguistic paradigms.[9]

When possible, inviting a colleague to talk about Chinese rhetoric is a way of acknowledging the limits of my own cultural knowledge and modeling intercultural dialog. An understanding of Chinese rhetoric enables students to discuss the limits of their cultural knowledge and how new knowledge changes their reading of the text. It also highlights how the characters' shifting positions change their understanding of both societies, themselves, and each other. We explore their realization that their identification with the new culture blinds them to their cultural conditioning. Students reflect on how their ideas about the target culture similarly enable and limit their interpretations.[10] The novel thus provides students with "opportunities ... to ... better understand ... their own multiple cultural, personal, and disciplinary identities" (Dimitrov and Haque, 450).

In Bernhardt's theory of second language reading, students' prior knowledge, especially of first language literature, either helps or interferes with their understanding of the literature depending on its appropriateness, and with what she calls "*authentic* interpretation" (202–203; my emphasis). My view is that if interpretation is based on an effective understanding of the text, no one interpretation is more authentic than another, hence the importance of a sequenced approach that goes from comprehension to interpretation. My view aligns closely with Dimitrov and Haque's that "a diversity of views, prior knowledge, backgrounds, assumptions and approaches to learning ... are an asset to learning" (444). Indeed, this diversity helps students to learn from each other how their cultural knowledge impacts their understanding.

Nevertheless, Bernhardt and Dimitrov and Haque agree on the importance of accessing students' prior knowledge and applying the easy to hard principle to tailor the level of linguistic, literary, and cultural difficulty to their abilities (Bernhardt, 204; Dimitrov and Haque, 444–46). Indeed, we must develop activities that attend to students' diverse cultural and linguistic backgrounds, so we tap into the educational resources of this diversity to benefit all participants. For example, I ask students for one word summarizing their reactions to the reading. Then we examine what those words reveal about the class responses. Imagining an ending also reveals how students' preconceptions shape their interpretation. It improves their understanding of their own and their peers' interpretive lenses. Furthermore, the difficulty of literary texts is often understood as linguistic, but Bernhardt includes conceptual or narrative difficulty. For her, focusing on a theme or genre lightens the cognitive load (204). A chronological corpus of first-person narratives helps students to learn how the tropes of identity and difference evolve over time. Graffigny's *Lettres* combines simplicity of plot and form with increasingly difficult philosophical meditations. *Ourika* allies linguistic simplicity with the complexity of intersecting literary movements. *Les Lettres chinoises*' clear style contrasts with the difficulties of Chinese rhetoric and multiple narrators. Studying two versions of *Le Horla* deepens students' understanding of narrative structures, while *Béni* poses linguistic challenges: the narrator's naïve voice offsets Begag's mix of languages, registers, and humor. In the culminating task, students take on the role of intercultural critic as they produce a pedagogical edition of *Lettres chinoises* for American learners of French. As they introduce this doubly foreign novel and make a case for its relevance to this readership, they become spokespeople for diversity and inclusion. Foreign literature pedagogy and ITC's approaches to prior knowledge and task difficulty help to rethink scaffolding, sequencing, and peer-work to enhance diversity and inclusion. As students become authors and editors throughout the course, a feeling of belonging to a community of readers—of the works studied and of each other's work—and writers strengthens their engagement with the materials and with each other.

Combining foreign literature pedagogy and ITC's insights about *how* and *what* we teach results in an inclusive learning community that values diversity. Because these novels encourage our identification with protagonists who struggle for inclusion and provide moments revealing their blind spots, they teach us how our socio-cultural positions and learning about the target culture conditions our interpretation. Teaching diversity and inclusion has to entail studying representations of the exclusionary mechanisms societies are built on; how characters respond to this exclusion; which tactics lead to inclusion and what alternative, inclusive, models of identity they propose. The novels also guide us as teachers of diverse and inclusive classrooms, since they allow us to reflect on the kinds of communicative interactions that illustrate both a sensitivity to others and a failure of responsibility toward others. They show that intercultural communication, which is at the heart of an inclusive foreign literature pedagogy, succeeds when participants interact in an open, respectful way, with an awareness of the limits of their knowledge. The narrative structures of the five novels teach us to tend to the interactions between the sender and the receiver of the letters or stories. More specifically, the novels compel us to pay attention to how unfamiliar experiences change people and to the importance of reciprocity and timely communication about these changes if a healthy relationship is to be maintained. They also dramatize the limited access each character has to other characters' experiences and how one can read traces of those experiences in their communication and silences. In teaching, this translates to the importance of timely communication, regular feedback, and attention to student progress as well as the danger of making assumptions. We must be aware of what goes on among students and beyond the classroom and acknowledge that life affects us all, impacting our performance in the classroom. The novels' more inclusive models of identities and their critique of binary exclusionary models of identity encourage us to move beyond the teacher-student dyad toward a multilateral dynamic where all participants learn from each other about our respective worldviews, strengths, and vulnerabilities to form an inclusive diverse learning community. Our classrooms then become spaces where we experiment with transforming traditional modes of identity construction to make them more inclusive and open to diversity.

## Notes

1 Lack of training to teach foreign language literatures remains an issue in graduate programs. For a good starting point, see Bernhardt 2001. Thank you to Hakim Abderrezak for his feedback on this chapter.
2 Examples for this chapter are taken from an introductory course on the novel in French.
3 For an excellent study of these questions, see Romanowski.
4 De Raedt's article is very useful on this topic.
5 The Julian-Damazy illustrations help students to understand difficult passages.
6 Thank you to Nasrin Qader for helping me think through this point and for her general feedback on this chapter. Sathy and Hogan similarly recommend we "[c]onnect with students through course content."

7  Only the first three novels are translated. Translation of the last two titles are mine.
8  Bernhardt suggests experimenting with dramatic readings (204), which we integrate with earlier texts also. Students role-play Zilia and Déterville's long exchanges or the characters of *Lettres chinoises* having a long-distance conversation. A clip of an adaptation of *Ourika* helps students to imagine their staging of key scenes (Théâtre à Vif).
9  This paragraph is adapted from Licops and Sun.
10  See Licops and Breslin (31–32).

## References

Begag, Azouz. *Béni ou le paradis privé*. Seuil, 1989.

—. "*Interview FIG 2011*." www.youtube.com/watch?v=LZbZ8r7HyOY, 2011.

Bernhardt, Elizabeth. "Research into the Teaching of Literature in a Second Language: What It Says and How to Communicate It to Graduate Students." In *SLA and the Literature Classroom: Fostering Dialogues*, edited by Virginia M. Scott and Holly Tucker, Cengage Learning, 2002, pp. 195–210.

Chen, Ying. *Les Lettres chinoises*. Leméac, 1993.

—. "Interview with Ying Chen." UBC French, Hispanic and Italian Studies, 2014, www.youtube.com/watch?v=lO32IKcu3iQ.

de Duras, Claire. *Ourika*, edited by Virginie Belzgaou, Gallimard Folioplus Classiques, 2007. De Raedt, Thérèse. "Ourika in Black and White: Textual and Visual Interplay." *Women in French Studies*, vol. 12, 2004, pp. 45–69.

de Graffigny, Françoise. *Lettres d'une Péruvienne*, edited by Thierry Corbeau, Flammarion, [1747] 2005. [*Letters from a Peruvian Woman*. Translated by David Kornacker, The Modern Language Association of America, 1993].

Dimitrov, Nanda and Aisha Haque. "Intercultural Teaching Competence: A Multi-Disciplinary Model for Instructor Reflection." *Intercultural Education*, vol. 27, no. 5, 2016, pp. 437–456.

Hargreaves, Alec. "Introduction." In *Shantytown Kid*. By Azouz Begag, University of Nebraska Press, 2007, pp. xv–xvi.

Licops, Dominique and Jili Sun. "Decoding Ying Chen's Les Lettres chinoises to Become Better Global Readers." The 24th International Conference of the International Association for Intercultural Communication Studies, DePaul University, Chicago, July 2018.

Licops, Dominique and Paul Breslin. "Des tempêtes à tout casser? Enseigner Césaire et Shakespeare au XXIè siècle." In *Reading Communities: A Dialogical Approach to French and Francophone Literature*, edited by Oana Panaïté, Cambridge Scholars Publishing, 2016, pp. 8–34.

Little, Roger. "Préface." *Ourika*. By Claire de Duras, U of Exeter P, 1998, pp. vii–xii.

Maupassant, Guy de. *Le Horla: Oeuvres complètes illustrées de Guy de Maupassant, dessins de Julian-Damazy*. Illustrated by Julian-Damazy, Ollendorff, 1908. gallica.bnf.fr/ark:/12148/bpt6k54033050.

Maupassant, Guy de. *Le Horla*, edited by Christine Bénévent, Gallimard Folioplus Classiques, [1908]2003.

Rogers, Sheila. *Azouz Begag, Le Gone du Chaâba*. University of Glasgow French and German Publications, 2008.

Romanowski, Sylvie. *Through Strangers' Eyes: Fictional Foreigners in Old Regime France*. Purdue UP, 2005.

Ruggia, Christophe (director). *Le Gone du Chaâba* [*The Kid from Chaaba*]. Les films du jour, Doriane Films, 1997.

Sathy, Viji and Kelly A. Hogan, "How to Make Your Teaching More Inclusive." *The Chronicle of Higher Education*, July 22, 2019, www.chronicle.com/article/how-to-make-your-teaching-more-inclusive.

Smith, Sidonie and Julia Watson. *Decolonizing the Subject: The Politics of Gender in Women's Autobiography*. U of Minnesota P, 1992.

Théâtre à Vif. "Ourika (extraits)." www.youtube.com/watch?v=lhlIfroOA80.

Zabus, Chantal. *The African Palimpsest: Indigenization of Language in the West African Europhone Novel*. Rodopi, 1991.

# 12
# THE MAKING OF THE OTHER AMERICAS

Discovering the Francospheres of Latin America

*Lowry Martin*

Several years ago as part of the University of Texas system's core curriculum requirement, the university asked departments to think of new and innovative courses that might not normally be a part of a department's curriculum but that had strong interdisciplinary underpinnings. Living in the United States' largest binational city, El Paso, Texas, I wanted to create a course grounded in French studies but that would also make connections with the Spanish colonial heritage of the Southern hemisphere. Having taken graduate seminars in Francophonie, my experience of French and Francophone Studies in the American Academy tended to focus on the Metropole and its former French colonies, with particular attention on the Maghreb, West Africa, followed by Canada and the Caribbean to a lesser extent. In a geographically unique city straddling two nations and two distinct cultures, I asked myself: how could I make French more relevant to my students and how might we rethink French Studies?

The goal of University of Texas El Paso's core curriculum courses within the Languages, Philosophy, and Culture Block are designed to expand students' knowledge of the human condition and human cultures, especially in relation to behaviors, ideas, and values expressed in works of human imagination and thought. These courses underscore the university's belief that "through study in disciplines such as literature and philosophy, students engage in critical analysis and develop an appreciation of the humanities as fundamental to the health and survival of any society." We are also tasked with integrating research, argumentative writing, and collaborative works in these courses. My department created this course as a means to expose students to French and to attract new majors. While the genesis of this course is rooted in interdisciplinarity, it can be easily adapted to an upper division French class. For this essay I have chosen to discuss modules, assignments, and exercises from both the Core curriculum and

DOI: 10.4324/9781003126461-13

my adaptation of that course to an upper-level French course to provide an overview of how versatile these materials can be.

In researching this course, I learned that France's colonial aspirations and influence permeated Central and South America well beyond France's disastrous incursion into Mexico in the 1860s. As I researched and investigated French involvement south of the Rio Grande, I discovered not only various ways in which France informed cultural life in Mexico and Latin America, but I also discovered important currents of reciprocal influence, collaboration, and discovery.

With this knowledge incorporated into the primary learning goals of the course, "The Making of the Other Americas" attempts to expand the traditional limits of French Studies in the United States. Instead of discussing a Francophone world often based on imperial conquest, colonization, and decolonization, the course is anchored in the concept of interculturality, which is often comprised of "Francospheres": spheres of French influence that are based on cultural and intellectual contribution and collaboration. The second goal of this course is to encourage closer consideration of the intertwined histories of France and Latin America as well as to supplement learners' knowledge of French influence in the United States beyond the American Revolution, Lafayette, the French Indian War, and the Louisiana Purchase.

This essay will first briefly describe some of the ways that we might rethink French studies in terms that transcend Metropolitan France, conquered lands, and the Francophone postcolonial world. This course is not intended to privilege literature over other cultural artefacts even though students do read literature such as Marie Vieux-Chauvet's *Love, Anger, Madness* and Aimé Césaire's *Notebook of a Return to the Native Land*. Indeed, students look at a variety of cultural objects from literature and art to cartography, music, and legal cases. The class is a series of explorations of ideas and geographic regions held together by the questions of how did France influence or become influenced by these peoples and regions. The course begins with French exploration of the New World and wends its way to the Mississippi River and Texas, across the Caribbean, through Mexico and even down to Argentina. Units explore such diverse topics as French influence on Latin American architecture, particularly in Mexico City and Buenos Aires, the Haitian Revolution, and French literary representations of Mexico, jazz, Storyville, and Josephine Baker.

Space constraints do not permit detailed discussions about the variety of assignments and exercises, but I would like to make a few general comments about how the course is organized. This course is organized to be a flipped classroom so that students are more responsible for their own learning. They often work in small groups to discuss, process, and engage with course materials. At various points in the semester students create maps, write film reviews, response papers, and short stories as well as write a ten-page research paper for their final project. Some of the course modules focus on French colonization throughout the Americas, the Haitian Revolution, French Writers in Mexico,

Caribbean Writers and Citizenship, The Panama Canal, and French economic and cultural expansion in Latin America. These heterogeneous but interlocking subjects reveal the expansiveness of French influence on the historiographies of the Western hemisphere.

## Francosphere

It was working on a prospective book chapter on *cinéma-monde* (world films) that I first encountered Bill Marshall's idea of Francospheres (Marshall, "Cinéma monde?" 36). This intellectual move transcends the binaries of postcolonialism. It looks not at French influence in formerly occupied and colonized lands but rather contains an ethical turn that is linked to "gestures of solidarity" and "interest to others" (Marshall, "Worlds within Worlds" 323). At the very heart of the idea of Francospheres is the idea that French language, culture, and history are entanglements of an "unstable and changing continuum of universal culture and living-in-the-world marked by profound inequalities of power" (324). By expanding what has traditionally been the *carte de la francophonie* (map of the French-speaking world) to include those regions that developed deep intellectual, political, or cultural engagement with France that was based neither on language nor conquest, we are able to rethink French studies and what it might mean. This is not to say that traditional colonial cartographies are excluded: we study France's empire building in Canada, the United States, and the Caribbean. However, framing the course in terms of spheres of influence allows students to make connections between France, its language and culture, and the predominantly Spanish-speaking world of Latin America. For those of us who teach in French departments, the very charter of our discipline has traditionally been defined by language and physical presence, whether we are in the Hexagon and its territories or its former colonies. Going beyond these traditional markers organically opens up broader questions regarding colonization, migration, and citizenship. More importantly, Francospheres fits nicely into what J. G. M. Le Clézio calls "interculturality," especially given his idea of meaningful dialogue and uncoerced sharing of another culture's wealth.

This course diverges from traditional French courses in that it puts in dialogue those obvious French connections with more subtle French reverberations in non-French-speaking cultures. For instance, students are asked to think about the French ideals of "Liberty, Fraternity, Equality" and how these French revolutionary cries were taken up in Latin America after 1810. One of the pedagogical goals of this course is to discover lesser-known French connections to the Americas and to formulate questions about how those connections help us to reconsider hegemonic historiographies in Canada, the United States, or even Latin America. In addition to exploring French historical influence in the Western Hemisphere, the curriculum connects readings, both literary and philosophical, with contemporary issues such as race, citizenship, and language in a hemispheric context. This story begins with France's earliest attempts at colonization in the New World.

## Decentering Colonial Cartographies

The first day of class students receive a map of the Western Hemisphere, and I ask them to shade in every place that France attempted to colonize. I have rarely had a student who knew that French is spoken in South America and that French Guiana is part of France, the westernmost point of the European Union. I then ask them to write on the reverse side all that they know about colonization in the Western hemisphere, and in particular which European countries claimed territories and approximate dates. Most classes are surprised to learn that France attempted to colonize current-day Brazil with settlements such as Fort Coligny in 1555 or that a dispute exists as to whether Jean Cousin arrived in 1488 in Brazil, four years before Christopher Columbus "discovered" the New World. Likewise, the French settlement at Fort Caroline in present day Florida in 1564 predated the English settlement of Jamestown by almost a half a century. Thus, from the first class, students are challenged to rethink and deconstruct dominant historiographies—these narratives of conquest and history that they believe to be true. Approximately one fourth of the semester focuses on French colonization from Canada to Brazil.

To provide context and orient the students to the time period, we watch three different films about French colonial efforts in New France until the French-Indian War. We begin with *Black Robe*, followed by *New France*, and *Last of the Mohicans*. These films allow us to examine three crucial elements of early French colonization: the role of the Catholic Church, treatment of Amerindians, and contrasting strategies of colonization between France and Great Britain. Reading excerpts from McShea's *Apostles of Empire: Jesuits and New France*, quickly introduces students to the more brutal realities of French colonization. They also learn how France's treatment of Native Americans as part of its colonization strategy was quite different from Great Britain's. France had a more mercantile view of colonization through market expansion and exploitation of natural resources. Creating subordinated trading partners and creating new revenue streams was more important than actual displacement of peoples and occupation of lands.

The instructional design of this module incorporates varied exercises from interactive map design to creative writing assignments. Their interactive maps feature two parts. The first map must locate at least six French forts and create legends for each fort, which encourages them to research more French colonial history as well, create narratives, and explain their motivation for their geographic choices and the relevance of each fort. The second maps show what has become of that area, whether it is still inhabited, its demographics and economy. This exercise also introduces our students to the use of digital maps through the Bibliothèque Nationale de France and further anchors their works with original historical drawings. Early depictions of colonial life allow students not only to analyze images but also to put them in dialogue with historical writings and fiction studied in class. Using the French web site www.gallic.fr we look at maps of the colonial period beginning with a map by André Thevet in the 16th century and comparing his map to later maps in the 17th and 18th centuries. Students are stunned at the detail and relative accuracy of these maps. After students have presented their maps, they have an in-class writing assignment to list all of the purposes for maps. Few of them think of treasure maps, but this idea provides a perfect segue for the following unit on French colonization in the Caribbean and the colonization of Haiti as we explore the role of French Buccaneers such as Jean Fleury, François Le Clerc, and later pirates such as Jean Lafitte.[1] The (de)centering of colonial cartographies teaches students that behind the boundaries and frontiers on a map lie much richer geo-political narratives involving French cultural exchange and influence that are often forgotten or overlooked in the American academy.

## Francophone Authors and (De)colonization:

Borders and frontiers are a part of daily life in America's largest metropolitan binational city so teaching about cultural hybridity is an easy concept to grasp. Despite a predominantly Hispanic and bilingual student population, our students often have only the most cursory knowledge about Caribbean colonization. Many students are often shocked when I tell them that French is spoken throughout the Caribbean. By mid-semester we have studied Haiti, Guadeloupe, Martinique, and other French islands, and thus we turn to the philosophical and literary production of authors from these lands and how they contributed to postcolonial thought. Beginning with Aimé Césaire and the Negritude movement, we next study Franz Fanon's *Black Skin, White Masks* and its critiques of French colonialism. Their works open discussions of 20th-century French colonization in our hemisphere and also a broader discussion of decolonization in Latin America. Central to these discussions are the issues of race and the treatment of indigenous peoples, particularly in Mexico.

Thinking about Fanon's thesis that colonialism requires the Black to remain in an inferior status within a colonial order, we explore how ideas of race still inflect political and cultural life in the Western Hemisphere. Having studied the Haitian diaspora and its tremendous impact on the further francization of Louisiana, we look at how French Creole communities continued to shape American culture. Because of my legal background, I integrate the legal case of *Plessy v. Ferguson* into our discussions. This landmark Supreme Court decision vividly illustrates the problems of epidermalization, because what is often overlooked in discussion of the Plessy case is that the plaintiff was of French descent and a light-skinned man of color who did not present as African-American.[2] As we discuss the far-reaching impact of this case that further entrenched Jim Crow laws and made "separate but equal" the defense for institutionalized racism, students research French digitalized newspaper articles from the US Library of Congress, such as French newspaper *L'Abeille de la Nouvelle Orléans*, that chronicle these events. These articles provide us with a very distinct point of view that is nuanced by language, French culture, and Louisianan hybridity. The *Plessy* case serves in addition as a sturdy chronological bridge between discussions about race, *Créolité*, and pigmentocracy in colonial and post-revolutionary Haiti and anchor later discussions about how race is portrayed in *Love, Anger, Madness*.

Thus, studying how race was playing out in the United States at the dawn of the 20$^{th}$ century provides a continuation from prior discussions of pigmentocracy in colonial Haiti where skin color determined social status. Linking these historical events to contemporary issues of racism in the United States, France, and Latin America, students write a short paper of three to five pages to discuss and relate their own experiences and observations related to differential treatment based on skin color along the US–Mexican border, within Mexico, and even in South America. This is followed by analysis of an article on race construction and race relations in Latin America using data from Brazil, Colombia, the Dominican Republic, and Panama. Reading their experiences against sociology data, students discover how "race" is both physical and cultural "with country variations in racial schema that reflect historical and political trajectories" (Telles, 865). By the midpoint of the semester, students have already been exposed to and are questioning these kinds of historical and political evolutions and the role of racial stereotypes in our hemisphere. Students quickly learn about the fallacy of a colorblind French Republic, but they are curious as to how France viewed Latin America, and particularly Mexico. I turn to literature to provide a framework for this inquiry.

## Mexico through the eyes of French Literature: Dumas, Artaud, and Le Clézio

Most students will have heard of the dream of El Dorado, the mythical City of Gold, which was much more associated with Spanish colonization than with France. However, French writer, Alexandre Dumas repurposes this myth in one of the few French mid-19$^{th}$-century novels to focus on the United States and Mexico in his work, *The Journal of Madame Giovanni* published in 1856 right after the California Gold Rush and California's induction into the United States.

This fictionalized travelogue/novel paints a uniquely French perspective of the California Gold Rush, the first days of California statehood, and Mexico on the verge of another revolution. Dumas's ethnic sketches of Chinese, Americans, Mexicans, and the French in San Francisco always initiate a great deal of discussion about stereotypes and myths about national personalities. What students find most fascinating is that Madame Giovanni was a real character—a former swindler from France sentenced to an English penal colony in Tasmania, a spy, and an eventual piano teacher who died in San Antonio, Texas!

Even though this novel offers an adventurous window into French representations of the US and Mexico, I use more contemporary French authors to tease out other cultural and intellectual links between Latin America and France. However, we focus primarily on how Mexico served as an inspiration for two very important 20th-century French authors, Artaud and Le Clézio. We begin with a poem by Antonin Artaud, who went to Mexico in 1936 to get in touch with the "red earth." His poem "Indian Culture" is dense, and students spend about thirty minutes in groups working to analyze the images, vocabulary, and structure. He calls Mexico the "land speaking of blood" and this poem is juxtaposed with his scenario of "The Conquest of Mexico" in his last manifesto for the *Theater and Its Double*. In the former, Artaud articulates his ideas of quest versus conquest as well as his anti-colonialist and anti-imperialist stances, which anticipates in many ways Le Clézio's formulation of interculturality. Artaud, and later Le Clézio, imagine Mexico as a land of "culture in action." Artaud's works illustrate how Mexico not only influenced and refined his thinking about theater but also how he conceived of Mexico as a "space of peaceful spirituality and the healing power of Aztecs" as opposed to violent European cultures driven by material greed (Su, 3). Mexico functions as a double negative exposure in which the bloody and brutal European colonization overlays an image of a primordial Mexico that is spiritually harmonious and full of the mythic arcane (Artaud, *The Peyote Dance* 20). After working through "Indian Culture" and "The Conquest of Mexico," students read excerpts from Artaud's *Selected Writings* wherein he states:

> what I came to look for on the soil of Mexico was precisely an echo, or rather a source, a real physical source of this revolutionary force .... In short, we expect from Mexico a new concept of Revolution, and also a new concept of Man which will serve to nourish, to feed with its magical life this ultimate form of humanism.
>
> *(368)*

Artaud distinguishes the difference between contemporary revolutions, such as the Bolshevik Revolution of 1917 and the Mexican Revolution by asserting that the Mexican Revolution was "a revolution of the indigenous soul, a revolution to win back the indigenous soul as it was before Cortez" (369). For Artaud, the El Dorado myth is not about the venal materiality of gold and wealth but a spiritual richness and harmony that is deeply rooted in indigenous cultures of Mexico.

Decades later, Mexico also held a great fascination for Nobel Prize winner Le Clézio. His long essay *The Mexican Dream* (*La fête chantée*) in which he discusses the richness of Mexico and its impact on his creative process ends this module on Mexico. Reading this essay allows us to explore how Le Clézio's philosophy/theory of interculturality works in his own artistic production. To aid students with his essay, they also read Martha van der Ritt's interview with Le Clézio. She defines interculturality as a:

proportional relationship between the interaction of disparate cultures and the resulting mental, verbal, and creative dialogues. It is a term that lies at the heart of numerous disciplines across the humanities, arts, and sciences with the objective of examining the expression and consequences of cultural encounters and dialogues on individuals and cultural expression.

*(128)*

Although Le Clézio has refused to define this term, he has stated that he understands interculturality as an ideal that enables peoples from different cultures to share their ideas and wealth (Van der Ritt, 129). He further asserts that working with this concept is more difficult in France because of its insistence on the idea of a singular French culture and language (128). Having already studied some writers of the French Caribbean, students must unpack this assertion and put it into dialogue with works by Césaire, Fanon, and Condé. Has France's insistence on a "colorblind" republic made it more resistant to multiculturalism? We ask ourselves how do Mexico and the United States embrace multiculturalism? Where are the advances for multiculturalism and how do we see resistance to it? We brainstorm as to ways in which we have seen progress in Mexico and the USA—such as the inclusion of Tex-Mex/Mexican cuisine as part of American cultural life or the acceptance of children speaking Spanish to each other in American schools. To develop these ideas, students write an eight-page essay discussing the importance of linguistic diversity as part of multi-culturalism and how they see multiculturalism at work in the United States, Mexico, and France. Often students will write about the proliferation and valorization of Spanish-speaking television, radio, and Latina/o literatures in the US and compare this with France's slow integration and support of minority languages such as Breton within its borders and Mexico's recent attempts to include living Native languages in Mexican education.

For some French writers Mexico is a land of dreams and passion, a privileged place of mystery and legend, but in what ways has France influenced Mexico? Space constraints prevent a more detailed analysis of the interculturality of Mexico and France; however, some of the areas that students investigate are how France impacted and shaped some of Mexico City's most famous architectural sites such as the Palacio de Bellas Artes, the Angel of Victory monument, and the reconstruction of Paseo de la Reforma into a French-styled boulevard. France's architectural heritage has contributed to architectural histories from Washington, DC to Mexico City to Buenos Aires.[3] Likewise, because of France's desire to expand markets and exert influence in Latin America, we study French economic projects such as France's financing of Honduras's Interoceanic railroad and the Panama Canal project. The role of French education in Mexico and Latin America highlight how language and culture were deployed as "foundation stones to build influence and pursue national goals in foreign lands" (Schoonover, 92). French efforts to promote its language and culture appealed to the elite of each Central American country, which were considered Francophile, except for Guatemala (93). With this in consideration, students are polled as to how they perceived France growing up in this region and acquiring French. Among Hispanic students, French is almost always viewed as a marker of class, sophistication, and education. Many students comment that it is the second language of "fresas," a term used to describe a snobby bourgeois class in Mexico.

Although French cultural and economic interventions in Latin America have not always been noble, they have created a rich intertwined history with Latin America that is often over-looked in French Studies. Many believed that France, as a Latin republic, had natural affinities with the Spanish-speaking countries of Latin America that would provide for mutually beneficial economic, scientific, and cultural exchanges (93). The exploration of these interconnections provides a rich field of inquiry for this course and for future scholars.

As the importance of the humanities and language acquisition continue to be questioned, this course emphasizes how multiculturalism, interculturality, and intellectual curiosity can create new world perspectives that highlight common bonds and histories of various regions and nations. Every module in this course could be expanded as a stand-alone class, but the purpose of this Core Curriculum course is to expose students to human cultures and conditions. In this course we travel both in time and space from the $16^{th}$-century eastern seaboard of Canada and the United States to contemporary French regions of the Americas to Mexico and Central America. During this intellectual journey, students realize how much French culture is woven into the patchwork of national cultures from Canada to Argentina, and the frontiers of interculturality expand beyond just our binational border.

## Notes

1 These discussions are taken up later in the semester when we study how French writers have represented Mexico and Mexico's influence on those writers.
2 To foster deeper discussions, students must find, read, and incorporate a scholarly article on diverse language inclusion in either France or Mexico. As a guide, I require that they read "Indigenous Language Policy and Education in Mexico" by Lourdes de Léon.
3 During the Porfiriato, Mexico City was often referred to as a "little Paris," and it was during this period that the first department stores were established in Mexico, most of them founded by "barcelonettes" (people from the French arrondissement of the same name).

## References

Artaud, Antonin. *The Theater and Its Double*. Translated by Mary Caroline Richards. Grove, 1958.
—. *The Peyote Dance*. Translated by Helen Weaver. Farrar, Straus & Giroux, 1976.
—. *Selected Writings*. Edited by Susan Sontag. U of California P, 1988.
Audebert, Cédric. *La Diaspora haïtienne*. Presses universitaires de Rennes, 2012.

Baudin, Jean, director. *Nouvelle France*. Performances by Gérard Depardieu. Lionsgate, 2004.

Beresford, Bruce, director. *Black Robe*. Samuel Goldwyn Company, 1991.

Césaire, Aimé. *Notebook of a Return to the Native Land*. Wesleyan Poetry Series, 2001.

De León, Lourdes. "Indigenous Language Policy and Education in Mexico." In *Language Policy and Political Issues*, edited by Teresa McCarty and Stephen Springer, 2017, pp. 1–19.

Dumas, Alexandre. *The Journal of Madame Giovanni*. International Collectors Library, 1945.

Edison, Paul. "Conquest Unrequited: French Expeditionary Science, 1864–1867." *French Historical Studies*, vol. 26, no. 3, 2003, pp. 459–495.

Fanon, Franz. *Black Skin, White Masks*. Grove Press, 2008.

Le Clézio, J. G. M. *The Mexican Dream; Or, the Uninterrupted Thought of Amerindian Civilizations*. U of Chicago P, 1993.

Mann, Michael, director. *Last of the Mohicans*. Performances by Daniel Day Lewis and Madeleine Stowe, Twentieth Century Fox, 1992.

Marshall, Bill. "Cinéma-monde? Towards a Concept of Francophone Cinema." *Francosphères*, vol. 1, no. 1, 2012, pp. 35–51.

—. "Worlds within; in the world." *Cinéma-monde: Decentered Perspectives on Global Filmmaking in French*, edited by Michael Gott and Thibaut Schilt. Edinburgh UP, 2018, pp. 323–335.

McShea, Bronwen. *Apostles of Empire: The Jesuits and New France*. University of Nebraska Press, 2019.

Merrin, Jean. *Histoire des corsaires*. Louviers, 2003.

Said, Edward. *Orientalism*. Pantheon Books, 1978.

Schoonover, Thomas. *The French in Central America: Culture and Commerce, 1820–1930*. Scholarly Resources, 2000.

Su, Tsu-Chung. "Artaud's Journey's to Mexico and His Portrayals of Land." *Comparative Literature and Culture*, vol. 14, no. 5, 2013, pp. 1–9. doi:10.7771/1481-4374.2151.

Telles, George. "Who Is Black, White, or Mixed Race? How Skin Color, Status, and Nation Shape Racial Classification in Latin America." *American Journal of Sociology*, vol. 120, no. 3, November 2003, pp. 864–907.

Thevet, André. "Le Nouveau Monde découvert et illustré de nostre temps." *Gallica*, Bibliothèque Nationale de France, Guillaume Chaudière, 1581. https://gallica.bnf.fr/ark:/12148/btv1b8469653q.r=André%20Thevet?rk=64378;0.

Van der Ritt, Martha. "*Why Interculturality? Interview with Jean-Marie Gustave Le Clézio*." *Contemporary French and Francophone Studies*, vol. 19, no. 2, 2005, pp. 128–139.

Vieux-Chauvet, Marie. *Amour, colère, folie*. Gallimard, 1968. [*Love, Anger, Madness*. Modern Library Torchbearers, 2010].

# 13
# CONNECTING FRENCH STUDIES TO THE WORLD THROUGH GLOBAL FOODWAYS

*Lauren Ravalico*

Food studies in the French classroom offers an innovative way to create an inclusive learning environment that engages students in critical thinking about the relationship between the politics of eating and the fluid meaning of collective national identity. In 2010 "the French gastronomic meal" was inducted into the UNESCO list of world heritage as part of the "intangible cultural heritage of humanity" ("Intangible"). This formal acknowledgment of the communal family ritual and social practice of eating a multi-course meal to celebrate special occasions in France provides the central point of critical inquiry in the upper-level cultural studies course on food I will discuss in this chapter. On the one hand, the UNESCO designation promotes the idea that shared food practices are a meaningful and joyful common denominator of what it is to be French. On the other hand, it tends to preserve the cultural stereotype that Frenchness is synonymous with the white elitist mystique of good taste.[1] The establishment of a sense of common culinary heritage is a valuable practice of national cohesion and a marker of cultural identity that nonetheless minoritizes certain histories of gender, class, and ethnic diversity. The course examines the relationship between French food history and its lesser-known histories to understand their mutually constitutive role in the ongoing creation of a national culture.

The short, quasi-sociological video that the French government submitted to include "the French gastronomic meal" in the UNESCO list of world heritage spotlights the culinary practices of an intergenerational, white family to emphasize the French "ritual" of purchasing high-quality, local food from specialized vendors, of preparing it together, and of including children in the generational "transmission" of culinary knowledge, ritualized eating practices (setting the table, consuming dishes in a fixed order), sensory pleasure, and conviviality around the table. While the video insists on the universality of these practices as part of

DOI: 10.4324/9781003126461-14

France's "living patrimony," it acknowledges that gastronomy honors the diversity of the country's *terroirs* and, with a noticeably brief—one might even say token—glimpse inside a halal market, "contributes to the acceptance of the Other" ("Intangible"; my translation). The video's breezy suggestion that food can surmount the politics of difference is, of course, magical thinking that must be unpacked critically. The idea of French gastronomy as generational transmission (values, tradition, and ritual), "*l'art de vivre*" (pleasure, good taste, and conviviality), and acceptance of the Other anchor the study of the modern history of French food as a narrative that glides over the complex, and sometimes fraught story of a nation's cultural identity.[2]

I designed "The Culture of the French Table" to focus on the cultural and political history of food in France from the 18$^{th}$ century to the present because it reveals the degree to which gender, class, and ethnic diversity has influenced the country's culinary tradition and thereby complicates the meaning of Frenchness. Questions of gender, class, and ethnic diversity, of course, point to the problem of exclusion from the creation of History. Engaging critically with diverse histories was a primary goal of the course; creating an inclusive learning environment to support that kind of learning was then a pedagogical imperative. The relationship, including the tension, between students' personal experiences and the process of learning about the Other is foundational to the inclusive praxis of food studies in the classroom: "We leave neither our needs for nor our interests in food at the classroom door. The interdisciplinary field of food studies emphasizes that these things come with us; they are us" (Murphy, 18). Using food "to think with," as Lévi-Strauss famously advocated, invites students to ruminate on their own lives, tastes, and family traditions while opening them up to the study of cultural histories and identities that could be quite unfamiliar (89).[3] Indeed, the practitioners of food studies in the classroom negotiate a challenging balance between validating students' personal experience—which can be instantaneous and reactive, yet deeply engrained—and the work of cultural analysis and critical thinking to continue in the vein of Lévi-Strauss's work: "Food becomes a lens through which we may explore the stratified realities of a society, its ideas about worth, about class, sex/gender, race, religion, and even nationality and humanity" (Bonnekessen, 280).

One effective method for encouraging a productive encounter between the personal and the critical is to create high-impact learning opportunities that pair sensory and hands-on experiences like cooking and tasting with intellectual reflection. In the following discussion about teaching gender, class, and ethnic diversity in "The Culture of the French Table," I highlight how each of these units was connected to an aspect of "Global Foodways," a campus-wide, yearlong program of thirty courses and fourteen events that I directed to engage the academic and regional community in an interdisciplinary exploration of food from the perspective of global humanities, a critical field for the advancement of ethical, engaged citizenship and cross-cultural literacy.[4] My goal for Global Foodways was to foster interactions of diversity among humanities scholars, practitioners, and audiences to enable a deeper understanding of food as a complex and at times paradoxical touchpoint of cultural memory, human creativity, and the history of the unfolding present. The term "food*ways*" suggests that both variation and movement are integral to the story of cuisine. My course and the program underscored this dynamism by emphasizing the intersecting paths of production, consumption, sustainability, and Diaspora.

## Gastronomic Transmission and Gender

The establishment of the French gastronomic tradition in the 18th century is anchored in the gendered division of public and private spheres. Professional male cooks working primarily in Paris "codified" the ingredients, preparation methods, and techniques of their cuisine with cookbooks, almanacs, and cooking schools to establish a stable system for the transmission of a shared gastronomic culture (Brown, 1; my translation; Davis, 9–11). The rise of public cooks and the guilds to which they belonged went on to shape the sexual politics of professional cooking in the modern restaurant as it emerged in the 1760s and flourished after the French Revolution (Davis, 12). This masculine history of the establishment of French gastronomy tends to overshadow the alternate, concurrent feminine history of gastronomy (from *gastro*: stomach, and *nomos*: law) with the practice of breastfeeding. While the course focused on gendered food history in France, a complementary Global Foodways event, "Women in the Kitchen," was planned to bring together a diverse local group of women whose professional work in various international culinary traditions and food journalism puts into contemporary perspective the outmoded stereotype of women's work being limited to the domestic sphere.[5]

In 18th-century France the question of whether a mother transmitted milk from her own body or outsourced this labor to a wet nurse was polemical. Wet nursing became a thriving occupation by the mid-18th century, when the majority of Parisian infants from all classes were eating out, so to speak, whether to enable their mothers to "ply their trades" or to liberate them "for the numerous social obligations incumbent upon highborn ladies" (Yalom, 106).[6] Indeed, Enlightenment debates about the value of maternal breastfeeding emphasize the central role of gastronomic transmission in the social conceptualization of the French Republic.

Rousseau notoriously railed against the "denatured" social practice of wet nursing in *Emile, or On Education*, arguing that it represented a corruption of the primal, essentially nourishing, nurturing, and sentimental function of motherhood—a "first education"—that forms compassionate, ethical men (37–46)[7]: "But let mothers design to nurse their children, morals will reform themselves, nature's sentiments will be awakened in every heart, the state will be repeopled" (46). Rousseau's insistence on "the poetics of mothers as a redemptive social force and the politics of egalitarian breast-feeding" reflects a broader Enlightenment ideology of gender roles that idealizes motherhood and thereby limits women's civic engagement to suckling (Yalom, 111). Students read excerpts from the first and fourth book of *Emile* alongside content and breastfeeding imagery I cull from Yalom and Brace to discuss the role of the first human food in the Enlightenment conceptualization of citizenship and the democratic State.[8] We then examine articles in the contemporary French press and excerpts from contemporary philosopher Elisabeth Badinter's *The Conflict: How Modern Motherhood Undermines the Status of Women* to debate whether mother's milk is still involved in the idealization of women's "natural" role in society and, in some sense, synonymous with a healthy body politic. The juxtaposition of past and present emphasizes the complex legacy of the Enlightenment's equivalence of women's supposed biological destiny with the moral, social, and political good.

This transhistorical unit is a fruitful opportunity to understand both how the past inflects the present and to include personal experience in a historical and philosophical discussion about how food culture and sexual diversity are inseparable. Badinter opposes current trends in global public health advocacy, especially "advocating [a mother's] on-demand breast-feeding for as long as the child wants it" (107). She argues that this monopoly on women's time is culturally imposed: a fundamentally sexist and classist movement "dressed in the guise of a modern, moral cause that worships all things natural" (5). She cites breastfeeding advocacy groups like the American La Leche League as enthusiastic inheritors and promoters of Rousseau's "traditional model" (105, 5). Students have grown up amidst endless feminist debates about "women having it all," and reading Badinter's work in historical context gives them the opportunity to debate whether innovations in outsourcing milk production—from the practice of wet nursing to technologies of artificial milk and bottle feeding—are socially progressive or regressive. Because the topic provoked lively classroom discussion, I added the history of nursing and baby-food technologies in France (with the option for a global comparative study) to a list of possible small-group research topics for oral presentation to the class.

## *L'Art de vivre* and Social Class

Our study of French food culture in the 18$^{th}$ century has, by this point, focused primarily on generational transmission in terms of gender and biological food production. We subsequently circle back to the invention of the modern restaurant and the culture of eating out in 19$^{th}$-century Paris, where the practice originated, to study the relationship between class and consumption (Sprang, 2–3). Brillat-Savarin's *Physiology of Taste*, with its pithy and enduring "Aphorisms of the Professor" ("a lifetime of one-liners" as Buford calls them in his introduction to the English translation, viii), provides historically contextualized food for thought to use as a warm-up activity for the unit: "Tell me what you eat, and I shall tell you what you are" ("Aphorisms" 2, 15). Students brainstorm a list of dishes and drinks they typically consume in everyday situations and at a traditional family meal. They exchange their lists anonymously, and each student tries to identify the author's regional, ethnic, religious, and class identity from the list. We then discuss the supposed connection between food and identity: do the readers' categorizations reflect how the authors see what they "are" through what they consume? Beyond the biological factors that give limited credence to the truism "you are what you eat," what, indeed, is the impact of the consumption/identity metaphor on the systemic categorization of people?

Brillat-Savarin (1755–1826), who was not a historian, chef, scientist, or professor, but rather an appellate judge (viii), is partly responsible for promoting the idealistic notion that the rise of the restaurant reflected post-Revolutionary "cultural democratization" in Paris (Sprang, 141). In reality, restaurants were prohibitively expensive for most Parisians in the 19th century, and so it became a public site of pervasive class inequality rather than haute cuisine for all (141–45). We focus on the zero-waste sub-culture and black-market economy of re-plating the leftover food of upper-class Parisian restaurant-goers for working-class locals and even poor provincial French people that emerged as a result of this inequality (Beizer, 373). The composite plates of leftovers, known as "harlequins" (*arlequins*), problematize the "you are what you eat" truism, for they were at once a sign of class difference and a site of intimate proximity between the rich and the poor.[9]

Eaters of leftovers appear in a smattering of realist novels in the 19th century, most notably in Zola's *The Belly of Paris* [*Le Ventre de Paris*] and in Eugène Sue's *The Mysteries of Paris* [*Les Mystères de Paris*], where they are stereotyped as lowlifes and criminals frequenting sinister, dirty locales that serve up greasy plates of unfinished "poultry drumsticks, fish tails, meat bones, crusts from pâtés, fried foods, cheese, vegetables, heads of woodcocks, crackers, and salad" (Sue, 14–15).[10] Enjoying a harlequin plate or soup—which one enthusiastic consumer in Sue's novel compares to an "omnibus"—means, of course, violating the gastronomic order the dishes were intended to respect, and providing, instead, decomposing haute cuisine-as-carrion for poor people (14).[11] It also emphasizes the intense stigma surrounding leftover food, which, according to Beizer, continues to prevail in French culture, "even in contemporary soup kitchens, where the unemployed and the homeless accept charitable dinners but often have difficulty accepting the offer of supplementary food to take away" (373).[12]

Because the consumption of leftover food touches upon so many historical and contemporary issues of cultural specificity, class, sustainability, and food insecurity, I put it at the center of a two-day Global Foodways event. The first was a public lecture and panel discussion about the culture, history, and politics of leftovers that brought together Janet Beizer, who is completing a book about "harlequin eaters," along with three leaders and activists working to combat food insecurity at the university, local, and regional level. The event emphasized cultural differences between France and the US as well as the efforts that contemporary food pantries and banks make to remove stigmatization and shame from the lived realities of poverty and hunger. Beizer, for example, showed the audience a shocking photograph from the 19th century that plays with angle and perspective to suggest that a group of Parisian restaurant-goers are vomiting on the harlequin eaters on the street below their perch at balcony tables. This signposting of poverty as disgusting stands in stark contrast with the work of the panelists, who described collaborating with restaurants and supermarkets to provide food-pantry menus that give patrons choice and dignity in eating.

A public screening of Agnès Varda's documentary *The Gleaners and I* [*Les Glaneurs et la glaneuse*] followed this event on the second day. The film reflects on shared practices of gleaning amongst different classes of urban and rural French people, including the various scavengers that gather leftover food after the close of the outdoor markets, artists, hoarders, farmers, and the filmmaker herself. The documentary approaches all of its subjects with curiosity and respect, which helped to inspire an interesting post-viewing discussion. A graduate student in Environmental and Sustainability Studies shared her experience as a gleaner. She described with pride her practice of local "dumpster diving" and arriving at the end of university receptions to recover uneaten food in a successful effort to reduce waste while fulfilling her goal to never buy food.

My intention with this interdisciplinary event was to draw together diverse groups of people from the university and local community. Survey data revealed a total of eighty-eight attendees, the majority of whom were undergraduate students in French Studies and Environmental and Sustainability Studies, but also included faculty, staff, and others unaffiliated with the university. Beyond the outside funding I had already secured and my department's partial sponsorship and in coordination with the Office of Sustainability, we offered a "zero waste" French food buffet at the first event.[13] We also joined forces to promote the event. This helped to diversify the audience.

## Acceptance of the Other, Colonial History, and Ethnic Diversity

The units on mother's milk and leftover restaurant food provide uncommon, but essential ways to problematize the notions of generational transmission and *l'art de vivre* that are hallmarks of the French gastronomic tradition according to the UNESCO video submission. The last unit I will discuss examines the relationship between food culture and, as the video proposes, "acceptance of the Other." The video optimistically, yet provocatively suggests that enjoying the food of former French colonies promotes tolerance. The conceptual equivalency here among physical incorporation, pleasure, and cross-cultural empathy offers a tantalizing, almost utopian vision of the power of food. We investigate its claim critically. We focus, first, on the importation of sugar, coffee, and chocolate from European colonies to understand the historical role of slavery in the "Frenchification" of these aliments in modern French gastronomy. Excerpts from Voltaire's satirical *Candide: Or Optimism* alongside François Boucher's genre painting *Breakfast* serve as cultural artifacts to understand the hidden history of slave labor in the development of fashionable cuisine and the idea of good taste. In particular, Candide's encounter with a partially dismembered Black slave during his stay in the Dutch colony of Surinam, whose abuse at the hands of his "master" is, the latter says, "what it costs, supplying you Europeans with sugar," uses wry humor to reveal dark truths (68).[14] Boucher's genial picture of his well-to-do family enjoying hot chocolate from the opulent urn located at the compositional center of the canvas provides a much more oblique reference to the Black bodies whose liquified labor is being consumed leisurely and with pleasure by women and children at the French table (Ravalico).

The ongoing, often brutal realities of the alimentary supply chain as well as the efforts of some manufacturers to produce food ethically became the topic of a complementary Global Foodways lecture with a guided twelve-course chocolate tasting that was attended by eighty people. Carla Martin, Founder and Executive Director of the Fine Cacao and Chocolate Institute and a Lecturer in the Department of African and African American Studies at Harvard, joined Bethany Nunn Moore, Founder of Cocoa Academic, a local chocolatery, to lead this high-impact learning opportunity for a mixed crowd of students, faculty, staff, and community members. Martin is a social anthropologist whose current research focuses on ethics, quality, and politics in cacao and chocolate. Her lecture provided a historical overview of the international chocolate business that enabled students to understand the exploitation of the fragile human and environmental ecologies and economies of the developing world in the global marketplace to satisfy the massive demand for chocolate candy. Moore, an ethical entrepreneur, provided a counterpoint to this postcolonial business structure. She paired her talk with an individually plated twelve-course taste tour of international cacao varieties to guide the audience through the "bean to bar" process of making small-batch, high-quality chocolate.

Couscous, like chocolate, is what Durmelat calls "an edible site of memory" that "makes perceptible the bits and pieces of an unfinished colonial past that are woven into everyday life" (394). I have used this North African dish as a teaching tool to think through diasporic foodways and the complicated emergence of French "couscousmania," as one language textbook brands the ubiquity of the dish in contemporary gastronomic culture (Mitchell and Tano, 385). In "The Culture of the French Table," we pair our study of Abdellatif Kechiche's film *The Secret of the Grain* [*La Graine et le mulet*] with the communal preparation of the dish at my home. The film features a contemporary working-class family of Tunisian origins whose withered patriarch emigrated to Sète in the 1970s and who endeavors, with the help of his family, to open a couscous restaurant after being laid off from his construction job at the port. The harrowingly bungled opening-night effort to secure financial backing for the restaurant unfolds in a sequence that emphasizes the "churlish manners" and almost pornographic "decadence" of the "European French" who wait impatiently for the family members to plate their meal, tongues practically hanging out as a voluptuous young woman belly dances to distract them from the delay (Abramson, 274). The film contrasts the family's immense and intimate pleasure in sharing a traditional Tunisian couscous together with the limits of that pleasure to construct a cultural bridge of tolerance and acceptance between French people of European and North African descent.

As a challenge to this deeply pessimistic view of the power of foodways, I set out to create a high-impact opportunity for students that would allow them to collaborate in the preparation, consumption, and communal serving of a traditional Tunisian couscous as part of a Global Foodways service project. A group of students joined forces with a local women's club to serve dinner at the Children's Hospital to families with convalescent children. We researched recipes and spoke to a Tunisian woman using the TalkAbroad.com second-language acquisition resource to finalize our version of the dish. Along with participation from faculty and students in Chinese Club, French and Francophone Studies, Hispanic Studies, and History, thirty-one of us prepared, tasted, and/or served an international meal to eighty-five people at the hospital. While it did not, of course, solve the problem of "acceptance of the Other," it succeeded as a high-impact method to make international food traditions enjoyable and reciprocally meaningful for members of the campus community and the local community.[15]

My intention in sharing the bounty of a French food studies course, especially when offered under the umbrella of a program like Global Foodways, has been to demonstrate that it provides a captivating conceptual hook as well as a personal way to understand the underrepresented role of diversity in the process of collective identity formation. Including gender, class, and ethnic diversity in the food studies curriculum is at once a comprehensive mode of cultural historiography and a pedagogical method for encouraging equal participation and an ethos of exchange in the classroom. In that sense, it practices what it preaches. The addition of high-impact learning opportunities, many of which incorporate the sensory experience of tasting and cooking into the study of a larger intellectual problem, then prompts students to understand holistically the concept of cultural relativity. Opening minds beyond the fast-food satisfaction of stereotypes is an essential and essentially challenging mission of humanities and foreign language departments. Food studies is a dynamic and fundamentally student-centered method to teach students that national identity is not a solid structure, but rather a fluid concept that must be reinterpreted.

## Notes

1 The first French application to have "French gastronomy" included in UNESCO's World Intangible Heritage list in 2008 was indeed rejected on the grounds that it was too culturally exclusive. In the second application, the "gastronomic meal of the French" appeared as what Durmelat calls a "more modest … euphemism" to sidestep the previous criticism (393).

2 Parkhurst Ferguson reminds us that "gastronomy" (*gastronomie*) emerged as a new term in 19th-century Paris that privileges "living to eat" over "eating to live" (3). She refers to Brillat-Savarin's famous aphorism from his *Physiology of Taste*: "Animals fill themselves; men eat; but only wise men know the art of eating" (15).
3 Murphy contrasts the "essential" aspect of food studies with the pejorative view that they are "basic," meaning simple and perhaps even frivolous because they are personal (20–21).
4 See "Global Foodways." To engage both the academic and regional community on a grand scale could require fundraising, depending on a particular institution's commitment to the project.
5 The event had to be canceled because of a mandatory hurricane evacuation.
6 By 1780, wet nurses fed about ninety percent of Parisian babies. They were effectively unionized in a "bureau" to secure pre-payment for their services (Yalom, 106).
7 Daughters are excluded from Rousseau's discussion of civic education. See Brace 363–64 for a discussion of wet nursing as "denatured."
8 Because this is an advanced course conducted entirely in French, I aim to keep reading and viewing material almost exclusively in French as well. I do make excerpts of certain English-language texts available on the course website as optional readings, but I tend to lecture on them as they relate to material the students have prepared for class.
9 The most affluent Parisians bought harlequins as "doggie bags" for their pets (Beizer, 373). For an explanation of how the harlequin economy worked, see Beizer (380–82).
10 Beizer discusses Mlle Saget's shaming in *The Belly of Paris* because she eats harlequins (379–80).
11 The term "omnibus" comes from the original French and is a simile for the harlequin rooted in 19th-century urban history (42). The English translation renders it as "smorgasbord" (14).
12 Aron emphasizes that in the 19th century, soup became ignoble as low-class food (206).
13 At the lecture and panel discussion, representatives from the Office of Sustainability presented how they coordinate with the university catering service to create events with no food left to waste and entirely recyclable and compostable materials.
14 Pangloss's cheerful acceptance of syphilis as a kind of minor disadvantage to colonization, which, after all, brought "chocolate and cochineal dye" to Europe, is another useful excerpt (12).
15 See also Perkins.

# References

Abramson, Julia. "French Food on Film: Beyond Gastronomy in *La Noire de ..., Chocolat, and La Graine et le mulet.*" *Contemporary French Civilization*, vol. 42, no. 3–4, 2017, pp. 259–278.

Aron, Jean-Paul. *The Art of Eating in France: Manners and Menus in the 19th Century*. Translated by Nina Rootes. Harper & Row, 1975.

Badinter, Elisabeth. *The Conflict: How Modern Motherhood Undermines the Status of Women*. Translated by Adriana Hunter. Metropolitan Books, 2011.

Beizer, Janet. "Why the French Hate Doggie Bags." *Contemporary French Civilization*, vol. 42, no. 3–4, 2017, pp. 373–389.

Bonnekessen, Barbara. "Food Is Good to Teach: An Exploration of the Cultural Meanings of Food." *Food, Culture and Society*, vol. 13, no. 2, 2010, pp. 279–295.

Brace, Laura. "Rousseau, Maternity and the Politics of Emptiness." *Polity*, vol. 39, no. 3, 2007, pp. 361–383.

Brillat-Savarin, Jean Anthelme. *The Physiology of Taste; Or, Meditations on Transcendental Gastronomy*. Translated and Edited by M. F. K. Fisher, introduction by Bill Buford. Vintage, 2011.

Brown, Becky A. *À Table: The Food Culture of France*. 2nd ed. Hackett, 2017.

Davis, Jennifer J. *Defining Culinary Authority: The Transformation of Modern Cooking in France, 1650–1830*. Louisiana SUP, 2013.

Durmelat, Sylvie. "Making Couscous French? Digesting the Loss of Empire." *Contemporary French Civilization*, vol. 42, no. 3–4, 2017, pp. 391–407.

"Global Foodways." https://blogs.cofc.edu/global-foodways.

"Intangible Cultural Heritage of Humanity: Gastronomic Meal of the French." UNESCO, https://ich.unesco.org/en/RL/gastronomic-meal-of-the-french-00437.

Kechiche, Abdellatif, director. *La Graine et le mulet*. Pathé Renn, 2007.

Lévi-Strauss, Claude. *Totemism*. Translated by Rodney Needham. Beacon P, 1963.

Mitchell, James G. and Cheryl Tano, editors. *Espaces: Rendez-vous avec le Monde Francophone*, 4th ed., Vista Higher Learning, 2019.

Murphy, Deirdre. "Toward a Pedagogy of Mouthiness: The Essential Interdisciplinarity of Studying Food." *Transformations: The Journal of Inclusive Scholarship and Pedagogy*, vol. 23, no. 2, 2012–2013, pp. 17–26.

Perkins, Erin. "Global Foodways Program Adds Cultural Perspective." *The College Today*, October 19, 2018, https://today.cofc.edu/2018/10/19/global-foodways-program/.

Ravalico, Lauren. "Global Foodways." *Skirt: Charleston's First Women's Magazine*, November 2018, pp. 10–11, www.skirt.com/global-foodways.

Rousseau, Jean-Jacques. *Emile, or On Education*. Translated by Allan Bloom. Basic Books, 1979.

Sprang, Rebecca. *The Invention of the Restaurant: Paris and Modern Gastronomic Culture*. Harvard UP, 2001.

Sue, Eugène. *Les Mystères de Paris*. Edited by Francis Lacassin, R. Laffont, 1989. [*The Mysteries of Paris*. Translated by Carolyn Betensky and Jonathan Loesberg. Penguin, 2015].

Varda, Agnès, director. *Les Glaneurs et la glaneuse*. Ciné Tamaris, 2000.

Voltaire. *Candide: ou l'Optimisme*. Translated by Burton Raffel. Yale UP, [1759] 2005.

Yalom, Marilyn. *A History of the Breast*. Ballantine, 1997.

# 14

# LESSONS IN DIVERSITY FROM THE STREET

## A Course on Hip-hop Cultures

*Kathryn St. Ours*

A course on hip-hop cultures is perfectly suited for the 21$^{st}$-century French-speaking classroom. Inherently interdisciplinary owing to its three main pillars—dance, art and music—such a course encourages language students to pursue (in French) various areas of inquiry from multiple perspectives: historical, musicological, ethnological, artistic, linguistic, anthropological. More importantly, a course on hip-hop places questions such as diversity, inclusion, and social justice at the forefront. Originating in the depressed, gang-ridden, violent Bronx neighborhoods of the 1960s, this counter-cultural movement has since spread to marginalized communities virtually everywhere, consistently challenging dominant power structures. The depth and breadth of the Francophone connection allows us to explore the emergence of hip-hop not only in the Hexagon but also in France's former colonies. Taught at the 300-level (mostly juniors and seniors), the course presumes prior knowledge of France's colonial past (gained in a required two-hundred level introductory course).

The legacies of colonialism today—racism, discrimination, inequality, poverty, immigration—affect both France and its erstwhile possessions. Within what has now become a diffuse and frontierless hip-hop nation, however, the particular geopolitics of each former colony spawn a variety of novel adaptations to social, political, and linguistic realities at the regional, national, and even municipal levels. This course takes students to France, Senegal, Gabon, Belgium, Tunisia, and Algeria, using transnational hip-hop as a powerful tool with which to pedagogically tackle the pressing issues of diversity and inclusion.

The framework for the course is provided by the English-language edition (published between 1998 and 2010) of French historian Pierre Nora's monumental seven-volume opus *Les Lieux de mémoire* [*Realms of Memory*], from which students read the preface and the final chapter "The Era of Commemorations" in Volume III. These texts present the utmost interest for the study of hip-hop cultures, for Nora's

DOI: 10.4324/9781003126461-15

initial project—focused on the monuments, sites, and symbols that crystallized the French heritage—changed over the course of more than a decade. Indeed, the historian came to recognize that "The object 'France' no longer makes sense as a persuasive unit of study. Whether one looks at economic factors, cultural practices, or mental evolutions, no unity is apparent; the existence of a France 'one and indivisible' has become purely problematic" (632). Nora goes on to define *lieux de mémoire* more broadly than earlier as "any significant entity, whether material or nonmaterial in nature, which by dint of human will or the work of time has become a symbolic element of the memorial heritage of any community" (xiii). As he and his contributors were hard at work, in fact, the burgeoning hip-hop scene in France had become the voice of the marginalized "Frances," eager to transform alienating spaces into memorial places where individual and community identity could flourish.

To put these opening readings into perspective, I ask the students about their prior experience studying French. What *lieux de mémoire* do they consider quintessentially French? Can they envision that street art or rap music might someday rightfully stand as *realms of memory* beside the Eiffel Tower, Verdun, or "La Marseillaise"? Can something originally not French become part of the national inheritance? Moreover, is there a US identity that we would all agree upon? What monuments, statues, sites, songs, or flags represent this country? Given the current climate, they quickly recognize that racial, economic, generational, and political factors have problematized the concept of a common cultural heritage.

What criteria would I apply to organize a course on Francophone hip-hop around a politically charged, socially significant construct that evolves over time? I intended to expose my students to significant foci of resistance that challenge the status quo in order to promote social justice. It was important to sensitize them to issues of race, power, and perspective so that they might become more compassionate, empathetic, and informed citizens. I also wished to advance the belief that creative endeavors can help to change the world. And although I wanted to underscore the continued vitality of the French language today (and to include primarily Francophone artists), it was also useful for my students to realize that other (non-)official languages as identity-markers were often key to the creation of *realms*.

Ultimately, the course was structured in three parts. In the first, we examine how hip-hop cultures dismantle traditional, no longer relevant *lieux,* such as patriarchy, sexism, and Frenchness. In the second, we study hip-hop as a multilayered form of expression that finds inspiration in traditions and histories that have been stifled or effaced. The third and final division highlights new *realms* that lay the groundwork for societies where we can proudly "talk the talk and walk the walk" of social justice.

## Toppling Traditional Realms of Memory

Nineteenth-century politicians sought to justify colonization as the vocation and mission of France to civilize "inferior" cultures. Over a century later in 2005, conservatives proposed to affirm the positive role of colonization in French history books. This did not happen, of course, due to vehement opposition from within and beyond the Hexagon. Meanwhile, whereas hip-hop cultures have been deconstructing France's glorified past for decades, hip-hop artists in the former colonies have only recently felt empowered to denounce the yoke of autocratic patriarchy. We concentrate here on the hip-hoppers in Europe and the Maghreb whose contrapuntal practices recount the somber stories behind the master narratives.

Many rap musicians evoke the colonial heritage and its far-reaching consequences. Beginning with music allows us to discover how colonization is portrayed in the language and/or corresponding video clips. We might first analyze the text of a song and then compare the lyrics to the visual images or contrarily, watch the muted video and interpret the visuals. The linguistic exegesis also provides the opportunity to appreciate a rapper's poetics.

By virtue of the transnational dimension of our course, I focus first on the Belgian rapper Isha, whose latest album *La Vie augmente* [*Life Increases*] (Volume III) was released in 2020. After reading a dossier devoted to this Francophone country's colonization of the Congo aptly entitled "L'Histoire nous raconte des histoires" ["History has been telling us stories"], students analyze the lyrics of the song "Les Magiciens." Isha's case is extremely interesting because as the son of a Belgian Congo historian, he possesses the factual knowledge upon which to foreground his commentary. As the song begins, one of the vanquished marvels at the white man's "magical" ability to subjugate the Congolese:

> Fire came from their boats, on the beach, blood flowed/
> They took the gold and the diamonds, they left the magic book/
> All those who saw them up close say that their eyes were the color of the sky/
> They all carried a dead man attached to an iron cross.
> (Le feu est sorti de leurs bateaux, sur la plage, le sang a coulé/
> Ils ont pris l'or et les diamants, ils ont laissé le livre magique/
> Tous ceux qui les ont vus de près disent que leurs yeux ont la couleur du ciel/
> Ils portaient tous un homme mort attaché à une croix de fer).

The students consider Isha's depiction of history and portrayal of the central African peoples' encounter with the whites. They appreciate the eyewitness point of view as an alternative to official history and point to the fact that the colonized lack the words to describe the weapons and religious beliefs of the conquerors. The title of the song, they remark, effectively captures the state of bewilderment that the words communicate. Many draw comparisons with what happened in the Americas. An appropriate assignment at this stage is the analysis of another rap song and/or video clip on the subject of colonization.[1] Some students prefer to focus on the poetics of the language, others on the aesthetic qualities of the film. Most explain how sound and image work together to powerfully denounce colonization as a crime against humanity.

Unfortunately, the independence of the former colonies did not put an end to injustice and inequality. Autocratic regimes maintained many of the ills of colonialism like discrimination, political repression, and economic disparity. We turn our attention next to the rap music produced under the post-colonial dictatorship in Tunisia. How has rap music contributed to undermining the memorial heritage of political and religious patriarchies? Even before the Tunisian Revolution in 2010, rapper El General (Hamada Ben Amor) condemns the then president and dictator Zine el-Abidine Ben Ali in the song, "Raïs le bled" (Head of state), in which he sings, "Mr. President, your people are dying." Targeting the autocracy, Ben Amor repeats several times that he speaks in the name of the Tunisian people, who suffer from poverty, hunger, lack of hospitals, schools, lodging, freedom of speech: "I see too much injustice and have decided to send this message despite repercussions." Students are encouraged to reflect on the capacity of rap to denounce systemic injustice. Can they cite any US rappers with a similar commitment? Has transnational hip-hop become a mainstay of oppositional networks throughout the world? Many of my students cite rappers from non-Francophone cultures, as well. This discussion offers a perfect opportunity to promote intercultural understanding.

Then, as a prelude to studying the rap that has been dominant in the aftermath of the Arab Spring, my students read Tahar Ben Jelloun's chapter on Tunisia in *L'étincelle* [*Revolts in the Arab Countries*]. Several years after the deposition of Ben Ali, Tunisians struggle to keep the promise of the overthrow alive. So just as they did under the former dictatorship, rap groups like Armada Bizerta now rage against the rise of conservatism that poses a threat to freedom of speech.[2] The obscurantist wave is criticized in "Wake up the Dead": "Désobéir est un devoir … Arrache ta liberté … L'urne est pourrie … L'islam politique est une maladie" ["Disobedience is a duty … Seize your freedom … The ballot box is corrupt … Political Islam is a disease"]. In the clip sung in Arabic, the captions in French are superimposed upon the relentless images of a zoo. The plight of the caged animals, along with a backbeat from a song about the Israeli occupation of Palestine by the famous Arab singer Fairuz, is an injunction for the Tunisian people to continue the fight to democratize their country.[3] Students definitely relate to rap's vocation to speak the truth to power (I first taught the course amid the 2013 Black Lives Matter protests). Future class participants would also be interested in a July 10, 2020 report on NPR's *All Things Considered*, entitled "Black Lives Matter Protesters March to Rap Songs by Local Heroes."

And how do Arab women who reject conservative Islam and anti-democratic governments fight to escape from the yoke of religious and political patriarchal systems? Are there feminists who show the courage to challenge patriarchy as a no-longer acceptable "element of the memorial heritage" (realm of memory) in their countries? As we undertake these issues, the class views the 2017 documentary *Fleurs du Bitume* [*Blooms in the Concrete*], in which three Tunisian female street artists—Shams (a slammer), Chaima (a hip-hop dancer), and Ouména (a graffitist)—use their talents to claim women's rights in the post-revolutionary period. As these women garner the support of brothers, fathers, and male friends, their ability to weaken traditional chauvinist political systems increases. My female students, in particular, find that this empowering film advocates for feminist humanism.[4]

## Realms of Memory from the Margins

The previous section concentrated on realms of memory shared by the dominant cultures into which subversive hip-hoppers have no desire to assimilate. Indeed, what can the Republic's motto "Liberty, equality, fraternity" or the "tri-color" mean for immigrants to France or even worse, for their descendants who continue to be referred to as the offspring of immigrants (*issus de l'immigration*)? What makes discussions about democracy and freedom on Tunisian television anything more than vacuous talk? We reflect on the difference between memory and history. Are there collective memories that are not part of official history? How important is connecting with *lieux de mémoire* from pasts that have remained untold, disconnected from lived experience, even forgotten? How can hip-hop help to reappropriate the past, thereby contributing to identity-formation and pride? I want my students to appreciate how rekindled *realms*—the retrieval of personal and/or collective histories—commemorate new generational, demographic, and ethnic trends in the Hexagon as well as in its former colonies.

Social scientists[5] have long taken an interest in the importance of roots for hip-hoppers. Ethnographer Claire Calogirou, for instance, relates the case of Franco-Algerian Kader Attou, who uses his art to reconstruct a *realm* for himself, his parents, and other immigrants. Choreographed in 2005, his performance "Douar" represents the difficulties of immigrating and of surviving in a new place: arrival, administrative red tape, search for employment, and feelings of alienation and solitude. The dance consists of various tableaux depicting waiting lines, boredom, moments of dejection but also of the happiness of shared community in a new place. As the spectacle ends, the dancers each hoist portraits of real-life individuals who exist and deserve to be acknowledged and legitimized. Such a quest for recognition is coupled with a thirst for re-membering—for what Nora calls "reconstitutive recovery" (626)—a vitally important element for those who feel incomplete as descendants and heirs of a particular cultural heritage.

What is important here is that Attou has willingly assumed his first-generational status and claimed it as a significant part of his identity, after a period of disinterest or negation (Caligourou 8); the dramatization of the past in "Douar" actually (re)creates a *realm of memory*. As a 2008 interview conducted at the *Hip-hop Exhibition* in Saint-Quentin-en-Yvelines indicates, the same dynamics are at work for dancer/choreographer Maria (102). She choreographed a piece after visiting her father's homeland, Senegal, where she was especially struck by the history of Gorée Island. It is there—in the House of Slaves, now a museum—that the "chattel" was held before being transported to the new world. Clearly, this *lieu de mémoire* is an important part of Maria's heritage as a French citizen. And she is not alone.[6] The ability to rejoin one's roots resonates with many of my students who, when prompted, express feelings of disconnect from the dominant culture. The ensuing discussion on how to communicate one's sense of marginalization creates a space for thoughtful interchange. What *realms* do they feel have been imposed upon them? What means to construct meaningful *realms* are at their disposal today?

The need to (re)cover disrupted *realms of memory* also prevails in former French colonies where rap musicians proliferate. The case of Gabon effectively epitomizes reappropriation of the past. Thanks to anthropologist Alice Aterianus-Owanga's monograph *Le rap, ça vient d'ci* [*Rap Comes from Here*], the interested reader discovers that "rap gaboma" has been busy reactivating the country's pre-colonial identity through music since the early 1990s. A group called Movaiza-leine (Bad Breath, i.e., candid and perhaps offensive lyrics) leads the way. Their recordings, videos clips, and live performances feature ritualistic practices, indigenous languages, the use of fetishes, tribal garb, and body paint, as well as traditional instruments. In "On détient la harpe sacrée" ["We possess the sacred harp"], students discover an appeal to Gabon's multiethnic and linguistic population to unite in an effort to preserve the country's vast bee forest and its immemorial spiritual secrets. The title belongs to a two-volume set that constitutes nothing less than an act of spiritual, spatial, and historical reclaiming of a significant Gabonese *lieu de mémoire*.[7]

## 21st-Century Realms of Memory

The rise of human rights movements everywhere gives voice to hitherto mute constituent groups. Hip-hop has succeeded in affirming subcultural identities within a globalized, interconnected, fast-paced world. This fact bears emphasizing and I encourage my students to think about the persistence of the ideals of equity and equality in times of constant change and upheaval. In future iterations of this course, we will look at the July 2020 fresco in the north of Paris honoring both Adama Traoré and George Floyd. The mural was itself vandalized with graffiti but quickly restored. Elsewhere, in Paris' tenth district, the well-respected "photograffeur" JR, famous for his photocollages—destined to peel off—also paid homage to Traoré and Floyd. Such is the fate of street art: it is inevitably subject to degradation. Most of my students agree that transience and transformation are not mutually exclusive and that perhaps the impermanence of street art constitutes its very value. Individual perceptions of street art create private memories. When adopted by a given community, these can become shared memories that circulate within fluid fields of energy.

Braving the hazards of streets around the world, JR has been advocating for racial/gender equality, social justice, and peace for decades. His widespread influence resulted in a 2011 TED talk, in which he maintains that street artists can change the world by changing the way we see it. Shortly after collecting the TED prize, therefore, he launched the *Inside Out Project,* creating sites that celebrate common ground, dialogue, and heritage building. Haitians participating in JR's *Inside Out Project* donned the walls of Port-au-Prince with portraits heralding its resilient citizens following the devastation of the 2010 earthquake (*Rising Souls Haiti*). We exist, we are still here, we are proud of our Haitian heritage, they all seem to be saying. On a broader scale, JR's tribute *Women Are Heroes* commemorates the "memorial heritage" of the undervalued members of our societies. Does this project not help to undermine history's predilection for male-dominated *lieux de mémoire?* [8]

Although short-lived, JR's projects are dependent upon technologies (such as the conspicuous photobooth truck) that are inaccessible in many less developed places. The graffiti artists in Senegal, for example, find it difficult to procure even spray paint. Nonetheless, this obstacle has not prevented them from covering the walls of Dakar, in particular, with paintings representing the common heritage that they seek to modernize. Set-Setal (meaning physical and moral cleansing in Wolof) is the ancestor of the current graffiti scene in Dakar. Following in the footsteps of their predecessors, they see their mission as that of reshaping the old collective ethos for a new urban environment. A member of the Art Collective Madzoo comments: "For everything that goes on here, the artist should be the guiding pole for his young people, for his population, his public" (Rabine, 97). Artists have transformed underground graffiti to communicate ethically-charged messages such as "Discipline," "Knowledge before action," "Future," or "Clean" (Rabine, 102–3)[9] and of course, more recently, the fight against the coronavirus (COVID-19).

Despite the intrinsically ephemeral status of street art, therefore, graffitists can adapt quickly to evolving circumstances. The polyvocality of the means and messages of hip-hop practices allows for diversity and inclusion. My students urge caution, however. Not all graffiti promotes the memorial heritage upon which our democracies are founded. A lively debate ensued around the issues of freedom of speech and political correctness. Although no conclusion was reached, most agreed that 21st-century *realms of memory* must represent and advance our shared democratic values.

We have seen desacralized *lieux* that no longer serve that purpose, revived memory spaces that do, and the timely creation of novel *realms*. The questioned validity of literary canons has enabled hip-hop music to infiltrate long-standing literary inheritances; rap/slam performers are poets with a growing memorial heritage of their own. Metaphor, rhyme, oblique literary/historical references, and word play are a few of the many devices that make Franco-Senegalese MC Solaar and Franco-Congolese Abd Al-Malik worth studying. I concentrate here on Al-Malik because of his lyricism and the rich possibilities his work holds for interdisciplinarity. The 2013 album *L'Art de la révolte* [*The Art of Revolt*]—an homage to Albert Camus—highlights many of the important milestones in the author's life and includes such titles as "Le Malentendu" ["The Misunderstanding"], "Stockholm" (site of his Nobel Prize acceptance speech), and "La Peste" ["The Plague"]. The relevance of the latter title goes without saying; the rapper employs the allegorical scope of the novel to evoke social problems in France today. This element of the course circles back to the discussion of hip-hop's ability to change the world.[10]

As the course ends, I ask my students to study the lyrics and video clip "Musique nègre" ["Black Music"] by Kery James, and to decide where they would situate it if they were to teach the course, i.e., does it 1) dismantle traditional and no longer relevant *lieux*; 2) rekindle *realms of memory* that have been overlooked or devalued; or 3) create new *realms*? They concluded that the song meets all three criteria: as a response to former 2017 presidential candidate Henry de Lesquen's racist condemnation of what he called "Black music," James and friends 1) refute that history has been made solely by the Europeans; 2) highlight the contributions to social justice of a vast array of Black activists, politicians, and extraordinary individuals like Martin Luther King, Jr., Malcolm X, and the Black Panthers, Thomas Sankara, Léopold Senghor, Rosa Parks, Muhammed Ali, the Senegalese *tirailleurs* (soldiers) of the French colonial army, and Black athletes at the 1968 Olympic Games; and 3) allow us to conceive of "musique nègre" as a *lieu*. Is Nora's project:

> whose ambition is to think about the nation without nationalism and about France without any universalistic a priori; whose inspiration is almost ethnographic; and whose method therefore consists in shedding light on the construction of representations, the formation of historical objects over time
>
> *(Nora, xxi)*

so different from James'?

## Conclusion

From its inception among the marginalized in New York City to its present global explosion, hip-hop has become a legitimate cultural movement. So much so that it has attained mainstream status. Urban art has been commercialized; upright or break dancing is taught in schools and studios; rap has become a billion-dollar industry. I challenge my students to reflect on the gentrification of hip-hop cultures. Is the movement destined to occupy a space in-between gentrification and institutionalization on one hand, and contestation and subversion, on the other?

As hip-hop continues to evolve, however, its roots must not be forgotten. In the words of sociologist Dieynébou Fofana, hip-hop cultural agents must use their particular "passports"——art, music, and dance—to mobilize civic action, to preserve their counter-cultural impact. The extra-territorial scope of hip-hop will allow further connections to be made, intersectional goals to be shared, and resistance movements to be sustained as its actors' struggle to "keep it real."

## Notes

1 Examples from France include MC Solaar, Kery James, Booba, or Black M, and from Belgium, Baloji, Damso, or Roméo Elvis. The lyrics to most of the songs mentioned in this essay can be found on genuis.fr.
2 https://www.youtube.com/watch?v=uz7rCCc32_Y.
3 For similar songs on unrest in the Mahgreb, see also "Bourguiba" (Alkpote), "Urban Resistance" (Armada Bizerta), and from the Algeria of Bouteflika, "La liberté" ["Liberty"] by Algerian Soulking, or by the censored and exiled Mouad El Belghouat, aka El Haqed (The Enraged) who burns his Moroccan passport before the camera in "Raka Taka" ("Hood Rat").
4 Other feminist voices from north and sub-Saharan Africa include rapper ZM from Niger, Senegalese graffiti artist Dieynaba Sidibie and rapper Moonaya, and from France, three international graffitists presented in an Arte production entitled "Kif le street art au féminin" [Love Those Women Street Artists], www.youtube.com/watch?v=k3t8Luo_IFQ.
5 Some examples: Karim Hammou, André Bazin, Alice Aterianus-Owanga, Corinne Plantin.
6 Fred Bendongué (former member of Traction Avant) returned to his African origins for the Biennale de la Danse de Lyon [Lyon Biannual Dance Festival]. He choreographed a piece about runaway slaves that included break dancing, tap, and modern dance. Furthermore, French rappers Mokobé et Booba recount a return to roots in "Maman dort" ["Mamma is sleeping"].
    https://genius.com/Mokobe-maman-dort-lyrics.
7 Those interested in hip-hop dance as the means to reactivate lost or fading realms of memory will be interested in The Dance for Freedom United Nations International Fund for Agricultural Development. Rwandan-born Sherrie Silver's initial choreography shot in Cameroon to the rap song "Freedom" by Mr. Eazi is the centerpiece of the "Dance for Change" [Bouge pour que ça change] campaign to promote and finance self-sufficient local farming.
8 Le Mouvement www.lemouvement.paris has launched a street art project devoted to social justice. The next time you are in Paris, pay attention to the conspicuous graffiti of umbrellas, intended to encourage people to open their hearts to 21$^{st}$-century immigrants. Students could be invited to research this collective.
9 Unfortunately, the hip-hop scene in Senegal virtually excludes women. Dieynaba Sinibe is one of the few recognized graffiti artists; likewise, female rappers are slowly emerging in a male-dominated practice.
10 After reading the first and last chapters of Franco-Rwandan author/rapper Gaël Faye's *Petit Pays* [*Small Country*], students write an essay comparing the text to the music video by the same name.

## References

Abd Al-Malik. *L'Art et la Révolte*, Château Rouge, 2013.
—. *Qu'Allah bénisse la France*. Albin Michel, 2004.
Aterianus-Owanga, Alice. *Le Rap, ça vient d'ici*. Maison des Sciences de l'Homme, 2017.
Bazin, Hugues. *La Culture hip-hop*. Desclée de Brouwer, 1995.

BBC News Afrique. "Des graffiti contre le Coronavirus." April 2, 2020, www.bbc.com/afrique/52120609.
Ben Jelloun, Tahar. *L'Étincelle*. Gallimard, 2011.
Calogirou, Claire. "Le motif des racines dans le hip-hop." *Ethnologie française*, vol. 43, no. 1, 2013, pp. 97–108.
Dieynébou, Fofana. "Émergence du hip-hop en France." In *Agora débats/jeunesses*, 2002, pp. 62–65.
Diouf, Mamadou. Gefame. "Wall Paintings and the Writing of History: Set/Setal in Dakar." *Journal of African Studies*, vol. 2, no. 1, 2005. http://hdl.handle.net/2027/spo.4761563.0002.102.
Faye, Gaël. *Petit pays*. Éditions Grasset & Fasquelle, 2016.
Hammou, Karim. *Une Histoire du rap en France*. La Découverte, 2012.
JR. *L'Art peut-il changer le monde?* French and European Publications Inc, 2016.
Morales, Karine and Caroline Péricard. *Fleurs de Bitume*. Keren Production, 2017. www.filmsdocumentaires.com/films/6076-les-fleurs-du-bitume.
Nora, Pierre. *Les Lieux de Mémoire*. Gallimard (Bibliothèque illustrée des histoires), 3 tomes: t. 1 *La République* (1 vol., 1984), t. 2 *La Nation* (3 vol., 1986), t. 3 *Les France* (3 vol., 1992. [*Realms of Memory*. Translated by Arthur Goldhammer, Columbia UP, 1998].
Plantin, Corinne. *Connaissez-vous vraiment la culture hip-hop?* Bookelis, 2017.
Rabine, Leslie. "'These Walls Belong to Everybody' The Graffiti Art Movement in Dakar." *African Studies Quarterly*, vol. 14, no. 3, 2014, pp. 89–112.
Le rap en France. "L'Histoire nous raconte des histoires, la colonisation belge au Congo vue par Isha." Dossier. http://lerapenfrance.fr/dossier-lhistoire-raconte-histoires-colonisation-belge-congo-vue-isha.

# 15

## "WE ARE ALL NEGROES"

Teaching Tolerance from a Haitian Literary Perspective

*Lovia Mondésir*

In his essay "Oneself as Another," Paul Ricœur presents the ethical intention of the self: "aiming at a good life lived with and for others in just institutions" ("Oneself" 172). However, how do we achieve such a life when facing injustice or while others are oppressed? How do we negotiate the act of living (well) when the structures meant to protect us coerce us instead? In other words, how much do unjust law, corrupt government, and legitimized discriminations impact our impetus to live well with and/for others? As teachers, we are regularly confronted with several versions of these sets of questions in our daily life and professional practice. Our answers to these questions may not only shape our life but also the lives of our students. Teaching and learning about tolerance and inclusivity is imperative in our contemporary world. This task is essential to both academic and personal growth because students "learn to critique current social relations and to envision more just and inclusive possibilities for social life" (Adams *et al.*, xvii). Through critical reading and discussion, they explore concepts that foster a better understanding of social and political issues while making a connection with occurrences in their personal lives. While topics such as racism, socio-economic inequalities, and religion may prove to be challenging and uncomfortable, approaching these questions with critical thinking, openness, and respect can help alleviate some of the discomfort. Ultimately, teaching and learning about these problems increases awareness and helps teachers steer their modules and activities toward fostering a more inclusive and safe classroom.

In this chapter, I take these reflections into account as I focus on the intersectionality of race/ethnicity, religion, and class, as portrayed by Jacques S. Alexis in *Les Arbres musiciens* [*The Musician Trees*] and Louis-Philippe Dalembert in *Avant que les ombres s'effacent* [*Until the Shadows Flee*]. Set during World War II, both texts are historical novels that offer a framework for interdisciplinary approaches

DOI: 10.4324/9781003126461-16

and a cross-disciplinary collaboration not limited to the field of literature, history, and religion. I teach the novels as a unit on Haiti in a more comprehensive course on Francophone Caribbean Literature and Culture. The main goal of the course is to provide students with opportunities to practice "intentional reading," "deep processing," and mindful writing in French (Svinicki and McKeachie, 30) with a focus on critical thinking and team-based learning. Both novels challenge conceptions of values such as diversity, inclusiveness, and tolerance. Alexis and Dalembert question the ethical basis for claims of superiority of one faith and race over all others. They also show the relevance of tolerance and justice for local communities and world peace. First, I analyze the ethical dimension of fiction and its pertinence to a quest for justice and inclusivity; then, I explore the interconnectedness of race, class, religion, and culture in Alexis's novel. Second, I investigate the fragility of identity through the relation between the self and the foreigner as well as the ethical implications of acknowledging our intrinsic strangeness. Third, I demonstrate the anthropological shift introduced by the Haitian Creole word "*Nèg*" (Negro) in Dalembert's work while showing that for him, tolerance is welcoming a plurality of identities and memories from oneself and from others. I conclude by confirming the relevance of both novelists' contributions to a study on tolerance and inclusivity for our students.

## Intolerance: Between Ethical Mistake and Patriotic Crime

How can teaching and reading literary texts sustain diversity, inclusivity, and tolerance? How can reading fiction incite us to be our best selves while pursuing unprejudiced interactions with others? Reflecting upon the correlation between fiction and life, Ricœur, in his book *From Text to Action*, offers the following assessment:

> […] we understand ourselves only by the long detour of the signs of humanity deposited in cultural works. What would we know of love and hate, of moral feelings, and, in general, of all that we call the *self* if these had not been brought to language and articulated by literature?
>
> *(87)*

The *self* is culturally constructed and, as such, can only be approached through language where it (the self) is inscribed. Consequently, literature provides us with the means to apprehend ourselves by "creat[ing] different mental experiments about ideas and values" (Rohden, 5). How does literature offer a critique of the real? According to Ricœur, a redescription of the real occurs when ordinary language is suspended and "discourse is raised to fiction" (*From Text*, 300). Moreover, this first interruption informs a second one that allows interpretation to take place. What is sought in interpretation, explains Ricœur, is not the author's intention "hidden behind the text but a world unfolded in front of it"

(*From Text*, 300). Consequently, interpretation is neither the "dismantling of structure" nor a subjective encounter between writer and reader; instead, interpretation is for the reader to know herself.

Paradoxically, this self-understanding occurs through a suspension of subjectivity. Indeed, self-understanding does not mean a projection of the reader's feelings onto the text but must be accomplished through questioning. In the philosopher's own words: "The critique of ideology is the necessary detour that self-understanding must take if the latter is to be formed by the matter of the text and not by the prejudices of the reader" (*From Text*, 88). Therefore, the ultimate meaning of interpretation is for the reader to know herself and to choose "among the multiple proposals of ethical justice brought forth by the reading" (*Time and Narrative III*, 249). Ricœur affirms that reading is "a provocation to be and act differently" (*Time and Narrative III*, 249).[1] Interpretation "becomes a way of living, of behaving in the world, hence of transforming it" (Abel, 374). In that sense, teaching/reading literary texts can be a tool for "anti-oppression and social justice education" (Adams *et al.*, xvii).

Caribbean novelists "in general share a tradition of being actively engaged in forming or transforming their societies through their work," notes Margaret Heady (49). In the presentation of his book, *Haiti and the United States: National Stereotypes and the Literary Imagination,* Michael Dash further describes Haitian literature as a "subversive" effort for Haitians to "rewrite themselves." He interprets Haitian literature as a means of "showing solidarity" (2). Alexis, for instance, used his Marvelous Realism theory for "Nation-building" (Heady, 46). His novel *Les Arbres musiciens* captures the involvement of two brothers in the "anti-superstition campaign" of 1942. The priest Diogène destroys Vodou temples and forcibly converts peasants to Catholicism, while Edgar, commissioned by the Haitian government, expropriates the same peasants. The seizing provides lands for a Haitian-American firm to cultivate rubber trees. Alexis delineates these events as a triple assault on religious freedom and racial and class equality. Staging the campaign as a family endeavor allows him to represent the interrelation between religious intolerance and economic inequalities, as well as the Haitian State's inherent contradictions. As the epitome of religious intolerance, this campaign shatters Haitian collective memory and re-enacts traumatic reminiscences from colonial times where slaves were punished for performing African rituals.[2] In his "Lettre ouverte à ce prêtre" ["Letter to this Priest"], Alexis explains that "the Haitian people were sacrificed to the vagaries of sectarian foreigners, infatuated by Western superiority to the point that they want to force their 'civilization' upon people who don't want it" (cited in Souffrant, 219).[3] The novelist emphasizes "the external threat of capitalist imperialism, the internal threats of corruption within the petit-bourgeois nationalist government" (Heady, 51). Planned by the French clergy established in Haiti, the campaign is carried out by Haitian politicians and priests to profit a Haitian-American firm. Alexis strives to show that these institutions are "sources of alienation in Haiti" (Heady, 52). In his depiction, he seeks to give a voice "to tens of thousands of human beings who were outraged, trampled upon, assaulted because they were impoverished, and illiterate Negroes abandoned by the official justice and their country" (Alexis, cited in Souffrant, 219).[4] Alexis considers the anti-superstitious campaign as a painful reality for all—a violation of human rights. Despite his Marxist attitudes toward religion, he takes a stand in the name of "intellectual probity" and tolerance. He observes that "the true human being must be ready to die if necessary to defend the right of his fellow man to profess opinions contrary to his own. That's what I call fraternity and you call love, this spirit of tolerance, of mutual respect, and understanding" (Alexis, cited in Souffrant, 215).[5] The concept of tolerance helps us to evaluate Alexis's position: he critiques Vodou as an alienating force but *tolerates* those who practice this religion. Furthermore, he interprets tolerance as a sign of progress, acknowledging the value of all human experiences.

In *Les Arbres*, race and ethnicity infiltrate almost every aspect of life. The racial question takes multiple forms: *mulâtromanie* (exclusive love of mulattos), colorism, and tensions between the French and the North-American clergy in Haiti. For example, renewing with colonial discrimination, President Élie Lescot only favors mulattoes in public administration. Thereby, he gives way to the development of colorist theories by the Black lower middle class. Nevertheless, Lescot's anti-Hitler politics contribute to improving his image. More precisely, following a nudge from the US government, Lescot imprisoned any German and Italian traders on Haitian soil that openly sympathized with Hitler and Mussolini. Furthermore, from December 8 to 12, 1941, Lescot's government officially (symbolically) declared war on the Rome-Berlin-Tokyo Axis. The narrator specifies: "People confusedly admitted that one could not violently oppose a government (no matter how corrupt!), that is participating in the great anti-Hitler crusade, whose outcome was instrumental for freedom around the world" (*Les Arbres* 158).[6] In addition, Alexis sketches the Haitian elite's alienating fascination for "everything" American. Dash shows that it is through the bourgeoisie that Alexis criticizes "America's presence in Haiti" (95).

Studying *Les Arbres*, students learn to situate Alexis in literary and cultural movements such as Indigenism, Negritude, and Marvelous Realism. They have the added opportunity to evaluate Alexis's rhetorical techniques, particularly his balanced use of Marvelous Realism and critical distancing effect. For example, to educate his readers and make them more lenient toward Vodou, he dissociates this religion from witchcraft practices and simultaneously critiques it as a sign of underdevelopment. To this end, he uses a plurality of points of view to describe the campaign by concurrently staging the perspectives of the perpetrators, the victims, and witnesses. By contrasting the Vodou chief priest Bois d'Orme with Diogène, Alexis seeks his readers' sympathy. Bois d'Orme is the forbearer of practical wisdom, who considers that all races, religions, and cultures are equal and claims the fraternity of all human beings. Besides, the character Gonaïbo—a model of inclusivity and Marxist consciousness—predicts the disappearance of

Vodou with the advent of education and technology. Because of the emphasis on religious freedom and economic and racial equality, in short, the "reimagining" "of being human" (Newman, 2) in *Les Arbres*, Dalembert's novel *Avant que les ombres s'effacent* [*Until the Shadows Flee*] proves a useful complement to Alexis's work.

## Tolerance or Seeing the Foreigner as Oneself

In his articles "La condition d'étranger" ["Being a Foreigner"] and "Étranger moi-même" ["A Foreigner Myself"], Ricœur asserts that the mistrust of native-born citizens toward foreigners is linked to the nature of identity itself, which is "fragile," "comparative," and "differential" ("Condition" 275). Its fragility comes from our difficulty in maintaining our sameness through time and in the face of change; so we continuously feel imperiled. Moreover, the foreigner threatens our self-understanding and forces us to ask the question, "Who am I?" ("Condition" 275).[7] This self-questioning may make us acknowledge our intrinsic strangeness. For instance, we may realize that: "The act of dwelling is an act of sharing the earth which is random and contingent" ("Étranger" 98).[8] Therefore, there is no necessary link between who we are and the space we inhabit. Conversely, we must recognize that we are also a *foreigner to the foreigner*. This reckoning compels us to be benevolent and acknowledge the *foreigner's right* to "universal hospitality," to be treated as a friend, not an enemy. Thus, hospitality is not about philanthropy, but rather about acknowledging the foreigner as our fellow, as *ourselves*. Hospitality materializes as the just protection of the "the right of foreign workers" or the "duty to help" refugees ("Étranger" 98).[9]

Dalembert's novel opens with Haiti's declaration of war on the Axis in 1941. The author stresses the 1939 Haitian Decree that naturalizes *in absentia* any Jew who wanted to flee Europe. As a result of the Haitian government's decision, hundreds of European Jewish families took on the Haitian nationality and took refuge in Haiti.[10] Born in Poland, Dr. Ruben Schwarzberg and his family flee to Berlin after the carnage of the Jewish community by the Polish army. At the rise of the Nazis, and after detention in the Buchenwald concentration camp, he takes refuge in Paris where he befriends Haitian writers Ida Faubert, Léon Laleau, and Roussan Camille. With their help, Ruben is released from the Argenteuil internment camp. Subsequently, he becomes a Haitian citizen in order to immigrate to Haiti. By extending the Haitian nationality to European Jews, Haiti gives a new meaning to the word community that transcends geopolitics' limits.

The narrator recalls that, shortly after claiming independence, Haiti adopted a similar measure to welcome any person fleeing slavery from the neighboring islands and the United States. Quoting the Haitian Constitution of 1804, the storyteller states: "any person who has been persecuted because of her ethnic origin or faith shall find refuge on the sacred territory of the nation" (Dalembert, 12). The narrator underscores: "at that moment, the young nation [of Haiti] had decided to put an end to that ridiculous notion of race, that all human beings were Negroes" (12). In fact, in Haitian culture, the Creole word *"Neg"* (or *Nègre* in French) refers not only to people of African descent but also to all humans. Dalembert emphasizes that to Haitians, there are "Black Negroes, blue Negroes, cinnamon or redhead Negroes, red Negroes under the skin or in general, Chinese Negroes with *slanting* eyes" (11–12).

Dalembert rightly describes this new meaning of the word "Nègre" as a result of Haiti's revolutionary history. Previously, French colonialists utilized skin color to deny Africans and their offspring any humanity or used skin shades to determine any non-European individual's worth. After its independence, Haiti redefined the word "Nègre" formerly used to annihilate people. The performative act of extending this designation to the human race is not a simple inversion but rather a transmutation of sense that is as radical as the Haitian Revolution itself. This anthropological shift constitutes another way for Haiti to realize the claims of both the French Revolution and the Enlightenment. Indeed, as shown by Michel-Rolph Trouillot, the slave trade increased during the French Revolution when political and philosophical debates on the rights of humanity were more vehement than ever (Trouillot, 80).

Thus, in the Haitian vernacular, "Nèg" universalizes humanness by rallying all races under this broad term, a single label that is actually not a racial epithet pertaining to any particular group. To account for the *"métissage"* and the "process of creolization" of the world (Glissant, 14–15), the narrator concludes: "One must not talk about racial purity, authentic identity, and all this nonsense. We are all bastards, period!" (Dalembert, 13). This statement appears as a direct answer to the Nuremberg Laws that condemn anyone with a "fraction of Jewish or Black blood" (Dalembert, 150). Ruben observes that: "The Jew and his Black accomplice, that's all the little corporal [Hitler] hated" (Dalembert, 150).[11] Both Frantz Fanon (69–74) and Édouard Glissant signal the structures of exclusion that Blacks and Jews face as minorities and migrants: starting with "the persecution of one and the enslavement of the other" (Glissant, 15).

## On Refugees, Languages, and Universal Hospitality

According to Ricœur, translation or studying a foreign language constitutes the perfect illustration of universal hospitality because of its equalizing effect; it makes us realize that the foreigner is an "other like [us]," both similar and different from us ("Étranger," 97). Far from any identity withdrawal, this reckoning creates a duty of assistance and mutuality. In Dalembert's work, reciprocity takes many forms: Polish assistance to the Haitian army during the Haitian revolution; Ida Faubert sheltering Ruben during his stay in Paris, Ruben delivering free care to his precarious neighbors; lastly, his grandniece's (Deborah) volunteering in Haiti, as a medical doctor after the 2010 earthquake. Witnessing the anti-superstition campaign, Ruben remembers the forced conversion of Jews to Catholicism throughout history. In reaction to this campaign, he participates in a Vodou ceremony, as a legacy to pass on to his children and grandchildren (Dalembert, 250). Thus, he enters the Haitian "symbolic world," to further "inscrib[e] himself in a 'we'" or a higher plane of his new community (Ricœur, *Reflections*, 88). His Vodou name *Moïse* retraces both his Jewish and Haitian heritages as it refers to the Tanakh patriarch, and a Haitian historical figure (Dalembert, 247). Moreover, Ruben's first-born son is named Jean-Jacques, to honor Haitian founding father, Dessalines.

Furthermore, Ruben's union to Sara El Khoury, a Christian Palestinian whose family migrates to Haiti at the end of the nineteenth century—makes manifest religious, racial, and cultural tolerance. This matrimony shows to a greater extent his adoption of a plurality of memories and identities as it gives way to Ruben's meditation on migratory movements from around the world. Thus, he tells his story to honor "millions of refugees, who even today roam desert, forest, and oceans seeking a land of refuge" (Dalembert, 201). This brings forth Dalembert's dedication of his novel to past and present refugees (11). Thus, students have a chance to reflect on the status of refugees seeking political asylum and the repercussions of mass migrations.

Reading *Avant que les ombres*, students learn to notice the rhetorical and creative choices a novelist inevitably makes. Dalembert builds intrigue around Haitian anthropologist Anténor Firmin's essay *De l'Égalité des races humaines* [*On the Equality of Human Races*] published in Paris in 1885.[12] The novelist imagines an impact of Firmin's book on the lives of the Schwarzberg-Livni family. Ruben and his sister reached proficiency level at reading (in French). This book, then, becomes a new foundational text for that Jewish family in addition to the Torah. *De l'Égalité* teaches them the equality of all races and religions, as well as an awareness of the diversity of the world. Indeed, *De l'Égalité* prepares the protagonists to face anti-Semitic behavior and gives them the necessary critical tools to refute the pseudo-scientific racism and religious intolerance of the Nazis. In the same fashion, the essay *Ainsi parla l'oncle* [*The Uncle's Tales*] by Haitian anthropologist Jean Price-Mars increasingly introduces Ruben to Haitian culture. Students can further fathom the complex intertextuality of Dalembert's novel achieved by integrating quotes from various French and Haitian writers. In the end, Dalembert not only depicts acts of tolerance and inclusivity but also speaks to the importance of literature and knowing a foreign language to cultivate diversity.

Students learn to recognize the polyphony of literary work through the author's diverse exploration of languages. The characters' utilization of Hebrew, German, English, Yiddish, French, and Haitian Creole may give way to a critical discussion about languages. Moreover, teaching students to take account of Dalembert's use of irony encourages them to grasp the richness of his work. Several examples can prove that point, including when a French policeman denied Ruben the fundamental right of a prisoner to make a phone call as he notes that France is the country of human rights. In addition, the Haitian oath of naturalization requires the naturalized person to be monogamous but a few pages later the narrator points out that compulsive male seduction is a national sport. The same incongruity is present when a Haitian calls Ruben, (a Jew) a "*Chrétien-vivant*" (literally a living Christian, which is another Haitian universalism for a human being) (Dalembert, 170). Beyond the ironic tone, this example presents the coexistence of conflicting realities and how the Creole meaning emerges in the French utterance and creates polyphony at the level of the word itself. An appraisal of these writing choices helps students to understand how the craft of language further inscribes the text in the realm of fiction at the same time that it grants the narrative its legitimacy.

Contrasting Alexis and Dalembert, students learn that, paradoxically, while the Haitian state showed tolerance toward foreigners, it did not extend the same protection to its native citizens during the anti-superstition campaign. Hence, in the Haitian context, the concepts of inclusivity, diversity, and tolerance do not refer to a set of well-honed practices but rather evoke an ideal. Besides, in *Les Arbres*, Alexis describes interracial relationships as a battle among all, whereas Dalembert emphasizes the founding of a new fraternity based on recognizing the humanity of the other and ethical responsibility toward the foreigner. Afterward, Ruben's ability—to negotiate and navigate between religious traditions such as Talmudic, Christian, and Vodou—makes explicit the need for their pacific coexistence. In Dalembert's writing, tolerance becomes the capacity to embrace religious, linguistic, and cultural proliferation.

Learning about tolerance and inclusivity enables students to explore topics that influence their lives. They can recognize biases, confront injustice, and critically examine race, identity, and diversity. They analyze the interpenetration of these constructs to grasp the subtleties of oppression. Reading fiction gives students the means to critique social institutions and the distribution of power to achieve self-understanding and to envision other possible worlds. Through critical reading and writing, students decipher the structure of a text or an idea to make relevant connections with other cultural productions while incorporating their findings within a broader context. They also perform tolerant behavior by modeling broad-mindedness and respect while discussing these difficult topics and collaborating with their peers from diverse backgrounds. Students will transfer these skills into real life situations, be it the workplace or the world at large. In conclusion, working on texts that incorporate inclusivity empowers them to better interact with others and build a more "just world." In that sense, tolerance resembles the ethical injunction of a good life lived with and for others.

## Notes

1 According to Ricœur: "narrative already belongs to the ethical field in virtue of its claim—inseparable from its narration—to ethical justice" (*Time and Narrative III*, 249).

2 The anti-superstition campaign equally contributes to the erasure of Haitian history since the ritual objects destroyed are mostly artifacts from colonial and pre-Colombian eras.
3 Le peuple haïtien "a été livré au caprice d'étrangers sectaires, infatués de la supériorité occidentale au point de vouloir imposer leur 'civilisation' aux gens qui n'en veulent pas" (Alexis, cited in Souffrant, 219). All translation of quotes from Alexis, Dalembert, and Ricœur's two articles into English are mine.
4 "Les voix de dizaines de milliers d'êtres humains outragés, foulés au pieds, violentés, parce que nègres, misérables, illettrés, abandonnés par la justice officielle et par l'État de leur pays" (Alexis, cited in Souffrant, 219).
5 "[L]'homme véritable doit être prêt à mourir, s'il le faut, pour défendre le droit de son semblable à professer des opinions contraires aux siennes … C'est ce que j'appelle la fraternité et que vous appelez, je crois l'Amour, cet esprit de tolérance, de respect mutuel et de compréhension" (Alexis, cited in Souffrant, 215).
6 "On admettait confusément qu'on ne pouvait s'opposer violemment à un gouvernement, aussi corrompu fût-il, alors qu'il s'était engagé dans la grande croisade antihitlérienne dont l'issue était décisive pour la liberté dans le monde" (Alexis, *Les Arbres*, 158).
7 "Qui suis-je?" (Ricœur, "Étranger," 97).
8 "L'acte d'habiter est un acte de partage de la terre qui est hasardeux, qui est fortuit. Il n'y a aucune nécessité à être 'ici'" (Ricœur, "Étranger," 98).
9 Quoting E. Kant in his *Projet de paix perpétuelle*, [*Perpetual Peace: A Philosophical Sketch*]. Ricœur affirms that hospitality is the right of the foreigner based on the common possession of the earth by all humans (Ricœur, "Étranger," 98).
10 Schwarzberg is representative of the hundreds of Jews from Austria, Poland, Belgium, and Germany who benefitted from the Haitian naturalization decree and immigrated to Haiti in 1937. For this little-known history, see www.franceinter.fr/histoire/juifs-et-haitiens-une-histoire-oubliee.
11 "Le Juif et ses comparses noirs, c'était tout ce que le petit caporal abhorrait, et il avait tenu à les associer dans les lois de Nuremberg" (Dalembert, 150).
12 *De l'Égalité des races humaines* is a response to Arthur de Gobineau's *Essai sur l'Inégalité des races humaines* [*An Essay on the Inequality of the Human Races*].

## References

Abel, Olivier. "Du sujet lecteur au sujet éthique." *Revue Internationale de philosophie*, vol. 225, no. 3, 2003, pp. 369–385.
Adams, Maurianne et al., editors. *Teaching for Diversity and Social Justice*. Routledge, 2007.
Alexis, Jacques Stephen. *Les Arbres musiciens* [*The Musician Trees*]. Gallimard, 1957.
—. "Du réalisme merveilleux des Haïtiens." *Présence Africaine*, vol. 165–166, no. 1, [1956] 2002, pp. 91–112.
Dalembert, Louis-Philippe. *Avant que les ombres s'effacent* [*Until the Shadows Flee*]. Edited by Sabine Wespieser, 2020.
Dash, J. Michael. *Literature and Ideology in Haiti, 1915–1961*. Springer, 1995.
—. *Haiti and the United States: National Stereotypes and the Literary Imagination*. Palgrave, 1997.
Fanon, Frantz. *Peau noire, masques blancs*. Seuil, 1981. [*Black Skin, White Masks*. Translated by Richard Philcox, Grove Press, 2008].
Firmin, Anténor. *De l'égalité des races humaines: anthropologie positive* [*On the Equality of Human Races: A Positive Anthropology*]. Librairie Cotillon, 1885.
Glissant, Édouard. *Le discours antillais*. Seuil, 1981. [*Caribbean Discourse: Selected Essays*. Translated by Michael Dash, U of Virginia P, 1992].

de Gobineau, Joseph-Arthur. *Essai sur l'inégalité des races humaines*. Kinoscript, 2012. [*An Essay on the Inequality of the Human Races*. Translated by Adrian Collins, Heinemann, 2020].

Heady, Margaret. *Marvelous Journeys: Routes of Identity in the Caribbean Novel*. Peter Lang, 2008.

Kant, Emmanuel. *Projet de paix perpétuelle*. 1795. Translated by Jean-Jacques Barrère and Christian Roche. Nathan, 2010. [*To Perpetual Peace: A Philosophical Sketch*. Translated by Ted Humpfrey, Hackett Publishing Company, 2003].

Newman, Scott. "From Marvelous Realism to World Literature: Rethinking the Human with Jacques Stephen Alexis." *Francosphères*, vol. 8, no. 1, 2019, pp. 1–21.

Price-Mars, Jean. *Ainsi parla l'oncle: Essais d'ethnographie [The Uncle's Tales]*. Parapsychology Foundation, 1954.

Ricœur, Paul. *Temps et récit*, III. Seuil, 1985.

—. *Du texte à l'action: Essais d'herméneutique, II*. Seuil, 1986. [*From Text to Action: Essays in Hermeneutics, II*. Translated by Kathleen Blamey. Northwestern UP, 2008].

—. *Time and Narrative III*. Translated by Kathleen Blamey, U of Chicago P, 1988.

—. *Soi-même comme un autre*. Seuil, 1990. [*Oneself as Another*. Translated by Kathleen Blamey, U of Chicago P, 1992].

—. *Le Juste*. Esprit, 1995. [*Reflections on the Just*. Translated by David Pellauer, U of Chicago P, 2007].

—. "Étranger, moi-même." [A Foreigner Myself]. *Semaines Sociales-L'immigration, défis et richesses*, 1997, pp. 93–106. www.ssf-fr.org/articles/54123-etranger-moi-meme.

—. "La condition d'étranger." ["Being a Foreigner"]. *Esprit*, March/April, no. 3, 2006, pp. 264–275.

Rohden, Luiz. "Ethical Assumptions and Implications of Hermeneutic Practice as Practical Wisdom." *Ricœur Studies/Etudes Ricœuriennes*, vol. 10, no. 2, 2019, pp. 5–20.

Souffrant, Claude. *Une négritude socialiste: Religion et développement chez J. Roumain, J. S. Alexis et L. Hughes*. L'Harmattan, 1978.

Svinicki, Marilla and Wilbert McKeachie. *McKeachie's Teaching Tips*. Cengage Learning, 2014.

Trouillot, Michel-Rolph. *Silencing the Past: Power and the Production of History*. Beacon P, 1995.

# 16
# INTRODUCING DIVERSITY INTO THE GRADUATE CLASSROOM

## Teaching Jewish Francophone Writers

*Nancy M. Arenberg*

In large research universities across the nation, there is a current trend to interpolate diversity into departmental strategic plans, hiring initiatives, and, above all, into the myriad of courses offered to both undergraduate and graduate students. One of the most daunting challenges, however, is to develop courses that will spark our students' interest in literature, while designing the class to align with recent university objectives, promoting diversity and inclusion as curricular components. In the last two years, I have contributed to the University of Arkansas's diversity and inclusion initiative by creating a new literature course for our MA students. *Jewish Francophone Writers* introduces students to a variety of Jewish writers from the French-speaking world. The underpinnings of this seminar focus on incorporating issues of ethnicity, compassion, and cultural hybridity into a survey of Francophone Jewish minority writers. As an effective method to present this literature, a multifaceted approach is useful to delve into the complexity of historical, cultural, and socio-political issues that permeate these various literary texts. It is also beneficial to expose students to some current theories on the Jewish Diaspora and Jewish "otherness" to enable them to interpret these works in a meaningful, insightful way.

The chapter focuses on how teachers can expand either their contemporary French literature classes or their Francophone literature courses to integrate underrepresented authors into their curricula, with the overarching objective of creating global citizens in their French programs. The pedagogical purpose of implementing a diversity course is to broaden students' existing knowledge of current issues such as gender, racism, and identity that they have encountered in more traditional works (across the humanities), while inviting them to discover intersections of similarity with regard to ethnicity and intolerance. In addition, it is important to generate student awareness and sensitivity to the plight of an overlooked, neglected group in

DOI: 10.4324/9781003126461-17

literature—French-speaking Jews. On a general level, this idea of awareness is also part of the mission of the humanities, an integral part of every student's educational experience. As Eric Touya de Marenne notes, "Individual and societal change can happen through critical thinking and critical awareness—a potential to connect the text with the world" (16). Touya de Marenne also emphasizes the value of exposing students to studying difference and otherness in a multifaceted way. As will be shown, these aspects frequently appear in the texts of Jewish minority writers and tend to concentrate, to some extent, on the authors' life experiences.

There are many noteworthy benefits associated with the creation of diversity and inclusion courses. In many universities, these classes serve to fulfill key learning outcomes such as the promotion of intercultural competence, increased synthesis of a wide range of material, and a heightened awareness of globalization. For graduate students, diversity classes focus on developing critical and analytical skills, which they achieve by a close study of selected texts by Jewish authors. As an organizational tool to examine the various readings, an interdisciplinary approach is an efficacious way to ensure an extensive analysis of these contemporary works. Ivanitskaya, Clark, Montgomery, and Primeau provide insight on the value of an interdisciplinary method: "To a higher degree than traditional single topic approaches, interdisciplinary learning fosters a problem-focused integration of influence consistent with more complex knowledge structures" (100). To apply this to a course devoted to minority Jewish writers, the idea of "complex knowledge structures" refers to the plurality of areas within the humanities that are germane to the comprehension of these texts. In other words, these literary productions cannot be read without delving into the historical and sociopolitical contexts in which they are situated. Most importantly, it is through this interdisciplinary approach that graduate students can amplify their interpretation by deploying a comparative strategy, enabling them to make contrasts and comparisons between the works to identify intertextual connections.

To study the rich tapestry of voices associated with Jewish minority literature, it is important to establish a classroom atmosphere in which everyone can freely express their ideas, with tolerance and respect towards the opinions of others. Melissa Morgan Consoli and Patricia Marin support the use of peer interactions to ensure the sharing of a variety of perspectives (150). In my classroom, I tend to maintain an open, informal atmosphere, which is conducive to creating a dialogue between myself and the students. To engender dialogue, I often post a short list of more complex questions, an assignment that enables the students to delve more deeply into the text. In this way, they can more readily engage in shared interpretations and impressions of the selected work. For variety, this activity can also be adapted into a discussion board format (via Blackboard) to create more student interaction. In the classroom setting, the students can then react to the posts of their peers to continue the conversation, an activity that engages each student in the ongoing dialogue. As many MA classes are small, individual oral presentations are also effective in eliciting reactions and opinions from others, while ensuring that the conversation is not teacher focused. For example, I ask the students to choose one critical article to apply to their analysis of one of the selected works to sharpen and develop their critical thinking skills. I often ask my students to end their oral presentations with a question for the group to foster additional discussion based on the exposition that they have shared with the class. Students can more fully develop these presentations in their final analytical essay, focusing on a selected work and topic of their choice.

As far as the general organizational format, it is not essential to structure the course chronologically, however, the syllabus can easily be divided between French works and Francophone texts. The latter organization permits students to trace the evolution of seminal Jewish themes such as identity, exile, and nomadism, all of which are related to the Jewish condition. To begin, it is useful to point out the importance of the Dreyfus Affair (1894–1906), as it provides a historical context for subsequent representations of the Jew in literature. Moreover, the scandal surrounding the Dreyfus Affair in France underscores the key problem of anti-Semitism, which has plagued Jews for centuries. This historical controversy also sets the stage for the first reading, which is Sartre's *Réflexions sur la question juive* [*Anti-Semite and Jew*], an essay in which anti-Semitism is at the core of his argument. Here, Sartre also studies the socio-political problem of Jewish exclusion from French society. In terms of race and ethnicity, Sartre underlines the "otherness" of the Jew, proclaiming the Jew a misfit in society, an absent being that has no country or history (111, 118). For Sartre, it is seemingly impossible for the Jew to assimilate in French society, which amplifies his view of the Jew as an intruder or an outcast from the societal perspective of the anti-Semite. Although Sartre's essay is dense and, at times, challenging for the students, the discussions of the reading can become more active by selecting a series of his statements on anti-Semitism and then asking the students to react to these remarks. The professor can conduct this activity on Blackboard by setting it up as a discussion board in which statements elicit student responses, which the professor later shares anonymously. To illustrate this idea, an effective example of a reaction statement is Sartre's concluding idea in which he proposes a radical solution, a socialist revolution, to end anti-Semitism in France.

After reading Sartre's essay, the second text, also non-fictional, is grounded in some of the same areas, mainly politics and sociology. Albert Memmi reprises some of Sartre's main topics but approaches these questions from an authentic Jewish perspective, one that is particularly effective as a minority writer from North Africa. Memmi, a Tunisian Jew, published *Portrait d'un juif* [*Portrait of a Jew*] in 1962. This text can be characterized as a hybrid work because it is, in part, theoretical, sociological, historical, and cultural. Here, the author not only studies anti-Semitism, also from a socio-political angle, but further/also delves into some key Jewish problems such as oppression, racism, difference, and identity. As the students begin to identify similarities and contrasts between these two theoretical works, it is important to underscore that Memmi examines anti-Semitism in a different way. In contrast to Sartre, he looks at it as widespread hostility directed at Jews, thus widening the scope from Sartre's focus on anti-Semitism in French society. Above all, Memmi takes a stance, condemning anti-Semitism as a universal form of oppression (53). It is the theme of oppression that provides the structural framework for *Portrait of a Jew* and is explored (quite often) from an autobiographical position. Within the body of the text, Memmi does, however, deviate from his own life experiences to examine the collective aspects of oppression, a fundamental crisis linked to the Jewish condition. At the same time, he compares Jewish oppression to, as he phrases it, *le malheur* (misfortune) of other minority groups, mainly colonized 'victims' like North Africans and West Africans (29). As shown in Sartre's essay, Memmi also integrates politics into his argument, emphasizing the marginalization of the Jew. For Memmi, the Jew is depicted as an invisible figure, as he is not recognized politically, thus is also hindered from participating in politics (268). In another noteworthy section of the text, Memmi studies the mythical representation of the Jew in which he examines certain biological characteristics of the Jewish people. Once again, he emphasizes that the representation of the Jew is constructed by socially imposed images of the Jew, which are predominantly negative, smacking of overt racism and intolerance. At the same time, he formulates an original term by stating that he studies *la judéité* or Jewishness, a concept linked to the quest to define his own identity. Here again, an interdisciplinary approach is useful in reading and discussing this work, as Memmi historically traces the problems of persecution and hatred toward the Jews, issues which hark back to the biblical plight of the chosen people. In any event, this initial study of Sartre's and Memmi's theoretical texts provides a framework in which the instructor can situate the subsequent postmodern readings.

To transition into the literary domain, the socio-political aspect of Sartre's and Memmi's theoretical works resurfaces, but the textual emphasis is shifted to the historical context of World War II. Patrick Modiano's *Dora Bruder* can be characterized as a hybrid work, fusing autobiography, fiction, and the detective novel, while rejecting the use of chronological narration. In fact, there is a constant alternating movement between the past and the present, facilitating the study of presence and absence as it relates to the complex question of Jewish identity. For the Bruders, this means hiding to escape deportation. Interestingly, Dora Bruder was an actual teenage girl who disappeared from a boarding school in Paris, where she was hidden during the Occupation. In 1985, the narrator inadvertently discovers her story in a 1941 issue of the newspaper *Paris Soir*, and, in turn, becomes obsessed by her disturbing disappearance. Through the unfolding events, the reader follows the narrator's search for traces of Dora Bruder, as he tries to reconstruct the pieces of her life, aided by some photos, and, in so doing, he attempts to give presence to this enigmatic figure. Most of all, the fact that Dora went missing alludes to the haunting absence associated with the Holocaust. It is Modiano's blend of history and fiction that enables the instructor to present the text from an interdisciplinary angle, while directing the students' focus to the hardship of life for French Jews during the Occupation.

Modiano's emphasis on the Occupation period provides an authentic context, one which creates a bridge to cross into Simone Veil's *Une jeunesse au temps de la Shoah: Extraits d'une vie*, [*Childhood during the Shoah: Excerpts of a Life*]. This text is the abridged version of Veil's lengthy autobiographical work, *Une vie* [*A Life*], which documented not only her imprisonment in the death camps but her extraordinary life experiences in public service. To retrace some of the key biographical events of Veil's life, she was deported from France in 1944 to Auschwitz-Birkenau with her sister and mother; she remained there until the camp was liberated by the British in 1945. She, in turn, was repatriated to France with her sister but suffered the loss of her beloved mother, who died in the camps. To chart her personal experiences, steeped in tragedy, the author follows a chronological trajectory by dividing the text into four cohesive sections: The Occupation, deportation, imprisonment at Auschwitz-Birkenau, and the postwar period.

As Veil's memoir provides the students with an example of a different genre, it is important to avoid categorizing the work as merely another historical documentation of the unconscionable events of the Holocaust. To widen the lens, the instructor can direct the students' focus to Veil's form of life writing by pointing out that she engages in the act of testimonial writing. From the opening pages of the text, the author, as a survivor, positions herself as a witness who wishes to share her painful life experiences with subsequent generations. In her role as a witness, Veil feels it is her social responsibility to relive her personal tragedy by transcribing her experiences into words on the page, thereby creating visible proof that she survived to tell her story to future generations. Above all, Veil envisioned her work as a pedagogical tool for her audience, with the intention of sparking global awareness of the Shoah. As an introduction to reading Veil's testimonial narrative, it is worthwhile to inquire if the students have read other Holocaust narratives. Since my university is located in the southern US, I was surprised to learn that some of the students, who come from rural areas of the state, had read *Night* by Elie Wiesel, which allowed them to compare the texts to develop a deeper understanding of Veil's account. To delve more into the nuances of testimonial writing, it is beneficial to propose some critical sources for supplementary reading. For example, the instructor can direct the students to Shoshana Felman's and Dori Laub's theories on testimonial writing and Wiesel's perspectives on witnessing, with emphasis on the importance of 'speaking up.'[1]

In studying Veil's memoir, it is important to expand the interdisciplinary angle of the previous works, which emphasized history and politics, to highlight the significance of gender roles in the narrative. The best example of this is situated in one of the main chapters of the text, *L'enfer* [*Hell*], which deals explicitly with internment at Auschwitz-Birkenau. Veil's recollection of her daily struggle to stay alive in the camps underscores the value of creating affective bonds with other women as a fundamental survival strategy. In fact, female solidarity in the blocks may have motivated women to live longer.[2] This interesting study of gender issues seeps into other layers of the narrative, most of which relate to the overarching theme of Jewish identity. Here, the instructor can bring Memmi and Sartre back into the discussion to point out that the "otherness" of the Jew is addressed from a woman's point of view. In sharp contrast to Sartre's and Memmi's theoretical positions, Veil recounts her experiences with intolerance, racism, and anti-Semitism in a highly personal way. In the concluding part of the text, she describes harsh encounters with her fellow French citizens who were overtly disinterested in the suffering of the former deportees. They treated the victims of the war as the "other," thus making it impossible for the returned to re-integrate into French society. With these recollections, Veil takes on a supplementary role as a socio-political spokeswoman, which is particularly evident in the final chapter of her text. She interpolates various political commentaries directed at the French government, one of which is her condemnation of the collaboration between the Vichy regime and the Nazis. With this reference, Veil reminds her French readers that the Vichy regime should not be absolved of their crimes. As shown here, the study of Veil's testimonial narrative plays a key role in fulfilling one of the main outcomes of a diversity and inclusion course—the expansion of the students' knowledge, in this case, of the Shoah. It is also important to read a Holocaust narrative in a certain way. On an ethical level, Elaine Scarry suggests that students study texts in the humanities with sympathy, compassion, and empathy (11). Moreover, if graduate students approach testimonial narratives with Scarry's reading strategies in mind, then they are more apt to achieve the objective of becoming global citizens of the world. For graduate students, this goal is obtained by raising their awareness and sensitivity to the tragedy of genocide and the isolation of "otherness," as shown in Veil's Holocaust memoir.

By the middle part of the semester, the students begin to explore more contemporary works, which can be read from a Jewish cultural perspective. The first fictional text is composed by a young, prolific writer, Eliette Abécassis, a descendant of Moroccan-Jewish roots. In her highly successful novel, *La Répudiée* [*Sacred*], the author invites the reader to discover the mysterious, hermetic world of Hasidic Jews, residing in the holy city of Jerusalem. Since this will be uncharted territory for most students, it is necessary to provide a brief explanation of Orthodox Judaism, with emphasis on Hasidic practices and customs. Within this insulated, highly conservative community, Abécassis focuses on the plight of Nathan and Rachel, a young couple struggling with the problem of infertility that threatens to destroy their marriage. To better understand this crisis, it is worthwhile to incorporate some critical sources on gender roles for men and women in Hasidic communities, including a discussion of Hasidic attitudes towards sexuality (Pitchon, 2017) I assign Eduardo Pitchon for this purpose. In general, graduate students find it interesting to examine the differences in gender roles between men and women, in this case, relegating Hasidic women, for the most part, to a domestic function. As noted above, these supplementary cultural sources constitute a new dimension of interdisciplinary approaches to enhance the students' interpretation of the text. Moreover, a Judeo-cultural discussion enables the class to understand the pressure for the protagonist to bear children, a divine duty for Hasidic wives. As the narrative unfolds, the students discover another manifestation of "otherness," as Rachel is repudiated as a wife because she cannot reproduce. To delve more closely into this critical question of "otherness," it is worthwhile to foster a comparative discussion, revolving around differences and similarities seen in Memmi's ideology of this conception. Once again, the instructor should encourage the group to make connections or to identify junctures of differences, which are inherently linked to the question of gender roles. In the concluding discussion, it is essential to examine Rachel's exclusion from the community and her marriage, as she is represented as a woman without a space or a place, a perpetual wanderer.

The theme of nomadism creates a fluid transition into Chochana Boukhobza's fictional work, *Un été à Jérusalem* [A Summer in Jerusalem]. Boukhobza is a Tunisian-Jewish author but identifies as an Israeli writer (she emigrated there at the age of seventeen). At the core of the narrative events, the unnamed protagonist (also the narrator) comes to Jerusalem from Paris to visit her family in 1983—a year after Israel's invasion of Lebanon. To trace the protagonist's trajectory, she lived in Israel three years prior to the family's arrival, but she became increasingly unhappy with Israeli politics and, in turn, decided to go back to France. When she returns to Israel for a summer visit, she is forced to grapple with her "otherness" amidst this climate of widespread violence in the region. The narrator's ongoing crisis of exile is defined by her sense of estrangement from her family, her religion, and the nation of Israel. As the narrative unfolds, the reader observes that the narrator launches a revolt against many cultural norms, including resisting the observance of mourning rituals for her beloved grandmother. As a backdrop, her parents are migrants from Tunisia; they are devout Jews who follow many customs grounded in North African Jewish traditions. The narrator, however, sets herself apart from her family by rejecting these cultural and religious practices; thus she is viewed as an "outsider." Since this novel is rooted in the Maghreb, a familiar area for previous Francophone readings, the instructor can invite the students to build on their knowledge of cultural hybridity, pertaining to the crisis of identity. Most importantly, the analysis of Boukhobza's work enables the students to compare and contrast key Jewish questions such as "otherness," wandering, exile, and intolerance, evoking the Jewish Diaspora. It is also interesting to return to the topic of space and place by discussing the image of the sacred city of Jerusalem. As the class will no doubt observe, Boukhobza depicts Jerusalem as a space of freedom for her protagonist, thus revealing a sharp contrast to Abécassis's cloistered representation of the old city in which Rachel is portrayed as a prisoner of the patriarchal order.

The overarching theme of nomadic peregrinations also reappears in Colette Fellous's *Aujourd'hui* [Today]. Like Boukhobza, she, too, is a writer of Jewish-Tunisian descent but emigrated at a young age to France. Although this work can be categorized as an autofiction, it can also be described as a visual collage, one that incorporates fragments of songs, art reproductions, photographs, and prose. At the locus of the work, the author explores her own cultural identity and Jewishness by revisiting her past in her native country, Tunisia. As seen in previous Jewish minority texts, she also examines exile, racism, and disenfranchisement, core elements within the fabric of this vibrant narrative. To initially present *Aujourd'hui* [Today], it is useful to underscore the importance of 1967 for Fellous, as this explosive period of the Six-Day War in Israel trickled into the Maghreb, creating tensions between Arabs and Jews in Tunisia. For these two ethnic groups, it also changed their harmonious way of co-existing together in Tunis as neighbors. For Fellous, this war is the catalyst that produces a sudden historical awareness of her "otherness" as a Jew living in a predominantly Arab country. Like other writers the students have read, this profound sense of difference, which harks back to Memmi, also vividly recalls the original Jewish condition—the Diaspora. In any case, Fellous's work adds a postmodern viewpoint to the common themes seen in other texts, mainly exclusion and intolerance.

The final text in the course sustains the focus on wandering but offers a different perspective and unique structural form. Monique Bosco's *La Femme de Loth* [*Lot's Wife*] introduces the group to a migrant Jewish text, as the author was born in Austria but was raised in France, and later emigrated to Montreal in 1948. As seen in Fellous's work, this novel is not structured chronologically; it is presented as a series of fragments that are numbered to create a sense of cohesion. In any case, the instructor can connect this work to the preceding novels by underscoring the overarching themes of diasporic meanderings, alienation, and exile. At the nexus of the narrative, Bosco creates a simple plot in which Hélène is abandoned by her lover, Pierre, after a lengthy affair, a traumatic loss that she is unable to forget. In the aftermath of the relationship, the narrator decides to compose a novel about her misfortune, while contemplating her suicide. To broaden the perspective on her loss, the protagonist identifies with the plight of many biblical figures found in the Book of Genesis. In studying Hélène's predicament, the students gain access to the biblical intertext within the narrative, a technique that highlights the signature style of the author. Most importantly, Bosco interpolates the biblical archetypes of Adam and Eve, the suffering of Job, the betrayal of Judas, and, above all, the story of Lot's wife to articulate the gravity of Hélène's loss. With this text, the students have the opportunity to not only make intertextual connections with the previous novels, penned by Francophone women, but can fulfill one of the main objectives of a diversity and inclusion course—an increased awareness of interculturalism.

As noted, the creation of a diversity course devoted to teaching underrepresented Jewish writers from the French-speaking world enables instructors to achieve their outcome—to produce global citizens of the world. In a graduate course, this concept of global citizenship is contingent on sensitizing students to current socio-political problems revolving around exclusion, immigration, displacement, and Jewish "otherness." At the same time, the inclusion of this type of literary course enhances our graduate students' overall knowledge and exposure to contemporary works, providing them with the tools to navigate in the world with a better understanding of cultural differences among diverse ethnic groups. Above all, the students benefit from a deeper cultural awareness of minority works, while ensuring the development of their intercultural knowledge of an absent voice, one which deserves to be heard—that of the silent Jew.

## Notes

1 Elie Wiesel discusses the importance of testimony with Henry Cargas.
2 See Hutton for details on women's relationships in the death camps.

## References

Abécassis, Eliette. *La Répudiée*. Livre de Poche, 2001. [*Sacred*. Aurora Metro Books, 2017].
Bosco, Monique. *La Femme de Loth*. BQ, 2003. [*Lot's Wife*. McClelland and Stewart, 1975].
Boukhobza, Chochana. *Un été à Jérusalem*. Points, 1988.
Cargas, Henry. *Conversations avec Elie Wiesel*. Justice Books, 1992.
Consoli, Melissa and Patricia Marin. "Teaching Diversity in the Graduate Classroom: The Instructor, the Students, the Classroom, or All of the Above?" *Journal of Diversity in Higher Education*, vol. 9, no. 2, 2016, pp. 143–157.
Fellous, Colette. *Aujourd'hui*. Folio, 2006.
Felman, Shoshana and Dori Laub. *Testimony: Crises of Witnessing in Literature, Psychoanalysis, and History*. Routledge, 1992.
Hutton, Margaret-Anne. "Female Identities in the Nazi Camps: French Deportees' Testimonial Accounts of the 1990s." *Romance Studies*, vol. 20, no. 1, 2002, pp. 55–64.
Ivanitskaya, Lana, et al. "Interdisciplinary Learning: Process and Outcomes." *Innovative Higher Education*, vol. 27, no. 2, 2002, pp. 95–111.
Memmi, Albert. *Portrait d'un juif*. Gallimard, 1962. [*Portrait of a Jew*. Orion, 1962].
Modiano, Patrick. *Dora Bruder*. Folio, 1997. [*Dora Bruder*. University of CA Press, 1999].
Pitchon, Eduardo. "Hasidic Attitudes Towards Sexuality." *Jewish Explorations of Sexuality*, edited by Jonathan Magonet. Berghahn Books, 1995, pp. 205–211.
Sartre, Jean-Paul. *Réflexions sur la question juive*. Folio, 1954. [*Anti-Semite and Jew*. Grove Press, 1962].
Scarry, Elaine. "Poetry, Injury and the Ethics of Reading." *The Humanities and Public Life*, edited by Peter Brooks. Fordham UP, 2014, pp. 41–48.
Touya de Marenne, Eric. *The Case for the Humanities: Pedagogy, Polity, Interdisciplinarity*. Rowman & Littlefield, 2016.
Veil, Simone. *Une jeunesse au temps de la Shoah: Extraits d'une vie*. Livre de Poche, 2010. [*A Life: A Memoir by Simone Veil*. Haus, 2009].

# 17
# PROMOTING MUTUAL UNDERSTANDING AND INCLUSION IN THE FRENCH CLASSROOM THROUGH FRENCH, ISRAELI, AND POLISH POST-HOLOCAUST LIFE WRITING

*E. Nicole Meyer*

> "A different language is a different vision of life."
>
> Federico Fellini

In an era of heightened misinformation, where ignorance and/or refusal to sift through fact and fiction can result in death from the coronavirus (COVID-19) or a simple neighborhood jog may prove fatal, our mission as teachers becomes all the more urgent. At institutions of higher learning and throughout society, anti-Semitism bubbles beneath speech resembling all too closely that of Hitler's rhetoric of the 1930s. To help students to move beyond stereotypes and the hate-filled speech of our current world, I created an interdisciplinary course that includes Israeli, Polish, and French narratives (including those of the Holocaust) in order to build mutual understanding.[1] Designed to inform and address an area where students are often misinformed, the course explores memoirs, autobiographical texts, short stories, and poems that voice pain and suffering, thus further providing an entry point to increased empathy. The impetus—and dare I say urgency—of proposing this course, came with a change in location. I am lucky to have a diverse student body, however, I discovered in 2014, when discussing a passage in Nathalie Sarraute's *Enfance* [*Childhood*] (236–37, 209), that the ignorance that this essay seeks to address was rampant. Indeed, when we discussed the aforementioned brief passage where Sarraute's father expresses his pride in being Jewish, I was immediately interrupted with the question "Are you Jewish?" No other author or artist other than those who are Jewish incite conflation between professor and writer. Yet, in every course in which I have taught where the Holocaust or a Jewish author appears, the question soon follows. Another factor in conceptualizing this new course was to pick an "other" who is not represented in our

DOI: 10.4324/9781003126461-18

student body. My hope is to deepen reflection on the complexities of othering and dehumanizing behaviors, to understand the erasure or minimization of our peers, and to comprehend the many conditions we have created that establish certain groups as the majority. Understanding what people experience when unsafe, unacknowledged, isolated, and worse, can help us all to recognize that systemic racism reaches beyond a single group. In so doing, students might enact a commitment to equity and social justice that extends outside the course and beyond their own perceived identity.

Rethinking essential teaching-related questions, such as how to engage students and promote mutual understanding and inclusion in the French curriculum, can help teachers to build French programs despite the challenges that currently face us.[2] In addition to expanding student audiences, such approaches integrate standards applicable to high school and university programs. The course I describe addresses multiple World-Readiness Standards, especially those of intercultural connections and comparisons.[3] Students can better understand distinctive viewpoints and cultural comparisons between language and especially culture through a course or unit(s) addressing issues of race, ethnicity, and gender in Israel and in France.

This chapter addresses the following three questions: 1) How can I engage students and promote mutual understanding and compassion through reading the experiences of others from places and backgrounds they have never experienced? 2) How do I expand our student audiences, attracting openly diverse students, thus building a more inclusive community? 3) What advice based on my course do I wish to share with you? In addition, it is my intention that such a course presents ways of articulating transferable skills to our ever-practical students, administrators, and fellow teachers.[4]

## Increasing Mutual Understanding

How does my "Reading across the Boundaries: Israeli and French Women's Autobiography" course featuring Israeli, Polish, and French post-Holocaust life writing contribute to the goals of increasing mutual understanding and empathy? The course introduces two Israeli autobiographical narratives, two Polish short stories, French post-Holocaust life writing, and two film adaptations, along with exercises and approaches designed to help students to better understand the dynamic complex relationship between culture, gender, and literary production. The course addresses language, identity, gender, geography, borders, exile and migration, homeland, and memory.[5] Historical and personal narratives naturally intertwine under these circumstances. Thus, on the first day of the course, we question "why autobiography?," "why women and gender considerations?," "why Israel?," "why French?," and "why post-1950 texts?" More questions and more answers follow during the semester.

Family and its traditions figure strongly throughout the course, as they do (whether directly or indirectly) in my students' own experiences. The different dynamics of Golda Meir's and Amos Oz's families, owing in part to generational differences and in part to religious and geographical considerations, provide a great beginning point to address any student preconceptions of how the other should be more like them. In order to progress from Andrew W. Ibrahim's "Fear Zone" where one avoids hard questions and talking to others who "think or look differently than me" to the "Learning Zone," where the student seeks out uncomfortable questions, becomes vulnerable about their own biases, and "listens" to those who think, look, and act differently, some background knowledge proves essential. Thus, the next task is to dive into historical background, including Carol Troen's brief overview of important dates and crucial events in Israel (422–23). A discussion of the students' own definitions of nationalism, as well as how Israelis view the concept, follows. Similarly to Lowry Martin's course described earlier in this volume, geographic maps combined with visual graphs of demographic information help students to visualize complex issues (peace, war, settlements) that concern Israel.[6] Readings and discussions reference the changing map of Israel as it became a country, the subsequent changes resulting from various wars, and the charts which reveal patterns over time of immigration of Jews and of non-Jews into the country. In addition, the Holocaust must be introduced and discussed before diving into the course, especially given its pivotal role in decisions abroad (in Great Britain, the United States, and Europe) which in turn encouraged the arrival of so many on the shores of tiny Palestine/Israel (pre- or post-1948). Carefully chosen excerpts of Golda Meir's *My Life*, supplemented by photos from "Picturing Golda Meir" and the rich archive at University of Wisconsin-Milwaukee enrich students' understanding of both events and the difficulties of establishing the State of Israel, as well as those of displacement due to being Jewish. Born in Kiev in 1898, displacement began early for Meir. Her parents, her beloved sister, and she reunited again in Milwaukee, Wisconsin in 1905. In 1921 the then married Meir, a committed Labor Zionist, joined a kibbutz in Palestine. Given her integral role in founding Israel, as well as her service as Prime Minister, *My Life*, functions both as personal and historical documentation, much as Rachel Fish describes:

> Personal diaries, letters of correspondence, and intellectual and political prose of individuals involved in the building of the nation-state comprised the first historical narratives for the State of Israel. The individuals who wrote were conscious of their role in history and were determined to document their actions and ideas.
>
> *(550)*

Meir's work thus presents a unique and compelling perspective to understanding the importance of nation building, the complexities of Israel, its relation to world anti-Semitism, and the intertwined narratives of family and nation.[7]

With Amos Oz's *A Tale of Love and Darkness*, we enter into questions of "Darkness and Silence: Mother and Motherland," the second module of the course. Carefully chosen autobiographical extracts complement the excellent film written and directed by and featuring Israeli-born Natalie Portman, which we watch after reading Oz. Discussions and written analysis supported by direct references and examples focus on the work's title, prominent motifs and images, notions of mother, family, and motherland, as well as the deliberate choice to rename oneself (Meir, Oz, and Portman all chose their surname).[8] The latter decision provides fruitful exchanges, as it can be considered in the context of the Nazi-imposed tattoos that dehumanize, strip of name, and violate religious practices of observant Jews. In addition, several students may point back to the renaming of their family upon entering the United States. Intentionally silencing one's own name of origin differs from having another name (or number) externally imposed. Combined with the analysis of the dark events of history, and especially the long-silenced story of Oz's mother's suicide, these distinctions enlighten the students' awareness of the intersectionality of systemic racism.[9] In other words, the notion that the latter reaches beyond one group may be new to some. Kimberlé Crenshaw's famed metaphor of standing in an intersection helps students to visualize the complexity of systemic racism through yet another lens:

> Discrimination, like traffic through an intersection, may flow in one direction, and it may flow in another. If an accident happens in an intersection, it can be caused by cars traveling from any number of directions and, sometimes, from all of them. Similarly, if a Black woman is harmed because she is in the intersection, her injury could result from sex discrimination or race discrimination.
>
> *(149)*

And, as this volume and my course reveals, many others enter into such intersections.

While, as Hanna Yablonka remarks, "mass murder was Germany's 'Final Solution' to the 'Jewish problem'" (1), there were many more victims. The murders included pets, the disabled, those determined by the Nazis to be LGBTQ, political resisters, or intellectuals deemed harmful to the Nazi agenda of purification and supremacy. The last course text provides a salient example of one experience of the Vichy collaboration in deporting such "undesirables" to the camps, many of whom never returned. The author Marguerite Duras recounts her agonizing wait for her husband, arrested along with his sister for being in the French Resistance.[10] In order to better understand multiple perspectives of the Holocaust, however, we turn first to assessing the significance of two autobiographical short stories by Holocaust survivors, both originally from Poland, and post-camp immigrants to Israel, Ida Fink and Sara Nomberg-Przytyk. These oft-displaced Jewish writers wrote multiple compelling stories recounting their concentration camp experience. Fink's "Scrap of Time" and Nomberg-Przytyk's "The Camp Blanket" provide absorbing tales that encourage us to ask questions such as: What questions should we ask? Why do the definitions of words such as Shoah, pogrom, Holocaust, and victim matter? Why are these texts published so many years later? In other words, the role of memory, narrative, and family (and arguably national) trauma are essential to asking good questions, perhaps the most important skill we can teach. "The teaching of the Shoah is first and foremost an action of ongoing soul search, within ourselves and through eternity" writes Abba Kovner. "In such a soul search the answers never appear before the questions" (Yablonka, 2018).

The use of carefully chosen images, concise presentations of each author, short articles such as the *New York Times* obituaries of Oz and Loridan-Ivens, and carefully placed images and quotes on the syllabus function to inspire connections, new questions, and subtly informed entry into the readings.[11] Thus, carefully selected quotes from Kovner, Colette, Carolyn Heilbrun, Sigmund Freud, and others pepper the syllabus. To assess student progress, the second of two exams asks the student to choose a quote from the syllabus that they have not used previously in their short papers. The task of this "Take Home Exam" is to reflect in one to two pages on how the quote relates to what they have learned in the course. The most innovative reflection, so far, resulted from a startling reading of the course through the prism of the following quote from Colette: "Is anyone imagining as he reads me that I'm portraying myself? Have patience, this is merely my model" (33). In order to ask new questions, modeling compelling questions through carefully designed reading, discussion, and essay prompts, the aforementioned techniques, and integration of collaboration throughout this process and course are essential. A frequent technique in my courses is to involve the students in writing exam questions (whether multiple choice, matching, or short essay). Working in small groups, they craft potential questions, select optimal examples which they then write on the classroom whiteboard. The whole class goes through the questions, evaluating whether they are "good" questions (e.g., clearly written, testing what they intended to test), determining point value in each case. The latter is important, as a two-point essay question requires a less complex answer than a ten-point essay question. Thus this task helps students to determine context, purpose, and pathways to success, which are transferable skills. This exercise opens the door to discussing what should be on the exam, and the importance of well-structured written analysis using direct references and examples.

The above-mentioned short stories and Marceline Loridan-Ivens *But You Did Not Come Back* voice the agony of loss (of so many loved ones, of a former sense of self and one's place in the world, of safety, and so much more). Combined with the current era, infused with COVID-19 and Black Lives Matter coming to the forefront of our students' consciousness and shaking them to the core, these readings permit increased empathy both for the loss and for the compelling ways of voicing it. Querying ways of depicting emotion, repeated motifs (darkness, hunger, time, remembering, forgetting) increase student awareness both of the past and of their present. Questions of who is narrating (survivors often carry the burden of the murdered in their task), of authenticity, memory, narrative representation, and recall of those now absent, as well as roles (perpetrator, participant, or collaborator), language (Hebrew, Polish, French), and the added (in)expressibility inherent to any recounting of such trauma, encourage deep reflection and the shifting of perspective. "Holocaust literature encompasses many languages, genres, and perspectives that mediate life and death, survival and memory, during and after the Nazi genocide," writes Sara R. Horowitz (429).

The question of various roles taken during these years, as well as the timing of the voicing of Holocaust trauma is raised by Yablonka, who refers to Yehuda Bauer's categories ("The Development" 1). Arguing that context and time matter, Yablonka delineates the three stages of building the telling of the story: "Information: 1945–1960; Knowledge: 1961–1973; Awareness: 1974–2013" ("The Shoah"). In other words, the cognitive process of understanding such traumatic experience takes time. While some Holocaust writing was immediate, from notes and stories scribbled in hiding, in transport or in the camps themselves, hidden to be found after the writer's imminent death, true awareness of the grand scale of atrocity came much later. In addition, time colors narration of the past in interesting ways. Yablonka offers the *Stanford Encyclopedia of Philosophy*'s definition of memory to better understand the process of remembering and its relation to both the present and to personal identity. "Memory" is the:

> diverse set of cognitive capacities by which we retain information and reconstruct past experiences, usually for present purposes. Memory is one of the most important ways by which our histories animate our current actions and experiences. Most notably, the human ability to conjure up long-gone but specific episodes of our lives is both familiar and puzzling, and is a key aspect of personal identity.
>
> *("Memory")*

One way to reinforce the personal understanding of the complexities of recounting memory is to ask the student to recall a long-ago argument with a sibling or close friend, in which they retold what happened to a parent or adult. The fact that each child retells their own recollection through their own individual prism, and the consulted parent reconstructs their own understanding of the story before meting out consequences, opens up interesting perspectives on the age-old question: What is truth?

## Expanding Inclusion in the Classroom

In addition to the student collaboration woven throughout the course design, the stretching of boundaries through inclusion of non-traditional students proves invaluable. Indeed, an 85-year-old student's response to Kovner's words: "I remember what I can't forget" (Yablonka, "The Shoah"), indelibly colors our understanding of the trauma he voices. This course welcomed five women over 80 years old, two others over the age of 62, and an auditor in her late 50s. In order to build such a diversity of ages and backgrounds, I contacted all of the regional rabbis, and several members of the local Alliance Française, described the course and its goals, and provided the flyer I had designed.[12] One rabbi's commitment to education and to his congregation resulted in many of the non-traditional students' eagerness to apply. No easy task, this involved hours of helping educated elders to complete the required freshman application (I will not describe their reaction to questions about their parents' financial support), provide student transcripts despite the impossibility of doing so through required direct electronic transmission, as universities (and high schools) did not start electronically storing such records back in the day, nor do they see the need to do so for students from that long ago. The knowledge, passion, and stories these women brought to our discussions were priceless, however. They also answered in compassionate fashion the inevitable "Are you Jewish?" question, and occasional unthinkingly anti-Semitic remark. While non-traditional students generally resist the notion of tests and papers, they promptly accepted the invitation to help the traditional students through participation in the collaborative exercises and tests. This collaboration between the traditional and non-traditional student strongly enhanced the learning experience of all involved, including that of the instructor.

## Conclusion: Lessons Learned

The collaborative design of the course combined with the rich selection of post-Holocaust narratives inspires rich questions and an opening of perspective for all involved. Anti-Semitism and ageism are combatted, and mutual respect established. The topics discussed above are in many ways "foreign" to the majority of my students raised in this predominantly (60%) African-American area. Thus, our traditional students can look at questions from new perspectives, build mutual understanding with others from different backgrounds and experiences, and process through an intersectional rather than a conflating lens. In short, this course includes those whose lives have been indelibly etched by the past and assures that those voices are not forgotten, whether they are located in the course material or in the classroom itself.

I gratefully acknowledge the Schusterman Center for Israel Studies Summer Institute for Israel Studies at Brandeis University for their generous grant that supported the creation of this course.

## Notes

1 I use the term mutual understanding rather than tolerance, an oft-used term, as the latter does not go far enough. A person may tolerate certain foods or people, however,

that may not include truly welcoming them or attempting to understand and relate to them, and certainly excludes the notions of equity and social justice.
2 See Meyer 2004, which addresses dealing with threatened enrollments, funding cuts, and more with suggested approaches to institutional, programmatic, and individual needs. One strategy that worked well to increase the number of French majors was to add occasional courses in English (with options of reading and writing in French for French students). In addition to those challenges of French program reduction or elimination in our introduction, see Meyer essay and the introduction to the volume (*Rethinking*). This volume's introduction addresses current challenges where additional reductions are often voiced as administrative solutions to the COVID-19 pandemic. In addition, it must be said that current speech (and iconography) propagating across the world, and certainly in the United States, reminds me of that of the Nazi (and Vichy) regime. I leave that for another article in preparation.
3 The American Association of Teachers of French is completing their retooling of the most recently articulated World-Readiness Standards for the French discipline. Their inclusion (both in can-do statements and in learning scenarios) of la Francophonie and questions of equity and social justice encourage this important work in the classroom.
4 In addressing transferable skills (sometimes called career connections), students perceive ways our courses build skills for their careers. This is an integral aspect of designing "transparent" assignments (TILT). Transparent, student-centered assignments help to create the growth mindset that Carol Dweck discusses in *Mindset: The New Psychology of Success*. And the growth we hope to see here includes becoming anti-racist, to use Ibram X. Kendi's term. Andrew W. Ibrahim's visual of this growth process can prove useful to our students and informs this essay.
5 While designed as an English language course, in part to entice non-French students into our program, parts of the course can be used as a unit within the reader's own courses. The texts written originally in French and the discussion and written assignments for the French language materials may be adapted to the French-speaking students' needs.
6 For maps, see Troen 165–66; Troen, Azaryahu and Golan 14; and Rabinovich and Reinharz 557. For charts of immigration, Troen, Azaryahu and Golan 28, 30; and Rabinovich and Reinharz 571–579. The materials for the introduction to Israel in the course were enhanced in part by a generous Schusterman Institute for Israeli Studies (Brandeis University) fellowship that supported this course. For anyone interested in a very short introduction to Zionism, please see Stanislawski.
7 Fish notes both the pivotal crisis arising from the "debacle of the 1973 war," and subsequent fall of the Labor Party (550–51) and states: "The primary concern during this stage of Israel's development was nation building, not only in terms of governance, infrastructures, and societal frameworks, but also in terms of narratives that formulated the identity and mentality of the policy and its people. The need to cultivate an identity unique and nationally distinct from that of any other sovereign state was a fundamental component of the early historiographical writings. This is not so dissimilar from other smaller countries whose histories and historians want to ensure and assert themselves for fear of being dwarfed by other nation-states" (550).
8 The discussion of choosing one's surname can be fascinating, especially when in the context of the process of immigration where some names were changed by those recording them, and thus not by the renamed person's choice. In other cases, the desire to assimilate, to silence one's Jewishness as a defining characteristic in dangerous times may come into play. Such renaming can complicate the tracing of one's genealogy as well.
9 To better understand intersectionality, I recommend Nira Yuval-Davis' "Intersectionality and Feminist Politics," in which she offers a brief history of the term, which originated from Kimberlé Crenshaw (140), as well as the inherent complexities

within (Yuval-Davis 193). Crenshaw's 1989 article offers the compelling metaphor of intersection I cite above (149). Soave's short "Intersectionality 101" provides it as well as further understanding of the term (59). "Social divisions are about macro axes of social power but also involve actual, concrete people," Yuval-Davis reminds us (198), adding that "there is a need to differentiate carefully between different kinds of difference" (199). "By incorporating these different kinds of differences into our analysis we can avoid conflating positionings, identities and values. We can also avoid attributing fixed identity groupings to the dynamic processes of positionality and location on the one hand and the contested and shifting political construction of categorical boundaries on the other" (200). The present volume includes identities in addition to those (age, disability, gender, race), which Yuval-Davis addresses "as being continually challenged and restructured both individually and socially" (201).
10 See Robert Antelme's *La Race humaine* [*The Human Race*], which shares his experiences.
11 For concise biographical background on Fink and Nomberg-Przytyk, see Horowitz ("Ida Fink") and Patterson. The *New York Times* obituaries for Amos (Kerschner) and for Loridan-Ivens (Rubin) help students see the richness of the lives that they led.
12 In Georgia, those aged over 62 can apply to attend university courses for no tuition. The application fee to do so is minimal, although the application and the robust dual security system for all computer access was daunting to most of these "new" students. Personal networking brought additional over 62-year-olds to the course.

## References

American Association of Teachers of French. "American Association of Teachers of French World-Readiness Standards for the French discipline," 2021.
Antelme, Robert. *L'espèce humaine*. Gallimard, 1957. [*The Human Race*. Marlboro/Northwestern, 1998].
Colette. *Break of Day*. Translated by Enid McLeod. Farrar, Straus, & Giroux, 1961. [*La naissance du jour*. Flammarion, 1984(1928)].
Crenshaw, Kimberlé Williams. "Demarginalizing the Intersection of Race and Sex: A Black Feminist Critique of Antidiscrimination Doctrine, Feminist Theory and Antiracist Politics." *University of Chicago Legal Forum*, vol. 1989, no. 1, 1989, pp. 139–67.
Duras, Marguerite. *The War: A Memoir*. Translated by Barbara Bray. Pantheon Books, 1986. [*La douleur*. Gallimard, 1985].
Dweck, Carol S. *Mindset: The New Psychology of Success*. Ballantine Books, 2016.
"Federico Fellini Quotes." *BrainyQuote.com* July 8, 2020, www.brainyquote.com/quotes/federico_fellini_106347.
Fink, Ida. "A Scrap of Time." In *A Scrap of Time and Other Stories*, translated by Madeline Levins and Francine Prose, Northwestern UP, 1995, pp. 3–10.
Finkiel, Emmanuel, director. *The War: A Memoir*. Music Box Films, 2017.
Fish, Rachel. "Zionism and New Israeli History." In *The Routledge Companion to Jewish History and Historiography*, edited by Dean Phillip Bell, Routledge, 2019, pp. 550–562.
Horowitz, Sara R. "Ida Fink." *Jewish Women: A Comprehensive Historical Encyclopedia*, 27 February 2009, Jewish Women's Archive, https://jwa.org/encyclopedia/article/fink-ida.
—. "Literature." In *The Oxford Handbook of Holocaust Studies*, edited by Peter Hayes and John K. Roth, Oxford UP, 2010, pp. 428–443.
Ibrahim, Andrew W. "Becoming Anti-Racist." www.surgeryredesign.com/current.
Kendi, Ibram X. *How to be an Anti-Racist*. One World, 2019.

Kerschner, Isabel. "Amos Oz, Israeli Author and Peace Advocate, Dies at 79." www.nytimes.com/2018/12/28/obituaries/amos-oz-dead.html.
Loridan-Ivens, Marceline. *But You Did Not Come Back. A Memoir.* Translated by Sandra Smith, Grove Press, 2016. [*Et tu n'es pas revenue. Suivi d'un dossier inédit d'Annette Wieviorka.* Editions Grasset & Fasquelle, 2015. Librairie Générale Française, 2016].
Meir, Golda. *My Life.* G. P. Putnam's Sons, 1975.
Meyer, E. Nicole. "Fractured Families: Program Growth through Innovative Teaching of French and Francophone Women's Autobiographies." In *Rethinking the French Classroom: New Approaches to Teaching Contemporary French and Francophone Women*, edited by E. Nicole Meyer and Joyce Johnston, Routledge, 2019, pp. 19–26.
—. "Shifting Contexts: Choosing Texts to Fit Institutional, Programmatic, and Individual Needs." *Modern French Literary Studies in the Classroom: Pedagogical Strategies*, edited by Charles J. Stivale, Modern Language Association, 2004, pp. 189–197.
Nomberg-Przytyk, Sara. "The Camp Blanket." In *Different Voices: Women and the Holocaust*, edited by Carol Rittner and John K. Roth, Paragon House, 1993, pp. 145–48.
Oz, Amos. *A Tale of Love and Darkness.* Translated by Nicholas de Lange, Harcourt, 2005.
"Picturing Golda Meir." https://uwm.edu/lib-collections/picturing-golda-meir/.
Portman, Natalie, director. *A Tale of Love and Darkness.* Universal Pictures, 2015.
Rabinovich, Itamar and Jehuda Reinharz, editors. *Israel in the Middle East: Documents and Readings on Society, Politics and Foreign Relations – Pre-1948 to the Present.* 2nd ed., Brandeis UP, 2008.
Rubin, Alissa J. "Marceline Loridan-Ivens, 90, Chronicler of Holocaust's Toll," *The New York Times*, New York edition, September 23, 2018, p. A28.
Soave, Robby. "Intersectionality 101." *Reason*, vol. 51, no. 3, July 2019, pp. 57–63.
*Stanford Encyclopedia of Philosophy.* "Memory." Winter 2012, https://stanford.library.sydney.edu.au/archives/win2012/entries/memory.
Stanislawski, Michael. *Zionism: A Very Short Introduction.* Oxford UP, 2017.
TILT Higher Ed. "*Transparency in Learning and Teaching.*" www.tilthighered.com.
Troen, Carol. "Glossary." In *Essential Israel: Essays for the 21st Century*, edited by S. Ilan Troen, and Rachel Fish. UP, Indiana UP, 2017, pp. 387–421.
—. "Timeline." In *Essential Israel: Essays for the 21st Century*, edited by S. Ilan Troen and Rachel Fish, Indiana UP, 2017, pp. 422-423.
Troen, S. Ilan and Rachel Fish, Indiana UP, 2017, pp. 387–423.
Troen, S, Ilan. *Imagining Zion: Dreams, Designs, and Realities in a Century of Jewish Settlement.* Yale UP, 2003.
Troen, S. Ilan *et al.* "Israel: Geography, Demography, and Economy." In *Essential Israel: Essays for the 21st Century*, edited by S. Ilan Troen and Rachel Fish, Indiana UP, 2017, pp. 12–39.
Yablonka, Hanna. "The Development of Holocaust Consciousness in Israel: The Nuremberg, Kapos, Kastner, and Eichmann Trials." *Israel Studies*, vol. 8, no. 3, Fall 2003, pp. 1–24.
—. "The Shoah and the Israelis: Memory History Identity." Schusterman Institute for Israeli Studies, Brandeis University, June 25, 2018. Lecture.
Yuval-Davis, Nira. "Intersectionality and Feminist Politics." *European Journal of Women's Studies*, vol. 13, no. 3, 2006, pp. 192–209.

# ESSENTIAL READS

Compiled by E. Nicole Meyer

With the participation of Nancy M. Arenberg, Tammy Berberi, Dominique Carlini Versini, Kathryn A. Dettmer, Brenda A. Dyer, CJ Gomolka, Eilene Hoft-March, Kris Aric Knisely, Kiki Kosnick, Dominique Licops, Lowry Martin, E. Nicole Meyer, Jessica S. Miller, Lovia Mondésir, Kate Nelson, Lauren Ravalico, and Kathryn St. Ours.

Abécassis, Eliette. *La Répudiée*. Livre de Poche, 2001.
"About Universal Design for Learning." CAST, April 23, 2019, udlguidelinescast.org.
Ashley, Florence. "Les personnes non-binaires en français: une perspective concernée et militante." *H-France Salon*, vol. 14, no. 11, 2019.
Aterianus-Owanga, Alice. *Le rap, ça vient d'ici*. Maison des Sciences de l'Homme, 2017.
Badinter, Elisabeth. *The Conflict: How Modern Motherhood Undermines the Status of Women*. Translated by Adriana Hunter, Metropolitan Books, 2011.
Bagieu, Pénélope. *Culottées*. Gallimard, 2018.
Blake, Felice *et al.*, editors. *Antiracism Inc.: Why the Way We Talk about Racial Justice Matters*. Punctum Books, 2019.
Crenshaw, Kimberlé Williams. "Demarginalizing the Intersection of Race and Sex: A Black Feminist Critique of Antidiscrimination Doctrine, Feminist Theory and Antiracist Politics." *University of Chicago Legal Forum*, vol. 1989, no. 1, 1989, pp. 139-167.
Cukierman, Leïla *et al.*, editors. *Décolonisons les Art!* L'Arche, 2018.
Dimitrov, Nanda and Aisha Haque, "Intercultural Teaching Competence: A Multi-Disciplinary Model for Instructor Reflection." *Intercultural Education*, vol. 27, no. 5, 2016, pp. 437–456. doi:10.1080/14675986.2016.1240502.
Dolmage, Jay T. *Academic Ableism: Disability and Higher Education*. U of Michigan P, 2017.
Dowd, Alicia C. and Estela Mara Bensimon. *Engaging the "Race Question": Accountability and Equity in U.S. Higher Education*. Teachers College Press, 2015.
Durmelat, Sylvie. "Making Couscous French? Digesting the Loss of Empire." *Contemporary French Civilization*, vol. 42, no. 3–4, 2017, pp. 391–407.

Edison, Paul. "Conquest Unrequited: French Expeditionary Science, 1864–1867." *French Historical Studies*, vol. 26, no. 3, 2003, pp. 459–495.

Firmin, Anténor. *De l'égalité des races humaines: anthropologie positive*. Librairie Cotillon, 1885.

Gannon, Kevin M. *Radical Hope: A Teaching Manifesto*. West Virginia UP, 2020.

Haddad, Raphaël. *Gender-Inclusive Language in France: A Manual*. Translated by Elsa Stéphan. Mots-Clés, 2019, www.motscles.net/ecriture-inclusive.

Hammou, Karim. *Une histoire du rap en France*. Éditions de la Découverte, 2013.

Ibrahim, Andrew W. "Becoming Anti-Racist." www.surgeryredesign.com/current.

Kendi, Ibram X. *How to Be an Antiracist*. One World, 2019.

Knisely, Kris Aric. "Le français non-binaire: Linguistic Forms Used by Non-Binary Speakers of French." *Foreign Language Annals*, vol. 53, no. 4, Winter 2020, pp. 850–76.

Kosnick, Kiki. "The Everyday Poetics of Gender-Inclusive French: Strategies for Navigating the Linguistic Landscape." *Modern & Contemporary France*, vol. 27, no. 2, 2019, pp. 147–161.

Lang, James M. *Small Teaching: Everyday Lessons from the Science of Learning*. Jossey-Bass, 2016.

Le Clézio, J. G. M. *The Mexican Dream: Or, the Interrupted Thought of Amerindian Civilizations*. U of Chicago P, 1993.

Lessard, Michaël and Suzanne Zaccour. *Manuel de grammaire non sexiste et inclusive. Le masculin ne l'emporte plus!* Éditions Syllepse, 2018.

Lewis, Amanda E. and John B. Diamond. *Despite the Best Intentions: How Racial Inequality Thrives in Good Schools*. Oxford UP, 2015.

Memmi, Albert. *Portrait d'un juif*. Gallimard, 1962.

Meyer, E. Nicole and Joyce Johnston, editors. *Rethinking the French Classroom: New Approaches to Teaching Contemporary French and Francophone Women*. Routledge, 2019.

Modiano, Patrick. *Dora Bruder*. Folio, 1997.

Murphy, Deirdre. "Toward a Pedagogy of Mouthiness: The Essential Interdisciplinarity of Studying Food." *Transformations: The Journal of Inclusive Scholarship and Pedagogy*, vol. 23, no. 2, 2012–2013, pp. 17–26.

Paiz, Joshua M. *Queering the English Language Classroom: A Practical Guide for Teachers*. Equinox, 2020.

Preciado, Paul B. *Un appartement sur Uranus: pour une révolution sexuelle*. Grasset, 2019.

Ricœur, Paul. "La condition d'étranger." *Esprit*, March/April, no. 3, 2006, pp. 264–275.

Saad, Layla F. and Robin J. DiAngelo. *Me and White Supremacy: Combat Racism, Change the World, and Become a Good Ancestor*. Sourcebooks, 2020.

Sathy, Viji and Kelly A. Hogan. "How to Make Your Teaching More Inclusive." *The Chronicle of Higher Education*, July 22, 2019, www.chronicle.com/article/how-to-make-your-teaching-more-inclusive.

Schoonover, Thomas. *The French in Central America: Culture and Commerce, 1820–1930*. Scholarly Resources, 2000.

Scott, Sally and Wade A. Edwards. *Disability and World Language Learning: Inclusive Teaching for Diverse Learners*. Rowman & Littlefield, 2018.

Stewart, Abigail J. and Virginia Valian. *Part I. An Inclusive Academy: Achieving Diversity and Excellence*. MIT P, 2018.

Swamy, Vinay and Louisa Mackenzie, editors. "Legitimizing 'iel'? Language and Trans Communities in Francophone and Anglophone Spaces." *H-France Salon*, vol. 11, no. 14, 2019, https://h-france.net/h-france-salon-volume-11-2019/#1114.

Tobin, Thomas J. and Kirsten T. Behling. *Reach Everyone, Teach Everyone: Universal Design for Learning in Higher Education*. West Virginia UP, 2018.

Veldwachter, Nadège. "Une 'dette d'honneur' impensée: Les réfugiés juifs et la République d'Haïti." *Cahiers d'études africaines*, vol. 233, no. 1, 2019, pp. 149–170.
Viennot, Eliane. *Le Langage inclusif: pourquoi, comment?* Éditions iXe, 2018.
—. *Non, masculin ne l'emporte pas sur le féminin! Petite histoire des résistances de la langue française.* Éditions iXe, 2017.
Waite, Stacey. *Teaching Queer: Radical Possibilities for Writing and Knowing.* U of Pittsburgh P, 2017.
Yalom, Marilyn. *A History of the Breast.* Ballantine, 1997.
Yang, Kao Kalia. *The Latehomecomer: A Hmong Family Memoir.* Coffee House Press, 2008.
Yuval-Davis, Nira. "Intersectionality and Feminist Politics." *European Journal of Women's Studies*, vol. 13, no. 3, 2006, pp. 192–209.

# INDEX

2Fik, 17–18

Abécassis, Eliette: *La Répudiée*, 174–75
ableism. 5, 65, 93, 188.
Académie Française: on *autrice*, 72; on French-language evolution, 15; on gender inclusivity, 58, 59, 60, 62, 69, 71
accessibility, 2, 88–89
adjectives: gender inclusivity and, 60–61, 64, 65
*African Psycho* (Mabanckou), 103–4
ageism: combating, 184
Alexis, Jacques S.: *Les Arbres musiciens*, 159–60, 161–63, 166
Algeria, 100, 113, 121, 149; colonial experience of, 109–10; Harkis in, 108
Al-Malik, Abd, 155–56
Alpheratz, 62, 63–64
American Council on the Teaching of Foreign Languages (ACTFL): on diversity and inclusion, 22; resources for teaching race of, 50–51, 89; standards and guidelines of, 87, 90
*Anti-Semite and Jew* (Sartre). See *Réflexions sur la question juive* (Sartre)
anti-Semitism, 184; in France, 171–72; Golda Meir on, 180; in modern United States, 178; Simone Veil's experience with, 174
*Apostles of Empire: Jesuits and New France* (McShea), 132

*Arab of the Future, The* (Sattouf). See *L'Arabe du futur* (Sattouf)
Arab Spring, 152
*Arbres musiciens, Les* (Alexis), 159–60, 161–63, 166
Artaud, Antonin: "The Conquest of Mexico," 135; "Indian Culture," 135; *Selected Writings*, 135
assessment. *See* Program Assessment Protocol; student assessment
audio processing disorders: French-language instruction and, 77, 78, 83, 84–85
*Aujourd'hui* (Fellous), 175–76
*Avant que les ombres s'effacent* (Dalembert), 159–60, 163–66

backward design: in curricular restructuring, 89
Badinter, Elisabeth: *TheConflict: How Modern Motherhood Undermines the Status of Women*, 142
Begag, Azouz: *Béni ou le paradis privé*, 121–22, 123; *Shantytown Kid*, 121
*Belly of Paris, The* (Zola). See *Ventre de Paris, Le* (Zola)
*Béni ou le paradis privé* (Begag), 121–22, 123
Ben Jelloun, Tahar: *Le racisme expliqué à ma fille*, 51; *L'étincelle*, 152
Berque, Jacques, 107
Best, Mireille, 104
Beurs, 108–9

Black Lives Matters (BLM): protests of, 106, 152, 182
Black Panthers: Kerry James on, 156
*Black Robe* (film), 132
*Black Skin, White Masks* (Fanon). See *Peau noire, masques blancs* (Fanon)
bodies: crip time and disabled, 39; gendered boundaries of, 30; marginalization of TGNC, in L2 instruction, 22; in queer pedagogy, 12–13;
Bosco, Monique: *La Femme de Loth*, 176
Boucher, François: *Breakfast*, 144–45
Boukhobza, Chochana: *Un été à Jérusalem*, 175
Brazil: attempted French colonization of, 132
*Breakfast* (Boucher), 144–45
breastfeeding, 141–42
Brillat-Savarin, Jean Anthelme: *Physiology of Taste*, 142; restaurant culture and, 143
Buddhism: Alexandre Jollien and, 34
burqa, 17; French law against wearing, 110
Business French: trans-focused materials in, 28

"Camp Blanket, The" (Nomberg-Przytyk), 181–82
Camus, Albert, 156; *L'Étranger*, 100
*Candide* (Voltaire): food culture in, 144–45
Caribbean Sea: enslaved French-speaking migrants from, 98; French colonization of, 129, 133; French language in, 130, 131, 133, 136, 161
cartography. See maps
Chaillou, Étienne, 16
Césaire, Aimé, 133, 136; *Notebook of a Return to the Native Land*, 130; "Pour une synthèse nouvelle…," 47
Chaima, 152–53
Chanterelle: "The Shuttle," 99
Chen, Ying: *Les Lettres chinoises*, 122, 123
*Childhood* (Sarraute). See *Enfance* (Sarraute)
*Childhood during the Shoah: Excerpts of a Life* (Veil). See *Jeunesse au temps de la Shoah: (Extraits d'une vie)*, *UneVie* (Veil)
*Chinese Letters, The* (Chen). See *Lettres chinoises, Les* (Chen)
Chinese rhetoric: as model of intercultural dialogue, 122–23
Chirac, Jacques: disability rights and, 35
chocolate: Othering and, 145; slavery and, 144
cis-normativity, 11–12, 13, 23, 24, 91; creep of, 25; expectations of, 28

civil discourse: French-language study and, 106–16
Civil Rights movement (United States): French decolonization struggle compared to, 102
classrooms: Eurocentrism in, 44; experimentation in, 65; as gender-affirming environment, 65; as foreign, to a disabled person, 36; queering of, in L2 development, 23–28. See also flipped classroom format
clothing nomenclature: queer pedagogy and, 17
coffee: slavery and,144
Colette, 182
colonialism: in French-language education, 88; legacies of, 149, 152; in New World by France, 132–33; race and, 44, 45, 49. See also decolonization
colonization: justifications for, 150–51; of New World, by France, 132–33
colorblind (to racial perceptions), 45; French Republic as, 134, 136
colors: stereotyping of, 25
communautarisme: use of, 108
*Conflict, The: How Modern Motherhood Undermines the Status of Women* (Badinter), 142
Congo: colonization of, 151;
"Conquest of Mexico, The" (Artaud), 135
contexts: in cultural discourse, 109–10
couscous: Othering and, 145–46
Cousin, Jean, 132
COVID-19 pandemic, 1–2, 178, 182; burqa use in, 17, graffiti in, 155; "social distance" in, 89
Crenshaw, Kimberlé: on "isms," 111; on systemic racism, 181
Creole: Haitian, 160, 164, 165, 166; speakers of, 101
crip time: as disability education strategy, 39
critical disability studies (CDS): on imperfection, 36
critical thinking: foodways and, 139, 140; Haitian literature and, 159, 160; in L2 pedagogy, 95; about race, 50; social justice and, 90, 95, 170; in student assessments, 17, 90, 95; skills, 171
critical tools: in civil discourse, 111–12
*Croisades vues par les Arabes, Les* (Maalouf), 48
Crusades: as subject of racial interpretation, 48
cultural biases: instructor's, recognizing, 49

cultural crossroads: French studies as, 103
curriculum: decolonization of, 97–105; diversification of, 87–96

Dalembert, Louis-Philippe: *Avant que les ombres s'effacent*, 159–60, 163–66
dance. *See* hip-hop culture
Daoud, Kamel: *Meursault, contre-enquête*, 100
Darrieussecq, Marie: *Truismes*, 72
debate: as civil discourse tool, 113
decolonization: of French studies curriculum, 97–105. *See also* colonialism
determiners: as tool for gender inclusivity in French, 63–64
Diallo, Rokhaya: on burqa use in COVID-19 pandemic, 17
Diaspora: Haitian, 133; Jewish, 169, 175, 176
Diop, Birago: "Souffles," 49
direct instruction: as guide to learning for students with learning disabilities, 81–83
disabled students, 88–89; in U.S. educational system, 36–37
disability education strategies, 39–42, 79–85
disability studies: in French classroom, 34–43, 77–86
discrimination: as colonialism's legacy, 149. *See also* racism
*Disintegration, The* (film), 112
diversity: in French curriculum, 87–96; in graduate classroom, 169–77; need for, in French classroom, 2, 170
*Dora Bruder* (Modiano), 172–73
Dracius, Suzanne: "La Montagne de feu," 102
Dreyfus Affair, 171
Dumas, Alexandre: *The Journal of Madame Giovanni*, 134–35
Duras, Claire de: *Ourika*, 119–20, 121, 122, 123
Duras, Marguerite, 181
dyslexia: French-language instruction and, 77–85

écriture inclusive, 58–60, 61, 68. *See also* *Manuel d'écriture inclusive*
El Dorado, 134, 135
*Enfance* (Sarraute), 178
English (language): French compared to, 64, 70, 82–83; as world language, 97
epicene words: as tool for gender inclusivity in French, 58, 59, 60–61, 64, 65, 72, 73
*été à Jérusalem, Un* (Boukhobza), 175

ethnic cleansing, 98–99
"étrange exil, Un" (Kane), 47, 51
Eurocentrism: in examining race, 47, 48; in French classroom, 44, 51
exclusion: of Blacks, 164; of Jews, 164, 171

Fairuz, 152
family: nomenclature, queer pedagogy and, 16–17; traditions, 179–80
Fanon, Frantz, 136; on exclusion, 164; *Peau noire, masques blancs*, 51, 133
*Fatima* (film), 111
Faucon, Philippe: films by, 111, 112
feedback: appropriate, 118; to students with learning disabilities, 83–85; timely and regular, 124. *See also* student assessment
Fellous, Colette: *Aujourd'hui*, 175–76
Felman, Shoshana: on testimonial writing, 173
feminists, 152; gender inclusivity in French and, 61, 68–69, 71–72
feminization, 58–59, 68–69; Académie Française on, 71
*Femme de Loth, La* (Bosco), 176
*fête chantée, La* (Le Clézio), 135–36
Fink, Ida: "Scrap of Time," 181–82
*Fleurs du Bitume* (documentary), 152–53
Fleury, Jean, 133
flipped classroom format, 93–94, 130–31
Floyd, George: fresco honoring, 154; murder of, 1, 106
Fondation Émergence, 30
foodways, 139–48
foreigners: Haitian state and, 166; in *Lettres d'une Péruvienne* (Graffigny), 119; mistrust of, 163. *See also* Othering
France: cultural influence in Latin America of, 129–38; disabled access in, 37–38; gastronomic tradition of, 141; New World colonization by, 132–33; as traditional center of inquiry, 97, 98
France Culture, 70, 110
Francophiles: historically and critically informed, queer pedagogy and, 13
*Francophone Heritage: Intercultural Studies* (textbook). *See* *Héritages francophones: Enquêtes interculturelles* (textbook)
Francophone literature. *See* French and Francophone literature: inclusivity in courses of,
Francosphere: as intellectual conception, 131–32
French (language): as growing and world language, 97; heritage speakers of,

100–102; among Hispanic students, 137; in Latin America, 136–37; native speakers of, 100–102; second-language learners of, 100
French 101. *See* introductory courses
French Academy. *See* Académie Française
French gastronomic meal, 139–40
French Guiana, 94, 132
French and Francophone literature: inclusivity in courses of, 99–100, 117–26, 159–166, 169–177, 178–179, 183
French studies: COVID-19 pandemic's effect on, 1–2; as cultural crossroads, 103; current status of, 1–2; identity politics in, 11; universalism in, 11
Freud, Sigmund, 182

Gabon: hip-hop culture in, 154
gastronomy. *See* foodways
gender (social construction): French gastronomy and, 141–42; as structural and political issue, 25, 28
gender-inclusive language: in curricular redesign, 92; in French classroom, 57–76; lack of resources for, 73–74; students' response to, 72–73
genders (grammatical and linguistic): English native learners' difficulty with, 70; historical evolution of, 41; queer pedagogy and, 15, 24–25
*Glaneurs et la glaneuse, Les* (documentary), 144
Glissant, Édouard: on exclusion, 164
globalization: awareness of, in learning outcomes, 13, 170; of identity structures, 12; *LesLettres chinoises* (Chen) as example of, 122; in queer pedagogy, 13
globally engaged polyglots: queer pedagogy and, 13
graduate classroom: diversity in, 169–77
Graffigny, Françoise: *Lettres d'une Péruvienne*, 118–19, 123
graffiti, 154; historical memory and, 155
grammar: as a linguistic concept in the language classroom, 69–70. *See also specific parts of speech*
Great Expulsion, The, 99
Guadeloupe, 133

*Haine et le pardon, La* (Kristeva), 35
Haiti: diaspora of, 133; French colonization of, 133; *Inside Out Project* in, 155; literature of, tolerance taught through, 159–68; pigmentocracy of, 134

Harkis, 108, 109
*Hatred and Forgiveness* (Kristeva). See *Haine et le pardon, La* (Kristeva)
Haut Conseil à l'égalité entre les femmes et les hommes, 71
Heilbrun, Carolyn, 182
*Héritages francophones: Enquêtes interculturelles* (textbook), 98
heritage speakers (of French): balancing the languages needs of, 100–102, 103
Hershey, Laura, 41
High Council for Equality Between Women and Men. *See* Haut Conseil à l'égalité entre les femmes et les hommes
hijabs, 17; French law against wearing, 110
hip-hop culture: diversity lessons from, 149–58; French memory and, 151
Hispanic students: French language and, 137
Hmong: integration into French-language classroom of, 94
Holocaust, the, 172; life-writing after 178–87; narratives of, 173–74
Honduras: French railroad funding in, 136
*Horla, Le* (Maupassant), 120–21, 122, 123
Huguenots, 98

*Identités Meurtrières, Les* (Maalouf), 110–11, 112
identity and identities: in civil discourse, 110–11; language and, 22, 103; Jewish identity, 169–172, 178–183
identity politics: in French studies, 11
immigration, 102, 177; as colonialism's legacy, 149, 153; to Israel, 180. *See also* migration
inclusion and inclusivity: as disability education strategy, 40–41; of gender, in French classroom, 57–67; in French literature studies, 99–100; 117–126, 159–166, 169–177, 178–182; need for, in French classroom, 2, 159, 170; racial, effects of, 46. *See also* gender-inclusive language
inclusive writing. *See écriture inclusive*
*Inclusive Writing Manual*. See *Manuel d'écriture inclusive*
"Indian Culture" (Artaud), 135
Individualized Education Plans, 36
inequality: in classroom, 117; as colonialism's legacy, 149, 152; in restaurants, 143
*Inside Out Project* (JR), 155
instructors: gender inclusivity manifesto for, 64–65; goals of, 77; recognizing racial

biases of, 49; self-reflections of, 102; students' self-expression and, 62
intercultural dialog, 122–23
interculturality 130, 137; Jean-Marie Gustave Le Clézio on, 131, 135, 136; Martha van der Ritt on, 135–36
Intercultural Teaching Competence (ITC) model, 117–18, 122, 123–24
interdependence and community: as disability education strategy, 39–40
internalized racism, 99
intersectionality, 120, 121, 159, 181; as critical tool in civil discourse, 111
interviews (live), 107; as civil discourse tool, 113–14, 118
*In the Name of Identity* (Maalouf). See *Identités Meurtrières, Les* (Maalouf)
introductory courses: queering of, 14–18; for students with learning disabilities, 78–85
Isha, 151
Islam: cultural practices of, queer pedagogy and, 17–18; in Philippe Faucon's films, 112; political, 152; secularity and, 110–11; women and, 152–53. See also Muslims
Islamophobia, 111, 112
Israel 175–176, 178–187

James, Kerry, 156
*jeunesse au temps de la Shoah: (Extraits d'une vie), Une* (Veil), 173–74
Jewish Francophone writers: life writing of, after the Holocaust, 178–87; teaching diversity through, 169–77
Jim Crow laws, 133–34
Jollien, Alexandre, 34–35, 42
*Journal of Madame Giovanni, The* (Dumas), 134–35
JR ("photograffeur"), 154–55

Kane, Cheikh Hamidou: "Un étrange exil," 47
Kechiche, Abdellatif, 112, 145–46
*Kiffe ta race* (podcast), 17
King, Martin Luther, Jr.: Kerry James on, 156
Kovner, Abba, 182, 183–84
Kristeva, Julia: on disability rights and social transformation, 35

L2 instruction: critical thinking in, 95; learning disabilities and, 78; needs of students in, 100, 102; range of content in, 95–96; trans, non-binary, and gender-non-conforming (TGNC) bodies in, 22–33
LaBelle, Sophie, 29
Lafitte, Jean, 133
laïcité, 110
La Leche League, 142
Lalonde, Michèle: "Speak White," 99, 101–2
*Lamsari et le trésor des Oudayas*, 48
language: in civil discourse, 108–9
*langage inclusif*: failures and imperatives of, 58–60
*L'Arabe du futur* (Sattouf), 104
*L'Art de la révolte* (Al-Malik) 155–56
*Last of the Mohicans* (film), 132
Latin America: Francospheres in, 129–38. See also specific countries
Laub, Dori: on testimonial writing, 173
learning disabilities: French-language education and students with, 77–86
learning management system (LMS): modifications for disabled students of, 79
Le Clerc, François, 133
Le Clézio, Jean-Marie Gustave: *La fête chantée*, 135–36; on interculturality, 131, 135, 136
leftovers (food), 143
Lejoindre, Eric, 114
*L'étincelle* (Ben Jelloun), 152
*L'Étranger* (Camus), 100
*Lettres chinoises, Les* (Chen), 122, 123
"Lettre de France" (Sembène), 48
*Lettres d'une Péruvienne* (Graffigny), 118–19, 123
*Lettres persanes* (Montesquieu), 48
LGBTQ+, 104; engagement with, 23, 29, 57; exemplification of, 92; Nazis and, 181. See also queer pedagogy
*Lieux de mémoire, Les* (Nora), 149–50
life writing: post-Holocaust, 178–87; Simone Veil and, 173
*Life Increases* (Isha). See *Vie augmente, La* (Isha)
*L'ingénu* (Voltaire), 48
listening: in civil discourse, 112–14
literature courses: of Haiti, 159–68; inclusivity in, 99–100, 117–26
Loridan-Ivens, Marceline: *But You Did Not Come Back*, 182; obituary of, 182
*Lot's Wife* (Bosco). See *Femme de Loth, La* (Bosco)

Louisiana: French culture in, 133–34
*Love, Anger, Madness* (Vieux-Chauvet), 130, 134

Maalouf, Amin: *Identités Meurtrières*, 110–11, 112; *Les Croisades vues par les Arabes*, 48
Mabanckou, Alain: *African Psycho*, 103–4
Macron, Emmanuel: on diversity and multiculturalism, 108
Malcolm X: Kerry James on, 156
*Manuel d'écriture inclusive*, 70, 72; essentialness of, 73; on gender inclusivity, 58, 59, 60, 68
*Manuel de littérature africaine (classe de 1ère)* (Ndiaye), 47–48
maps: pedagogical use of, 130, 132–33, 180
Maria (dancer/choreographer), 153–54
*Mariage pour tous* decision (2013), 16
marriage equality, 16–17
Marshall, Bill: Francospheres idea of, 131
Martin, Carla, 145
Martinique, 133
Marvelous Realism theory: applied to *Les Arbres musiciens* (Alexis), 161–63
masculine (grammar): as generic form, 57–59, 62, 68, 71
Maupassant, Guy de: *Le Horla*, 120–21, 122, 123
McShea, Bronwen: *Apostles of Empire: Jesuits and New France*, 132
MC Solaar, 155
Meir, Golda, 180, 181; *My Life*, 180
Memmi, Albert: *Portrait d'un juif*, 171–72, 174, 175, 176
memory: food and, 141, 145; French, hip-hop culture and, 150–56; Holocaust and, 182, 183
memorization: by students with learning disabilities, 78, 81, 82–83
*Mes Algéries en France* (Sebbar), 109–10
*Métamorphoses du handicap de 1970 à nos jours, Les* (Stiker), 35
*Meursault, contre-enquête* (Daoud), 100
*Mexican Dream, The* (Le Clézio). See *fête chantée, La* (Le Clézio)
Mexican Revolution: Antonin Artaud on, 135
Mexico: French intervention in (1860s), 130; French writing on, 135–36; multiculturalism in, 133, 136
Mexico City: French architectural influence in, 136

middot: as tool for gender inclusivity in French, 58, 59, 61–62, 68, 72, 73
migration: in French studies, 98–100, 165. See also immigration
Modern Language Aptitude Test (MLAT), 78
Modiano, Patrick: *Dora Bruder*, 172–73
"Montagne de feu, La" (Dracius), 102
Montesquieu: *Lettres persanes*, 48
Moore, Bethany Nunn, 145
"Mountain of Fire, The" (Dracius). See "Montagne de feu, La" (Dracius)
multiculturalism: discussions on, 50–51; Emmanuel Macron on, 108; in France, 136; in Mexico, 136; in the United States, 136
music. See hip-hop culture
*Musician Trees, The* (Alexis). See *Arbres musiciens, Les* (Alexis)
Muslims: in France, 17–18, 110–11, 114; misconceptions about, 48. See also Islam
mutual understanding: promoting, 178–83
*My Algerias in France* (Sebbar). See *Mes Algéries en France* (Sebbar)
*My Life* (Meir), 180
*Mystères de Paris, Les* (Sue), 143

nationalism, 156, 180
Native Americans: French and, 132; "Indian Culture" (Artaud), 135
native speakers (of French): balancing the languages needs of, 100–102, 103; grammar rules of, 72
Ndiaye, Papa Guèye: *Manuel de littérature africaine (classe de 1ère)*, 47–48
Nègre, 164
Negritude movement, 133, 162
neologisms: as tool for gender inclusivity, 58, 60, 62
neopronouns, 65; in queer communities, 24
New England: French speakers in, 99
*New France* (film), 132
New York City: hip-hop culture's origination in, 149, 156
*Night* (Wiesel), 173
noble savage, 48
Nomberg-Przytyk, Sara: "The Camp Blanket," 181–82
non-binary forms of speech, 62; chart of, 26–27
non-binary people. See trans, non-binary, and gender-non-conforming (TGNC) bodies

non-binary pronouns, 24–25, 63
Nora, Pierre: *Les Lieux de mémoire*, 149–50
normativity: cis-, 11–12, 13, 23, 24, 25, 28, 91; disabled students and, 36, 42
*Notebook of a Return to the Native Land* (Césaire), 130
nouns. *See* substantives
"Nuit de Sine" (Senghor), 47

Ojibwe: integration into French-language classroom of, 94
optimization: in higher education, disabled students and, 36
Organisation Internationale de la Francophonie (OIF), 97
Othering, 120–21, 140, 178–79; in the eighteenth century, 48; food culture and, 144–46; Jews and, 169, 174, 175. *See also* foreigners
Ouména, 152–53
*Ourika* (Duras), 119–20, 121, 122, 123
Oz, Amos, 180; obituary of, 182; *A Tale of Love and Darkness*, 180–81

PaCS legislation (1999), 16
Palacio de Bellas Artes (Mexico City), 136
Panama Canal, 136
Paris: restaurant culture in, 141, 142–43
Parks, Rosa: Kerry James on, 156
past participles: as tool for gender inclusivity in French, 62–63, 64
*Peau noire, masques blancs* (Fanon), 51, 133
perfectibility: in higher education, disabled students and, 36
*Persian Letters* (Montesquieu). See *Lettres persanes* (Montesquieu)
*Physiology of Taste* (Brillat-Savarin), 142
*Pig Tales* (Darrieussecq). See *Truismes* (Darrieussecq)
Pitchon, Eduardo, 174
Philippe, Édouard: on gender inclusivity in French, 58–59
*Plessy v. Ferguson* (1896), 133–34
podcasts: *Kiffe ta race*, 17; *France Culture*, 70, 110; value in queer pedagogy of, 18–19
*Portrait d'un juif* (Memmi), 171–72, 174, 175, 176
postcolonialism: food and, 145; in Francosphere, 130, 131, 133; race and, 45, 46
"Pour une synthèse nouvelle…" (Césaire), 47, 51

poverty: as colonialism's legacy, 149; among disabled people, 36; food pantries as signposts for, 144
Présence Africaine (publisher), 47–48
pride: as disability education strategy, 41
Program Assessment Protocol: use in curricular design of, 90–91
pronouns: in queer pedagogy, 24–25; as tool for gender inclusivity in French, 63–64. *See also specific types of pronouns*

Quality Matters standards, 2
Quebec: feminists in, 61; French speakers in, 99
queer pedagogy, 11–21; classrooms and, 23–28

race: in French classroom, 44–53; guidelines for discussing, 49–51; in Latin America, 134; materials for study of, 47–48; reasons for inclusion discussion of, 45–48
racial biases: recognizing instructor's, 49
racial capitalism: avoidance of, 47–48
racial justice, 51. *See also* Black Lives Matters (BLM)
racial literacy, 46
racism: as colonialism's legacy, 149; dismantling of, 45; internalized, 99; against Jews, 179; systemic, 45–47, 49–50, 106, 111–12, 179, 181
*racisme expliqué à ma fille, Le* (Ben Jelloun), 51
*Realms of Memory* (Nora). See *Lieux de mémoire, Les* (Nora)
*Réflexions sur la question juive* (Sartre), 171, 172, 174
religion: in cultural discourse context, 110, 159, 167–169, 177
*Répudiée, La* (Abécassis), 174–75
respect: need for, in French classroom, 170–71
*Revolts in the Arab Countries* (Ben Jelloun). See *L'étincelle* (Ben Jelloun)
rewording: as tool for gender inclusivity in French, 61
Richelieu, Armand Jean du Plessis Cardinal, 71
Ricœur, Paul: on the correlation between fiction and life, 160–61; on the ethical intention of the self, 159; on foreign

language study, 164–65; on mistrust toward foreigners, 163
rote memorization: difficulty with, among students with learning disabilities, 78
Rousseau, Jean-Jacques: on breastfeeding and wet nursing, 141–42

*Sacred* (Abécassis). See *Répudiée, La* (Abécassis)
Sankara, Thomas: Kerry James on, 156
Sarraute, Nathalie: *Enfance*, 178
Sartre, Jean-Paul: *Réflexions sur la question juive*, 171, 172, 174
Sattouf, Riad: *L'Arabe du futur*, 104
Schumann, John, 88–89
"Scrap of Time" (Fink), 181–82
Sebbar, Leila: *Mes Algéries en France*, 109–10
second language. *See* L2 instruction
second language reading theory (Bernhardt), 123
*Secret of the Grain, The* (film), 112, 145–46
secularity: in cultural discourse context, 110
*Selected Writings* (Artaud), 135
self, the: cultural construction of, 160–61; ethical intention of, 159
Sembène, Ousmane: "Lettre de France," 48
Senegal, 153; graffiti artists in, 155; *tirailleurs* from, 156
Senghor, Léopold Sédar, 103; Kerry James on, 156; "Nuit de Sine," 47
Set-Setal, 155
Shams, 152–53
*Shantytown Kid* (Begag), 121
"Shuttle, The," (Chanterelle song), 99
singular they: in queer communities, 24, 64
social inequalities: regress of, though language study, 106–7
"social solidarity" (Schumann), 89
*sociologue et l'ourson, La* (documentary), 16–17
"Souffles" (Diop), 49
speaking: in civil discourse, 112–14
speaking intensive courses, 107–8
"Speak White" (Lalonde), 99, 101–2
Stiker, Henri-Jacques: on psychology of inter-relationality with disabled people, 35
*Stranger, The. See* Camus
student assessment: in backward design, 89; equitable, 65, 118; in introductory courses, 17; linguistic inclusion and, 25; of students with learning disabilities, 83–85
Student Learning Outcomes (SLOs): American Council on the Teaching of Foreign Languages (ACTFL) guidelines used in, 89–90
subjectivity: suspension of, self-understanding and, 161; white male, 120–21
substantives: gender inclusivity and, 60, 64
Sue, Eugène: *Les Mystères de Paris*, 143
sugar: slavery and, 144, 145
*Summer in Jerusalem, A* (Boukhobza). See *été à Jérusalem, Un* (Boukhobza)
systemic racism, 45–47, 49–50, 106; colorblindness as contributor to, 45; as critical tool in civil discourse, 111–12; intersectionality of, 181; against Jews, 179

*Tale of Love and Darkness, A* (Oz), 180–81
Taubira, Christiane, 16
Taylor, Breonna: murder of, 1
teaching: as learning process, 77. *See also* instructors
TED Talks, 30, 155
testimonial writing, 173
textbooks (French), 98, 145; disabled people depicted in, 40; of *écriture inclusive*, 58; gender binarism in, 57, 59, 65, 73; learning disabled students and, 81; multiculturalism in, 88, 92. *See also specific textbooks*
Théry, Irène, 17
Théry, Mathias, 16–17
Thevet, André: map by, 133
they (singular): in queer communities, 24, 64
*Today* (Fellous). See *Aujourd'hui* (Fellous)
tolerance: need for, in French classroom, 159, 170–71
tokenization avoidance: racial, 45, 47–48; of trans, non-binary, and gender-non-conforming (TGNC) students, 24, 25
trans, non-binary, and gender-non-conforming (TGNC) bodies: connecting with, 27–28; in Frencophone communities, 24; inclusion in second language (L2) development classrooms, 22–33; respect for, 28–29
trans-affirming, queer inquiry-based pedagogies (TAQIBPs), 23–24, 25, 29, 30
transnationalism: hip-hop culture and, 149–58
Transparency Framework (Winkelmes): in curricular restructuring, 89
transphobia: in academic research, 28

Traoré, Adama: fresco honoring, 154
*Truismes* (Darrieussecq), 72
Tunisia: colonialism in, 152–53

upper-level courses: queer pedagogy and, 18–19
United Nations: on ethnic cleansing, 98; on gender-inclusive language, 57
United States: anti-Semitism in, 178; Civil Rights movement in, French decolonization struggle compared to, 102; French-language learners' diversity in, 100–102; multiculturalism in, 136
universal design (UD) principles: world language learning and, 38–39
Universal Design of Learning (UDL) framework, 78
*Until the Shadows Flee* (Dalembert). See *Avant que les ombres s'effacent* (Dalembert)

van der Ritt, Martha: on interculturality, 135–36
Varda, Agnès, 144

Veil, Simone: *Une jeunesse au temps de la Shoah: (Extraits d'une vie)*, 173–74
*Ventre de Paris, Le* (Zola), 143
verbs: gender egalitarianism of, 57, 65
*Vie augmente, La* (Isha), 151
Viennot, Éliane, 59, 61, 68, 71, 73
Vieux-Chauvet, Marie: *Love, Anger, Madness*, 130, 134
Voltaire: *Candide*, 144–45; *L'ingénu*, 48

WebQuest, 29
wet nursing, 141–42
white male subjectivity, 120–21
whiteness: French-language learning facilitation and, 88
Wiesel, Elie: *Night*, 173
women: burqa wearing and, 17; hip-hop culture and, 152–53
*Women Are Heroes* (JR), 155
World-Readiness Standards, 179

Zola, Émile: *Le Ventre de Paris*, 143

For Product Safety Concerns and Information please contact our EU representative  GPSR@taylorandfrancis.com
Taylor & Francis Verlag GmbH, Kaufingerstraße 24, 80331 München, Germany

www.ingramcontent.com/pod-product-compliance
Lightning Source LLC
Chambersburg PA
CBHW061348300426

44116CB00011B/2036